# JONATHAN KAUFMAN

"One hears the echoes of a world that

might have been." —*The Boston Sunday Globe*

National
Jewish
Book Award
Finalist

# A HOLE IN THE HEART
# OF THE WORLD

## The Jewish Experience in
## Eastern Europe After World War II

## Praise for *A Hole in the Heart of the World*

"Carefully researched. . . . Profoundly chilling. . . . It's clear that Kaufman's sympathies are fully engaged by the narratives he records, by the family histories so eventful they keep us reading with unflagging interest. . . . Consistently interesting. . . . We're grateful to Kaufman for introducing us to a number of exemplary—and memorable—characters."
—Francine Prose, *New York Newsday*

"Kaufman portrays these people with great feeling and compassion. . . . In Kaufman's book, one hears the echoes of a world that might have been."
—Zachary Karabell, *The Boston Sunday Globe*

"Kaufman makes good use of his rather large cast of characters to act out the tragic history of Europe in the twentieth century."
—Jonathan Kirsch, *Los Angeles Times*

"A snapshot of Jewish life throughout Eastern Europe at several moments in history."
—Jonathan Groner, *The Washington Post Book World*

"From Kaufman's accounts we learn what possibilities exist for the human spirit . . . Kaufman allows issues to emerge from the confounding complexities of changing beliefs, realities, hopes, and actions. For these lives are most fascinatingly and sadly strewn with confusion, intangibles, insecurities, blindspots. . . . I kept urging myself to slow down, to take in the gravity and the passions described, to read this book as I might a work of fiction, reading and rereading passages in order to observe the intricate and magical workings of language on history, biography, and, indeed, their telling in a journalistic style. . . . Instead the suspense pulled me through at a faster pace. . . . An invaluable collection of case studies."
—Patsy Baudoin, *The Boston Book Review*

"In plain but poignant prose, Kaufman tells the complex, tragic, but ultimately triumphant and—yes—inspiring stories of five such resourceful and lucky survivors, from the '30s to the present. . . . Kaufman is particularly good on Communism's simultaneous anti-Semitism and exploitation of the Jews against the right."
—Robert Eisner, *The Cleveland Plain Dealer*

"In this impressionistic portrait of a place and its people, Kaufman looks at the lives of those who survived."
—Neely Tucker, *The Detroit Free Press*

"Beautifully written. . . . Engrossing. . . . A balanced account of how and why Jews were disproportionately represented in the leadership of most Eastern European countries. . . . Unlike so many accounts that depict Eastern Europe as a kind of extensive cemetery for Jewish life and culture, this book provides real, if modest, evidence of Jewish resilience and renewal . . . a work of exemplary journalistic research and narrative."
—*Kirkus Reviews*

"Deeply engrossing . . . expertly crafted."
—*Publishers Weekly*

PENGUIN BOOKS

# A HOLE IN THE HEART OF THE WORLD

Jonathan Kaufman is a page-one feature writer for *The Wall Street Journal*. He was a Pulitzer Prize–winning reporter for *The Boston Globe*, where he was Berlin Bureau Chief. He is the author of *Broken Alliance: The Turbulent Times Between Blacks and Jews in America* for which he was awarded the National Jewish Book Award and the Present Tense/American Jewish Committee Award. He lives with his wife and children in Newton, Massachusetts.

Jonathan Kaufman

# A Hole in the Heart of the World

The Jewish Experience
in Eastern Europe after
World War II

PENGUIN BOOKS

For Barb, always

_____

PENGUIN BOOKS
Published by the Penguin Group
Penguin Putnam Inc., 375 Hudson Street,
New York, New York 10014, U.S.A.
Penguin Books Ltd, 27 Wrights Lane,
London W8 5TZ, England
Penguin Books Australia Ltd, Ringwood,
Victoria, Australia
Penguin Books Canada Ltd, 10 Alcorn Avenue,
Toronto, Ontario, Canada M4V 3B2
Penguin Books (N.Z.) Ltd, 182–190 Wairau Road,
Auckland 10, New Zealand

Penguin Books Ltd, Registered Offices:
Harmondsworth, Middlesex, England

First published in the United States of America by
Viking Penguin, a division of Penguin Books USA Inc. 1997
Published in Penguin Books 1998

10   9   8   7   6   5   4   3

THE LIBRARY OF CONGRESS HAS CATALOGUED THE HARDCOVER AS FOLLOWS:
Kaufman, Jonathan.
A hole in the heart of the world: being Jewish in Eastern Europe / Jonathan Kaufman.
p.   cm.
ISBN 0-670-86747-0 (hc.)
ISBN 0 14 02.5453 6 (pbk.)
1. Jews—Europe, Eastern—History—20th century.   2. Holocaust survivors—Europe,
Eastern.   3. Jews—Europe, Eastern—Identity.   4. Jews—Europe, Eastern—Social
life and customs.   5. Europe, Eastern—Ethnic relations.   I. Title.
DS135.E83K38   1997
947'.004924—dc20        96–25656

Printed in the United States of America
Set in Fairfield Light
Designed by Junie Lee

# Contents

*A section of photographs follows page 184.*

Early one morning, twenty people form a line outside a meat store in Moscow. The manager of the store comes out and announces, "Comrades! We will be short of meat today. All Jews leave the line!"

The Jews head home.

A few hours later, rain is falling. The manager comes out again. "Comrades!" he says. "We are still short of meat. Everyone who is not a loyal member of the Communist Party leave the line!"

Another group shuffles off. Only members of the Communist Party remain.

A few hours later, the rain has turned into a downpour. The manager comes out a third time. "Comrades!" he says. "I must be honest. We will have no meat today. You can all go home."

"It's always this way!" one Communist grumbles to another, as they stalk off in the rain. "The Jews always get treated better."

—A joke told in Moscow

*A local version of the same joke was told for forty-five years in Warsaw, Prague, Budapest, Bucharest, and East Berlin.*

# Introduction

*1989*

"You really should visit the synagogue," the concierge at the hotel in Budapest said one afternoon.

I had finished my interviews for the day. The plane did not leave for a few hours. So, like a dutiful tourist, I followed the maze of streets, head buried in my map, hoping I would be able to find this tiny remnant of Jewish culture before I headed off to the airport. The streets twisted and turned. I cut through a shopping arcade and rounded a corner. Suddenly there it was: the Dohany Synagogue, the biggest synagogue I had ever seen. The building spanned an entire block, with stained-glass windows set in the pale facade, gazing out over the busy streets below. Twin domes sat atop the beige brick building, each of them at least six stories high. The synagogue loomed over the busy main street like a fortress or a great cathedral. This was not a small, dusty prayer house tucked away down a narrow side street, the remnant of an insular culture that had filled the crevices of the city. This was a synagogue as grand as Saint Patrick's Cathedral in New York, located in the center of the city. Inside, there was seating for 2,500 beneath a massive domed ceiling etched with gold. Heavy wooden doors cut off the noise from the street. Two balconies ran along the perimeter of the room. The synagogue sat at a majestic angle, slicing the edge off a busy, traffic-choked plaza. It demanded notice and respect—which it deserved, since before World War II it was the chief synagogue for four hundred thousand Jews who had lived in Hungary, many of them in Budapest. Now the cavernous structure echoed with the footsteps of occasional tourists and the hammering of workmen repairing the roof to stop it from crumbling. The Nazis had killed most of Hungary's Jews, but there were still one hundred thousand left in Budapest—survivors of the Nazis, but also their children and grandchildren. They filled the synagogue to capacity on the Jewish High Holidays of Rosh Hashanah and Yom Kippur.

Soon after leaving Budapest, back in Berlin, I became curious about Berlin's synagogues. It was November. The Berlin Wall had just fallen. I took a taxi through what remained of the wall to attend Friday-evening Sabbath services at a synagogue in East Berlin. It had survived the ravages of Kristallnacht, the "Night of Broken Glass," in November 1938, when the Nazis set fire to the synagogues and smashed the windows of Jewish homes and stores in an anti-Semitic rampage, a state-organized pogrom. While hundreds of fires raged throughout the city that night and Nazi storm troopers hurled bricks through the windows of temples, homes, and stores, this synagogue had been spared by geographic luck. It was set back in a courtyard, surrounded and protected by adjoining buildings. The Nazis wanted to burn down the synagogues, not German homes.

The service I attended, sad and depressing, was held in a small room off the lobby, with eight rows of benches. There were a few tourists, some visiting Israelis and Americans, and a handful of elderly East German Jews, looking tired and threadbare. The prayers were led by a cantor; the synagogue had no rabbi. One seat was occupied by my German taxi driver, who had asked if he could come in; he remembered taking Jews to pray there in the 1950s, before the Berlin Wall had gone up. The prayer books were frayed and falling apart at the spine. Stickers inside their front covers logged who had donated them to the synagogue and when. No sticker bore a date later than 1938, the year of Kristallnacht.

After the service, I stayed to talk with the cantor, an elderly man who had lived his entire life under the Nazis and then under the Communists. I remarked how small the synagogue seemed. "Oh, this is the small chapel," he said, gesturing around the small room we had just prayed in. The main synagogue lay across the lobby. The Nazis, he said, had used it as a stable.

I walked through the wooden doors into the synagogue itself. Above me, the ceiling soared upward. The walls glistened bright white. As in Budapest, there were seats for more than two thousand people. The floors, where Nazi officers had once stabled their horses, were highly polished. Before the Berlin Wall fell, the Communists had spent hundreds of thousands of dollars restoring the synagogue to its prewar glory, hoping to impress American Jews, who they believed could open the door to the American government and win East Germany respectability. But the main synagogue was rarely used; there were not enough Jews to occupy it. The Communists reckoned there were no more than a few hundred Jews left in East Berlin, maybe a few thousand in all of East Germany. Even on the Jewish holidays of Rosh Hashanah and Yom Kippur, when the least observant of Jews felt obliged to put in an appearance, the temple never attracted more than a hundred congregants. They sat scattered among the old benches like expectant passengers in a cavernous train station. This was the largest synagogue left in Berlin, East or West. Before World War II, there had been ninety-nine synagogues in Berlin. Now just six remained.

A few days later, as I rushed down the streets of Prague in the chaotic days of the "Velvet Revolution" that toppled the Communists and brought Vaclav Havel to power, I suddenly heard a chorus of voices that came from a small, monastery-like building—gray stone with an orange high-peaked roof—set just off the street near Prague's fairy-tale-like Old Town Square. It sounded like the chanting of monks. I stopped to investigate, stepping down through a narrow doorway into a nave with windows set high into the wall. It was in fact a synagogue, dating back to the twelfth or thirteenth century. The sound I heard were the prayers of Jewish men, seated in ornately carved wooden chairs. Above their heads flew banners that the Czech Jewish community had first hoisted in public celebrations honoring the Holy Roman Emperor in 1357. Outside, across the alley, stood a pink building with a clock tower. Its two clocks could be seen for blocks around. One had Roman numerals; the other had Hebrew letters instead of numbers on the dial. This was the Jewish Town Hall, the heart of Prague's old Jewish community, located just a few blocks from the Old Town Square. The soft pink of the clock tower echoed the pastel colors of the palaces and merchant houses that lay around it. This was a community that saw itself sitting not in the shadow of the rest of the city, but alongside it as an equal partner.

We are all captives of the movies that play in our minds when we visit new places. As I traveled around Germany and Eastern Europe those days after the Berlin Wall fell, the movie in my head was *Fiddler on the Roof*. When I thought of Jews in Eastern Europe, I visualized Jews crammed into crowded villages, singing songs about tradition, busily trying to marry off their daughters by day, by night warding off the rage of local anti-Semites. Or I remembered the grainy black-and-white pictures of frightened Jewish women in head scarves, clutching their children as they were herded onto the trains for Auschwitz. None of those images prepared me for the richness and vibrancy, the wealth and power, that Jews had wielded in Germany and Eastern Europe before World War II. Berlin before Hitler was much like New York today. Over 150,000 Jews lived in Berlin, many of them extremely prominent and wealthy. Jews lived in the city's best neighborhoods and edited Germany's best newspapers. The big department stores that lined the Kurfürstendamm, Berlin's elegant main shopping street, were all owned by Jews. On the eve of Hitler's takeover in 1933, 75 percent of the plays opening in Berlin were written or directed by Jews.

In Warsaw before the Second World War, 40 percent of the lawyers were Jewish; in Budapest, Jews had been so instrumental in building up the country's banks and railroads that many were invited to join the nobility.

All this flew in the face of the images that danced through my head of Jews who were poor, deeply religious, and cloistered into ghettos or small villages. The pre–World War II Jews whose ghosts I now encountered—the Jews who thronged the big synagogue in downtown Budapest, who left their nameplates in the prayer books in Berlin, who stopped by the Jewish Town Hall on their way to the ancient and venerable synagogue in Prague— were more often than not middle class and assimilated. They went to the opera and voted for liberal political parties. They were Jewish on the Sabbath or when it came time for Passover or Hanukkah. But the other six days in the week, they viewed themselves as simply Hungarian or Polish, German or Czech. They were like many American Jews I know. They were, in a chilling way, much like me.

And now there was nothing. In East Berlin, a few Jews scattered in the seats in the synagogue, each empty seat and worn, long-unused prayer book a reminder of what had been lost; in Budapest, a plaque on an apartment house wall marking the border of the ghetto the Nazis had built to hold the Jews; in Warsaw and towns across Poland, cemeteries choked with weeds because there was no one left to care for them. If these had been small, marginal communities, perhaps the loss would be easier to bear. But all around Germany and Eastern Europe, from Berlin to Prague to Budapest to Warsaw, Eastern Europeans were throwing off Communism for freedom and democracy. They were insisting on being called "Central Europeans," so that people would no longer associate them with the Soviet Union and Communism and the gray monolith of the Warsaw Pact. They were trying to reclaim their role at the center of European life and world civilization. Yet something was missing. Destroying the Jews had not just wounded this part of the world. It had ripped out its heart.

Much has been written about what the Holocaust did to Jews. But little has been said about what it did to Germany, Czechoslovakia, Hungary, and Poland—how it deprived these countries of generations of artists, scientists, writers, entrepreneurs; even more, of an entire worldview.

Before the rise of the Nazis, Germans were the most frequent recipients of the Nobel Prize. Between 1901, the first year the prize was awarded, and 1933, six Germans won the Nobel Prize for medicine, more than scientists in any other country. After 1933, Germany's Nobel laureates were few and far between. One-quarter of the Nobel Prize winners in medicine after 1933 were of German-Jewish origin. None lived in Germany.

In Czechoslovakia before World War II, Jews shaped Prague's emergence as a cultural and literary capital. "Inside every citizen of Prague," Franz Kafka wrote, "there is a Czech, a Jew, and a German"—a testament to Prague's role as the cultural crossing point of Central Europe, where a German-speaking Jewish elite nurtured writers like Kafka and turned Prague into the hub of Central European culture. The Jews of Prague were the soil from which this creative explosion sprung. They were the readers who bought German books, the cognoscenti who attended German plays, the audience that dressed in black tie and lavish gowns and took the train to Vienna to see the opera. They fostered a cosmopolitan "Central European culture," which crossed from Prague to Vienna, from Budapest to Berlin, and then back to Prague, giving the region much of its identity.

But now the Jews were gone. And there was an emptiness in Central Europe—a hole—that haunted those who remained, even if they could not quite bring themselves to acknowledge what it was. In reunited Germany, scholars held conferences on "Why Germany Lacks a Sense of Humor," which droned on for days before acknowledging that a main reason was that most of Germany's great satirists and comedians before World War II had been Jews. In Poland, it became common to hear Poles lament, "We are trying to rebuild our country with our bodies, but we are missing the head." The Jews had disappeared. To understand the synergy of Central Europe and its Jews, to understand the energy that flowed through Budapest in 1900, Prague in 1910, Berlin in the 1920s, Warsaw in the 1930s, consider the role Jews played in New York in the second half of the twentieth century. And imagine what New York would be like—its culture, literary life, and politics—if the city were suddenly bereft of Jews.

Nor had the annihilation of the Jews of Germany and Eastern Europe been solely the work of the Nazis, as many wanted to believe.

Though most people today do not realize it, Hitler did not succeed in wiping out Eastern European Jews. Hitler had managed
within a few years to murder six out of every seven Jews in
Eastern Europe. But when the war ended, there were still
700,000 Jews left in Eastern Europe: 140,000 in Hungary; 51,000
in Czechoslovakia; 50,000 in Poland, plus another 250,000 who
had fled to Russia when the Germans first invaded; 428,000 in
Romania; even 25,000 in Germany—mostly spouses of non-Jews,
survivors of the concentration camps and death marches. Not a
large community by any means, but certainly enough to rebuild a
society leavened once again with Jewish influence and benefiting
from the richness of Jewish life, laughter, and achievement.

That never happened. The Communists, often with the enthusiastic backing of those they ruled, chose instead to hound Jews
from their countries, leaving a legacy of anti-Semitism and intoler-
ance that fermented long after the Nazis had left.

And yet, at the same time, Jews seemed to be everywhere after
the fall of the Berlin Wall.

Soon after visiting the sad synagogue in East Berlin, I returned
to see the ruins of another large synagogue, on nearby Oranienburger Strasse, once the grandest synagogue in Berlin, perhaps in
all of Europe. In the shadow of this great synagogue, offices for
three separate Jewish organizations had sprung up—one for East
German Jews who wanted to become part of the West German
Jewish community; another for East German Jews who wanted to
remain Communists; and a third for East German Jews who
wanted nothing to do with the first two groups. None of the
groups was talking to the others. They were feuding—always a
sign of a healthy Jewish community. There might be only four
hundred Jews in East Berlin, but now, with the Berlin Wall down,
they seemed to have four hundred and one opinions. They had
even set up rival kosher cafés.

In Prague under Communism, the Jewish community had
become so small that the city's Jews often scoured hotel lobbies
to search out Jewish tourists to complete a minyan, the ten
men required to start a Jewish service. Now, five months after the

collapse of Communism, there were two community seders at Passover. One was sponsored by the official Jewish community, whose average member was seventy-one years old. It was held downstairs in the kosher restaurant of the frayed Jewish community center, around the corner from the Jewish Town Hall. The other seder, crammed with young Jews from mixed marriages or Jews who had recently discovered they were Jewish or Jews who felt the old, established Jewish community was just too stodgy, was held upstairs. It was a boisterous and uproarious Passover seder, with people laughing and talking until late in the evening. They talked about inviting rabbis from other countries to teach them more Hebrew, so they could sing even more prayers and songs next year.

In Budapest, the Jewish community opened three Jewish schools. They became so popular that there were three applicants for every spot. Many of the applicants were non-Jews who wanted a good education for their children—and figured the Jews knew how to provide good schools. Jews taking advantage of the collapse of Communism and the end of censorship formed a new Jewish magazine. After a few months, several disgruntled staffers left to form a second Jewish magazine.

Like wildflowers that sprout from the ashes of a forest fire once the overhead brush falls away to let in the sunlight, Jews were emerging from the shadows and blossoming into life.

Even more stunning were Jews appearing at the top of the new non-Communist governments. In Poland, where the Holocaust had wiped out the largest Jewish community in Europe and there was supposed to be only a handful of Jews left, two of Lech Walesa's top advisers were Jewish—Adam Michnik, one of Poland's leading dissidents under Communism, and Bromeslaw Geremek, who now chaired the parliament's foreign affairs committee. In East Berlin on November 4, 1989, just before the Berlin Wall fell, three of the people who had spoken to the cheering crowd of one million calling for democracy and freedom were Jewish, including East Germany's leading dissident writer, its leading dissident lawyer, and the head of East Germany's feared spying network. Odd bedfellows indeed! In Romania, the new prime minister named after the fall of Nicolae Ceauşescu was Peter Roman, the grandson of a rabbi.

I had come to Europe familiar with the Holocaust but, like most Americans, ignorant about what happened afterward. Jewish life had been shrouded behind the Iron Curtain. That there were any Jews at all in Germany and Eastern Europe after Hitler and Stalin was remarkable. Who were these Jews who had survived Hitler and Stalin and forty-five years of Communism? Who were their children? Why had they stayed? How had they coped?

I decided to seek the answers to these questions through the lives of five families—four Jewish and one Catholic. Together, their stories reveal much of the hidden history of Jews in Eastern Europe.

Klaus Gysi was not the kind of man Jewish children in the United States learned about in Sunday school. He was a Communist and a top member of the East German government. Gysi had joined the Communist Party in the 1920s and climbed steadily, sometimes ruthlessly, through the ranks, becoming minister of culture and secretary of religious affairs. Everyone who had met him told me that Klaus Gysi was the most interesting Communist they had ever met—clever, witty, irreverent. And everyone traced that, somehow, to his being Jewish. Klaus Gysi, people said, was the kind of Communist who made Communism seem charming. His son, Gregor, was equally fascinating. He had become a lawyer in East Germany and in the 1980s found himself increasingly drawn to defend Communism's opponents. After the fall of the Berlin Wall, Gregor Gysi emerged as head of the new, reformed Communist Party in a reunited Germany and one of the most charismatic politicians in Germany. Neither Klaus nor Gregor Gysi had ever considered his religion important. Each was, on the surface, a good Communist atheist. But when Germany reunited and Gregor Gysi emerged as a leading political figure, he suddenly became the target of anti-Semitic hate mail. It rattled him, and he groped for answers. The story of the Gysis, father and son, spanned Germany's history from the rise of the Nazis to the collapse of the Communists. It touched on many of the twists and turns of Jewish life in Germany and Eastern Europe: the romance of many Jews with Socialism and Communism; the compromises Jews, like others, were compelled to make under a Communist regime; the uneasy future of Jews in a united Germany. It also opened a window onto a rich family conflict. Just as his contemporaries had rebelled against their parents in the United States in the 1960's, so Gregor Gysi had rebelled against his father. As the Communist minister of culture in East Germany, Klaus Gysi banned capitalist rock and roll; Gregor listened to it secretly at home. In the United States, teenagers had rebelled against the Vietnam War; in East Germany, against the 1968 Soviet invasion of Czechoslovakia. Gregor came to question many of the principles his father held dear.

Estrongo Nachama was a concentration camp survivor who became cantor of West Berlin's small Jewish community after the end of World War II and was one of the few people allowed free access between East and West Germany during the Cold War. He crossed through the Berlin Wall regularly to officiate at weddings and funerals in East Berlin, often smuggling food and medical supplies to the dwindling Jewish population there. His son, Andreas, was a historian who played a pivotal role in bringing Germans face-to-face with their history and the Holocaust. Both felt at home as Jews in Germany—until the Berlin Wall fell and attacks on synagogues and foreigners soared. Within days of the fall of the wall, a Jewish cemetery was desecrated in East Berlin. A few weeks later, someone sent a pig's head to the small Leipzig synagogue in East Germany.

Neo-Nazi gangs sprang up across East and West Germany, marching through the streets brandishing the Heil Hitler salute and distributing pamphlets emblazoned with the swastika. By 1991, Germany was awash in a flood of anti-Semitic and anti-foreigner violence. By 1992, there were 2,285 incidents of right-wing violence, resulting in seventeen deaths. Jews were targets, but so were Romanians, Turks, and Gypsies. Thirty percent of Germans responding to surveys said they "understood" the anger of the neo-Nazis. Estrongo Nachama became enraged; his son was worried and concerned.

Many of the attacks against Jews and foreigners were taking place not in East Germany, where people had lived under Communism for forty-five years and had never been taught the full truth about the Holocaust, where massive unemployment and disorienting political change were confusing teenagers and adults alike. They were occurring in stable, prosperous West Germany, in otherwise well-manicured towns like Solingen, famed for its fine Henkel cutlery, a place with neat rows of houses and clean streets—where in 1993 neo-Nazis firebombed a house and killed five Turks, including two small girls who had spent their entire lives in Germany and spoke German fluently. City officials insisted they had never had problems with anti-foreign feelings. But police found a swastika carved into the sandbox of the neighborhood playground. There were incidents in cosmopolitan West Berlin, with its large Turkish population and small but proud Jewish community—where many dark-skinned foreigners were now afraid to travel the subway at night for fear of running into neo-Nazi gangs. At the West Berlin synagogue where Estrongo Nachama had sung for forty-five years, they had long had a metal detector at the entrance to protect against Arab terrorism. Now the metal detector was exposing non-Jewish Germans armed with knives and brass knuckles, trying to attend Sabbath services. What was happening to Germany?

Estrongo Nachama urged his forty-year-old son, Andreas, to pack up his family and leave Germany. Andreas resisted but discreetly began looking into jobs outside the country—harking back to a time, fifty years earlier, when his grandparents had begun to plan their unsuccessful escape from the Nazis. The story of the Nachamas and their evolving attitudes toward Germany from the end of World War II through the fall of the Berlin Wall illuminate the complex, shifting, and always tortured history of relations between Germans and Jews in the shadow of the Holocaust.

Tamas Raj was a rabbi turned dissident in Hungary. After the 1967 Six Day War, he was dismissed from his pulpit by Hungary's Communist-controlled Jewish leaders, who considered him too popular and too supportive of Israel. Raj had survived World War II as a child and had been brought up under the totalitarian

Communism that descended upon Eastern Europe after 1945. The trauma of the Holocaust and the relentless persecutions by the Communists had turned many of the Jews remaining in Eastern Europe into victims—helpless before the changing political forces that swirled around them. Raj was a resister. For more than twenty years, he had waged an underground war to preserve and nurture Jewish life. Secretly, Raj taught Hebrew classes and classes in Jewish history in his living room. His students were ordinary Jews and political dissidents. His life underground in Hungary in the 1970s and 1980s shed light on the remarkable ways in which Jews had kept their faith and hope alive while most people in the West, and most Americans, were writing about the "disappearance" of Eastern European Jews.

Sylvia Wittmann was a 33-year-old Czech woman who looked and acted as if she belonged in funky Greenwich Village rather than in the historic streets of Prague. When I first met her, she was plastering the buildings of the city's old Jewish ghetto with flyers announcing her Jewish tour service. She was, she said, considering becoming a rabbi. She had started a Jewish congregation in the basement of her house. She was learning about feminism and Hasidism. Sylvia's embrace of Judaism reflected the rebirth of Judaism that was taking place among young people throughout Eastern Europe, liberated from years of Communism. It was all the more poignant because the men and women spearheading the eclectic revival were, like Sylvia, often the sons and daughters of parents who had striven to bury their pasts under anti-Semitic Communist regimes. Sylvia's mother had been imprisoned by the Communists in the 1950s as a "Zionist agent" and had never talked about her background to her daughter—until Sylvia, like thousands of others, stumbled upon it and began to fan the embers back to flame.

"The Jews have given up on the Germans. But they still hate the Poles," a Polish Catholic writer said to me one evening in his apartment. "Why is that?" Barbara Asendrych, a Pole and a Catholic, was an example of why. Like so many Poles, her family had borne silent witness to the sufferings of the Jews during World War II and in the years afterward. They had benefited by the destruction of the Jews. Barbara's godmother lived in a small town, Zelechow, in a house the Nazis had seized from Jews and then turned over to poorer Poles. In Warsaw after the war, Barbara's mother had moved to a larger apartment in what had once been the Jewish ghetto, after the last Jews were killed in the futile resistance of the Warsaw ghetto uprising. Barbara was not an anti-Semite, though she told the occasional Jewish joke. Who in Poland did not? But her life reflected the deep antagonisms between Poles and Jews that lasted even after there were hardly any Jews left for Poles to hate.

The story that unfolds here is divided into four parts. Part I traces the prewar history of the families and their experiences from the defeat of the Nazis in 1945 to the descent of the Iron Curtain and the triumph of Communist rule by 1948. Part II looks at the fate of these families and Jewish life under Communist rule from 1948 to 1968, when the Communists strove to complete what Hitler began: the extermination of Jewish life in Eastern Europe. In Part III, the focus shifts to the second generation, the sons and daughters of the survivors of the Holocaust. For them, the Soviet invasion of Czechoslovakia in 1968 marked the start of a political awakening and laid the groundwork for an astonishing rebirth of Jewish life through the 1970s and 1980s. Part IV looks at the fates of these families in the new world created by the fall of the Berlin Wall in 1989. The final chapter reflects on the experiences of both generations and what the future may hold.

Before the narrative begins, however, we describe a moment frozen in time—Thursday, November 9, 1989, the day the Berlin Wall fell. That day changed forever the lives of millions of Eastern Europeans. And it ripped down the screen that long had hidden Jewish life in Eastern Europe.

# Chapter One

# "They Will Have Their Ceremonies, and We Will Have Ours"

*West Berlin*

It was a cool day, the sky thick with clouds—a harbinger of the bleak winter that East Berliners call the "suicide months." The acrid stench of burning coal soured the air. The sky was gray; color would not return until April.

On Bornholmer Strasse, in the center of what had once been a united city, the gray face of the Berlin Wall—actually two parallel walls, with a grassy no-man's-land between—loomed up, splitting the street in half. On the eastern side, soldiers in twin guard towers kept watch over the no-man's-land and peered into the West through high-powered binoculars. On the western side, a Berlin police officer atop a wooden observation platform gazed back impassively.

It had been like that for twenty-eight years. No one saw any chance that it would change anytime soon.

Estrongo Nachama, who had survived the Nazi death camps to become the cantor for a West Berlin synagogue, left his office at the Jewish Community Center on Fasanen Strasse, climbed into his Ford, turned left out of the parking lot, and headed home. Although Nachama had lived in Germany for almost forty-five years, he refused to buy a German car. His family observed, out of his earshot, that the Ford he drove, like the Mercedes or the BMW he could easily have afforded, was made in Germany. But,

Estrongo Nachama insisted, those were *German* cars. At seventy-two, Nachama still cut an imposing figure, carrying himself like a man used to commanding attention. He was short, barrel-chested, with swept-back black hair and deep, penetrating eyes. When he was a young man, his face had been movie star handsome, and his clear baritone caused his family to believe that he might forsake the family grain business and study to be a cantor. Nachama was not German but Greek. The Nazis had rounded up his family in Salonika and sent them to concentration camps in Poland. His family was killed; miraculously, Nachama survived. He still carried the number from Auschwitz tattooed on his arm—116155. He ended up in Berlin after the war and never left. He had made his provisional peace with Germany. Nachama had nothing bad to say about the West Germans. He returned to Greece only for occasional vacations. Nachama had thought for a time of being an opera singer, but in 1947 he was pressed into service as the cantor of the still damaged synagogue on Pestalozzi Strasse in West Berlin's fashionable Charlottenburg district. Before the war, the synagogue had been home to a small Orthodox congregation. After the war, with most of Berlin's synagogues in ruins and the number of Jews reduced to a handful, the Pestalozzi Strasse synagogue slowly reemerged to become Berlin's preeminent temple, filled with the city's increasingly prosperous Jewish community. After services on the Jewish High Holidays, the congregation tumbled out the doors into a small courtyard in front of the synagogue, dressed in their fashionable coats and well-cut suits, their children scampering around noisily. Nachama's reputation grew as well. He sang every Friday night and Saturday morning, recorded traditional Jewish prayers on records, performed concerts, and broadcast Friday-night Sabbath services over West Berlin radio. Nachama still spoke the simple, accented German of an immigrant. But when he sang, his voice shook the room and reached down into people's souls.

From the looks of the Pestalozzi Strasse synagogue, or the streets leading to Nachama's home, Berlin seemed like any other bustling, prosperous European city. Shoppers thronged the streets, café tables spilled out onto the sidewalks. Here in the center of

West Berlin, the idea of the Berlin Wall seemed absurd—a twelve-foot-high wall dividing a city in half! From these fashionable streets the wall could not even be seen. But take a ride in any direction, and it always loomed up suddenly at the end of a street or around a corner, like the curtains at the side of a stage that abruptly remind actors, "What you are doing is not real life. Real life lies outside this curtain." The Berlin Wall did not just cut Berlin in half; it encircled West Berlin, creating a rich, sparkling enclave right in the middle of Communist East Germany. To get from West Berlin to West Germany, travelers had to cross through two separate checkpoints—once when they left the city and entered East Germany; another four hours later, when they finally crossed the East German border into West Germany again. These transit roads bridging West Berlin and the rest of West Germany were the fastest highways in East Germany but no match for the no-speed-limit West German autobahns, where cars regularly exceeded 100 mph. Nor was there much for West Berliners to do on the long car trips in and out of Berlin; they were not permitted to hop off at an exit and explore the countryside. Control towers with armed guards posted at off ramps saw to it that East and West did not come together. West German travelers had to stay on the highway, stopping only at approved roadside service stations that sold gas, liquor, and chocolate for West German marks—an efficient way for East Germany to get some much-needed hard currency. Living walled in made some West Berliners claustrophobic. Because West Berlin served an important political purpose for West Germany—it was the primary symbol of the Cold War—the West German government offered inducements to settle there. Money was lavished on concerts, cultural events, and parks. Compulsory service in the German army was waived for young residents. As a result, the city was an odd mix of pensioners, leftists, and members of the counterculture. It was in many ways the most un-German city in Germany—cosmopolitan, freewheeling, with a certain spirit that came from living in an absurd situation, on the edge of the Cold War.

For four decades, Nachama had been one of the few West Germans regularly permitted to go *nach drüben*—"over there"—to the other side of the Berlin Wall. Several times a month, he passed through the checkpoints to officiate at occasional bar mitzvahs or weddings and far more frequent funerals. Over the years, he had smuggled in medicines, and fruits and vegetables to Jews who needed them. He was a familiar figure at the border checkpoints, and the guards routinely waved him past. His radio broadcast of Friday-night Sabbath services could be heard in East Berlin and had a devoted following. When elderly Jewish ladies in East Germany recalled Nachama singing in the 1940s and 1950s, the years melted from their faces. They talked about Estrongo Nachama as if he were Frank Sinatra.

Though Nachama had been sent to Auschwitz, he did not hate the Germans. He had married a German-Jewish woman whose wartime experience had been as harrowing as his own. She had hidden in Berlin for the entire war, a teenage girl changing houses from one month to the next, fearful of being caught and deported. His son was German, married to an Israeli but living in Berlin. His grandchildren lived here too. Nachama was not one of those Jews in Germany who always "sat on packed suitcases," convinced the Nazis might return at any moment and force the Jews to flee. He had his music and his family and the love and respect of thousands of Germans—not just the Jews but Gentile Germans who listened to his radio programs and packed his concerts, finding solace in the traditional melodies that reminded them of the rich Jewish flavor that had once infused Berlin.

Today was a day packed to overflowing with significance: It was November 9, 1989, the anniversary of the night in 1938 when the Nazis unleashed their pogrom against Germany's Jews, burning synagogues, looting Jewish-owned stores, smashing windows in shops, synagogues, and Jewish homes. If anyone still had any doubts what the Nazis had planned for the Jews, Kristallnacht erased them. From that November night to the end of World War II, six and a half years later, the fate of the Jews in Berlin, and then across Europe, marched inexorably from terror to deportation to mass murder.

Dates and anniversaries carried special weight in Germany. When someone died before a landmark birthday—fifty or seventy-five or a hundred—newspapers often noted the passing with special sadness. November 9 was a landmark day for

Germans for many reasons. It was the anniversary of Kristall-nacht. But it was also the date Germany's Kaiser abdicated following Germany's defeat in World War I. It was also the date Germany had founded the ill-fated Weimar Republic. And it was also the date when Adolf Hitler launched his Munich beer hall putsch in 1923, the first attempt by the Nazis to seize control of the German government. The coup was crushed; the Nazis were voted into power nine years later. Some speculated that the Nazis chose November 9 for Kristallnacht in part to commemorate Hitler's putsch. One could argue that for German history, and for most West Germans, the creation of the Weimar Republic and Hitler's failed putsch were probably as significant as, if not more important than, Kristallnacht. But West Germany was the world's prime example of the maxim that history is written by the victors. West Germany was regularly, and correctly, forced to bow its head and acknowledge its catastrophic past. November 9, whatever its resonance for Germans, had become the day to commemorate Kristallnacht. It was the day West Germany remembered the Jews.

In recent years, November 9 commemorations in Berlin and elsewhere in West Germany had developed a routine, even ritualistic quality. West German politicians attended somber ceremonies, trying to convince constituents at home, and foreigners abroad, that the Germans had changed and put the past behind them. Many younger Germans chafed at always having to apologize for being German. Some especially chafed at having to apologize to Jews, when Israel, as they charged, was oppressing the Palestinians. Wasn't that as bad as what the Nazis had done? they asked. No matter what West Germans said or did, it never seemed enough. In America, in Europe, in their own self-reflective moments, the weight of the Holocaust smothered them, like the thick gray clouds in an autumnal Berlin sky. As they swept through Munich and Paris and London on business or traveled across Europe on vacation, buoyed by their powerful economy and swelling incomes, West Germans projected a robust self-confidence, even an arrogance. But most still became tentative and unsure when they met someone Jewish.

This year, 1989, had been no different. Indeed, in the first week of November, an incident took place that revealed the insensitivity and awkwardness of the Germans when they dealt with Jews, even when they tried to do the right thing. Helmut Kohl, the German chancellor, a hulking man of formidable size and iron will, had gone east to Poland to meet with the new, non-Communist government that had suddenly risen to power over the summer—the first crack in the Iron Curtain in almost forty-five years. Kohl had taken with him Heinz Galinski, then the leader of Germany's small Jewish community. As a gesture of reconciliation—ritualistic but important—Kohl planned that the two men visit Auschwitz, the German death camp in Poland where Galinski himself had been imprisoned. Kohl's aides scheduled the visit for Saturday, the Jewish Sabbath. Galinski, who like most religious Jews would not participate in a public ceremony on a Saturday, refused to go.

Fifty-one years after Kristallnacht, nearly forty-five years after the end of World War II, there was no one on the staff of the German chancellor to point out that it was insensitive to ask Germany's preeminent Jewish leader to visit Auschwitz on the Jewish Sabbath.

The visit of Galinski and Kohl to Auschwitz was rescheduled for Sunday, November 12.

Nachama shook his head when he heard of the episode. He tried to stay out of politics. On the afternoon of November 9 the mayor of West Berlin came to the Jewish Community Center on Fasanen Strasse for the Berlin commemoration of Kristallnacht, along with other officials. Nachama sang the haunting Jewish prayer of mourning in his rich baritone. He hated the politicians horning in on these Kristallnacht ceremonies with all their speeches. Why should they even be there? The Germans hadn't suffered, Nachama reasoned. The Jews had suffered! At times like this Nachama preferred the synagogues and ceremonies over in Communist East Berlin. During services there, the synagogue was virtually empty, of course. But at least there were no politicians giving speeches.

Nachama drove past the elegant Kempinski Hotel on the Kurfürstendamm and headed home. He climbed the four flights to the home he shared with his wife, a spacious, high-ceilinged

apartment filled with mementos of his decades of singing.
Nachama flipped on the television. So much had been happening
in the past few months. The Iron Curtain was beginning to
weaken; Poland had conducted its first free elections; Lech
Walesa and Solidarity had won a surprise victory. All summer,
thousands of East Germans had been taking trains to Hungary
and Czechoslovakia to escape into the West, embarrassing the
East German government. Then, the previous month, in October,
massive weekly demonstrations erupted in Leipzig. Each Monday,
tens of thousands of East Germans, in defiance of their Communist rulers, converged and, in a silent candlelight procession,
marched around the ring road that encircled the center of town.
As the demonstrations swelled in size, they became bolder. Soon
marchers were carrying signs reading "We Are the People" and
demanding free elections. Nachama's son, Andreas, who had
been visiting East Germany all year to set up a museum exhibit,
told his father that he sensed something big was happening. On
the other side of the wall, five days earlier, in the center of East
Berlin, a million people had gathered to demand an honest legal
system and the right to travel freely.

On television, a startled reporter was standing in front of the
Berlin Wall. The camera switched to images of East Berliners
streaming through checkpoints in their tinny, bright-colored
cars—green and orange and yellow—and on foot past apathetic
East German soldiers. West Berliners were pounding happily on
car roofs and spraying champagne on bewildered East Germans as
they flooded into the western sector.

The phone rang. Nachama's daughter-in-law was shouting over
the phone: "You won't believe what is happening!"

The Berlin Wall had fallen.

The German superstition about anniversaries had been confirmed again. Nachama watched the flickering television screen.
The irony was not lost on him. Now the Germans would forever
remember November 9 as the night the Berlin Wall fell; the Jews
would still remember Kristallnacht. They will have their ceremonies, and we will have ours, Nachama thought. The Germans
will celebrate. And we, the Jews, will mourn.

But Nachama was not upset. That would come later. Within a year, he would be enraged, terrified of the rise of neo-Nazi violence in a reunited Germany, urging his son and grandchildren to flee the country, lamenting that he and his wife were too old to adjust to a new life somewhere else. But on this euphoric night he, like most Germans, was happy—the Germans over in East Germany could now be free.

*East Berlin*

The apartment overlooking Leipziger Strasse in East Berlin was an abode of privilege, a reward for loyalty to the Communist regime. Many East Germans waited a decade or more to move from a one-room to a two-room flat. Klaus Gysi's apartment had three bedrooms and a spacious living room and dining room. The parquet floors were covered with woven wool carpets. But most striking were the books. The walls everywhere were lined floor to ceiling with bookcases—not just in the living room but in the hallways that snaked from room to room. There were books crammed end to end on the shelves, with more tucked in on their sides—artbooks, novels, nonfiction; in German, English, and French. The walls that did not contain books held carefully framed paintings and prints, all obviously original, many of them inscribed to Gysi or his wife.

But the Gysis' apartment was also a place of exile. Klaus Gysi, now 77, had sat at the levers of power in East Germany—as minister of culture and ambassador to Italy, most recently as secretary of religious affairs overseeing Communist control of East German churches. The tumult unfolding in the streets below did not surprise him. He had seen the fuse burning. For almost a decade, the church groups he was supposed to keep in check had increasingly chafed at any efforts to be controlled. Gysi sympathized. He had become friends with many of the men and women of the church, sharing their learned conversations and wide-ranging knowledge; they were so different from the Communist bureaucrats who did not know their Bible or their Marx. When Mikhail Gorbachev came to power in 1985, Gysi had hoped that change would follow. But it did not. The Politburo, his old Communist comrades, were too stubborn. It was as if they were caught in a time warp, still living in the Germany of the 1940s and the early days of the Cold War rather than in the 1980s.

Just a month earlier, in October, Gorbachev had visited East Germany to celebrate its fortieth anniversary, a grand pageant of red flags and missile launchers, ranks of goose-stepping soldiers and interminable speeches. Erich Honecker, the seventy-seven-year-old ruler of East Germany, had been Gorbachev's host. The crisis was building. All summer long, thousands of East Germans had been filling trains to Hungary and Czechoslovakia. They claimed they were going on vacation. But once in these countries, the East Germans were seeking political asylum and escape to the West. The Hungarians would not send them back, and the Czechs didn't know what to do. The East Germans crammed into the grounds of the West German embassy in Prague, demanding asylum; they filled the streets leading to the embassy entrance. East Germany was hemorrhaging people. Most damning of all was that these were not dissidents and malcontents; they were handsome young workers with families, and they told West German television stations that they would rather start over in West Germany with nothing than have their children brought up in the hopeless, stifling Socialism of East Germany. The Monday-night demonstrations in Leipzig had become an embarrassment, growing bolder every week, until East Germans were marching and chanting their slogans of protest right under the nose of the headquarters of the feared East German secret police, the Stasi. Honecker and his regime seemed paralyzed. Short of massacring the people marching in Leipzig—the Tiananmen option, the hardliners called it, referring to the Communist Chinese decision to call in tanks and mow down demonstrators in Beijing five months earlier—the Communists did not know what to do. As he accompanied Gorbachev to the airport on the last day of the Soviet leader's visit, Honecker prattled on about new Socialist housing construction and grand plans for East Germany's future. Gorbachev cut him off. "Those who wait too long," he warned, "will be overcome by history."

Three weeks after Gorbachev left, his warning became a

reality. The younger members of the East German Politburo, fearing Honecker's intransigence was threatening their own power, toppled the old man in a bloodless coup. They installed a young leader, Egon Krenz. But the demonstrations continued, spreading from Leipzig to East Berlin, where one out of every four people worked for either the Communist Party or the government. On November 4, Klaus Gysi's own son, Gregor, had spoken to a million people in the center of East Berlin. Bespectacled and balding, protected by his father's influence but also scorning it, Gregor Gysi was a loyal Communist. He had been trying for almost a decade to change the East German system from within. A lawyer, he had begun by defending dissidents in East German courts. It was a thankless job and one that seemed to radicalize him. He had become increasingly bold over the years, clashing with his father, taking on more and more "subversive" clients who were calling for democracy. And now, a few days before the fall of the wall, a million people had cheered as Gregor Gysi, son of the old Communist Klaus Gysi, called for the rule of law in East Germany, and the right of East Germans to travel freely.

Klaus Gysi had few illusions about East Germany. His friends said they always heard the best jokes belittling the Politburo at Klaus Gysi's birthday parties. But he had always been loyal to his country. He had hidden in Germany once, during the Third Reich. But not, he insisted, because he was Jewish. It was because he was a Communist and a fighter against Fascism. Indeed, it did not occur to him—nor would he think it odd years later—that in a country that had just a few hundred Jews, three of the people who had spoken at the giant anti-Communist rally in Berlin a few days earlier were Jews: his old comrade Markus Wolf, who had been East Germany's top spymaster; one of East Germany's best writers, Stefan Heym; and Gregor.

And now, on November 9, noises rose up from Leipziger Strasse into the apartment where the Gysis were finishing dinner. The Gysis fancied Italian wine, though a good French wine was always welcome. That night they were eating Chinese food, carefully cooked by Klaus's wife, Birgid. It was their wedding anniversary, and they had invited some friends to join them in a celebration.

Klaus Gysi turned on the television. This close to the wall, East Germans—even loyal Communist East Germans like Klaus Gysi—got their news from West Berlin television stations. The West Berlin broadcasters had long ago boosted their signals so that most East Germans could receive West German signals on their televisions and radios. The East Germans had given up trying to jam them years ago. Better that the East Germans be narcotized by the West German game shows and soap operas than have yet another reason to hate the Communist regime. The news Klaus Gysi saw told the same story Estrongo Nachama had just learned a few miles away: the Berlin Wall had fallen!

The Gysis and their dinner guests hurried to the balcony and peered down at the jubilant crowd surging along the street to cross through the wall into West Berlin.

Before World War II, Leipziger Strasse had led directly into Potsdamer Platz, the busiest intersection in all of continental Europe, Berlin's Piccadilly Circus. The young Klaus Gysi had walked up Leipziger Strasse, past the large department stores and bustling shops, many of them owned by Jews. He had passed through Potsdamer Platz on the way to a Communist Party meeting attended by Albert Einstein. But that was more than fifty years ago. The Nazis had murdered the Jews. The Communists had closed the department stores. A silent, windswept Potsdamer Platz now lay in a swath that stretched between the two concrete walls that made up the Berlin Wall. All the buildings in that "dead zone" had been leveled so armed East German guards in towers could have a better view of potential escapees. Dogs patrolled the barren plaza. Rabbits burrowed underneath. The only sign that there had once been life there was the stairway descending to the old Potsdamer Platz subway stop, its metal railing leading down to a hole full of rubble. A lively street on the western side dead-ended abruptly at the wall and was picked up on the eastern side by a tedious row of Communist housing.

The wall had slashed a deep scar across Berlin, cutting the city in half. Fifty years earlier, when Klaus Gysi started out on one end of Leipziger Strasse, he knew what awaited him at the other end. The Berlin Wall had changed that. Now no one in East Berlin knew what lay on the other side. The wall was crumbling, and the people behind it, like the Gysis, were heading into an uncertain future.

## Warsaw, Poland

Barbara Asendrych was at home and in bed. It had been a bad year for her, a bad decade. The doctors had told her that she might get better soon if she rested.

Barbara lived in a two-room flat on the top floor of a four-story building in Warsaw—through the front doors, up three flights, then past a metal grate to the final set of stairs, which led to the top of the building. The plants she had set out on the narrow staircase leading to her door fought to offset the gloom. It was a gloom endemic to Polish apartment houses, which were typically constructed of shoddy materials in impersonal clusters that snuffed out any attempts at individuality or stylishness. Just to have her own apartment was a boon for Barbara. As a child, she had been forced to retreat for hours to the bathroom while her mother entertained boyfriends in her one-bedroom apartment. For years, she and her husband and son had been forced by Poland's persistent housing shortage to cram into rooms carved out of other apartments, sharing bathrooms and kitchens with friends and relatives. Barbara's grandmother had been the most important influence in her life—making sure she attended Mass every Sunday, rousing her to attend religious classes. Barbara still had her first-communion photograph—a brown-haired girl in a white dress, looking slightly bewildered—in an album in the living room.

The past year had been tumultuous in Poland. The economy had slowed down, and the government had finally buckled and agreed to begin talks with Lech Walesa, the leader of Solidarity. The trade union had revolutionized Polish politics in 1980 and then was driven underground when the government sent tanks into the streets against its own people, arrested Walesa, and declared martial law in 1981. Barbara was not a political person. Her husband was more interested in politics than she was, but they both watched the turn of events warily. Too many people had disappeared in Poland over the years because of their interest in politics: too many imprisoned; too many killed.

Barbara was a short, dark-haired woman with a soft face that dissolved into light, childlike laughter. She worked as a computer programmer, although her illnesses kept her out of work and on disability much of the time. She had married and had a son, who had recently presented her with a grandchild, upon whom Barbara doted. It was as if a computer had combed through the files of middle-aged women in Warsaw and selected someone to represent "typical." Barbara Asendrych was a typical Pole with a typical job whose life had been devoid of extraordinary revelations—until recently.

For now Barbara lived with the dark secret of what her mother had done during the war, and as Communism passed and secrets began to come out, hers was emerging too.

Polish television reported the news of the fall of the Berlin Wall, and Barbara watched it from her bed. She felt uneasy. Born during the Second World War, she could remember Warsaw after the Germans had left—how her mother and her devoutly Catholic grandmother had ripped out the floorboards of the apartment they shared and burned them for heat. She remembered how Poles lined up for hours to get pitiful rations of food. The news that the wall had fallen made her anxious and suspicious. Ever since the war, Poles had cast a wary eye on a powerful and united Germany. It was a Polish trait. Some said it was one of the few traits that Poles shared with Jews.

The news and pictures flickering across the television screen washed over her. She had her own secrets and her own mission to complete.

### Budapest, Hungary

Tamas Raj rarely let politics enter his synagogue. He thought of himself as a man who seldom brought politics into his life at all. But for twenty-five years he had always been cast in the political maelstrom.

Raj had begun his career as a rabbi in 1962, out in the Hungarian provinces, in a university town where there were few Jews left after the war, and only the older ones went to synagogue. By reaching out to the young, Raj had increased the number of people who came to his synagogue, even the number who were prepared to step forward and acknowledge that they were Jews. He ran dances and discussion groups. He decorated meeting rooms with pictures of Israel. His efforts were making Judaism into a vibrant religion and way of life for the young, and the Jewish leadership in Hungary, controlled by the Communist Party, was furious. The Communists considered Raj a troublemaker. They wanted him stopped. Didn't he know that the Communists tolerated a small Jewish community in Hungary with the understanding that it was to be a dying Jewish community, a museum relic of elderly Jews there for tourists and worried American Jews to see. But the dances he had put on, the slide shows, these were unacceptable. Raj refused to bend. He would continue to preach Judaism as a living, breathing thing. He would continue to reach out to young people.

It had all come to a head when Israel won the Six Day War in 1967. Raj grew increasingly bold in his sermons and packed his provincial synagogue with people who came from both far and near to watch the plays he put on and to hear him speak. The secret police threatened him. The Communists put him in jail for a few days. Finally, the official Jewish community—at the behest of the Communists—took away his synagogue and his apartment. He was forced to move back to Budapest—to move in with his mother and eke out a living writing essays on obscure Hungarian writers.

But Tamas Raj was an obstinate man. He had refused to disappear, and now he had a synagogue again—a small, drafty temple with a ceiling that leaked, tucked away in a Budapest neighborhood. The young people were coming again, to hear this somber-looking man with bushy eyebrows and a deep, resonant voice, who could be foreboding and obstinate at one moment and then, in the presence of a child or a teenager, transform into a warm and engaging uncle. He was again being pulled into politics. Just as Poland that summer had cracked unexpectedly and allowed

Solidarity to seize the reins of government, so too Hungary's Communists were easing up, sensing change in the wind. They promised there would soon be free elections. The large, dim library where Raj had done his research during his years of internal exile had turned out to be a meeting place for other dissidents, fired from their jobs. Now they were urging him to run for parliament as an anti-Communist.

In the 1960s, before all the trouble, Tamas Raj had spoken from the pulpit of one of the most magnificent synagogues in Hungary, a huge domed building in a city far from Budapest that could seat two thousand and filled to overflowing with admirers from everywhere. This Friday night, November 10, 1989, he spoke from a small pulpit to the few that had gathered there. "The walls that divide us," Raj said, "are tumbling down. And although this particular wall coming down might arouse some unhappy memories in certain people—in spite of this, the will of the people and freedom is more important." After the service, an elderly man approached Raj and criticized him for celebrating on behalf of the Germans. He should be attacking the Germans for what they had done—not only to Hungary's Jews but to Raj and Raj's family.

"The situation is different than it was fifty years ago," said Raj. As he walked home, Raj could reflect on how different that situation had rapidly become: Two decades ago, he had arrived at this apartment unemployed; now he was trying to decide whether to run for parliament.

*Prague, Czechoslovakia*

By the time the tremors from the fall of the Berlin Wall reached Prague, Sylvia Wittmann was heading back there from Paris. She had watched reports of the fall of the wall on a friend's television set in the French capital. It was an appropriate place for a Czech to be. Even during the darkest days of Communism, when Czechoslovakia was under virtual occupation by Russian troops and sagged under the weight of Communist ideology, Czech intellectuals, unfurling a map, would point out to visitors that Prague lay *west* of Vienna. The message was simple: Czechoslovakia was neither historically nor geographically part of the monolithic "Eastern Bloc," locked into alliance with the Slavic Soviet Union. It was part of Europe. It lay at the center of Europe. The Holy Roman Emperor had ruled from Prague. Mozart had composed here. Verdi had premiered his operas to sophisticated audiences in Prague. The Czechs were not part of Eastern Europe. They were part of Central Europe, with Prague its cultural and spiritual capital, like Paris to the west. This whole business of Russian occupation and Communist totalitarianism, the Czechs seemed to say, was just a tragic mistake, a historical aberration. Few from the West paid much attention. In the forty-five years that Czechoslovakia lived under Communist rule, it sank from view, the golden spires of Prague hidden behind the Iron Curtain.

It was people like Sylvia Wittmann who kept the spark of Czechoslovakia alive. At thirty-three, she was dark-haired, with an exotic beauty that seemed part Middle Eastern. Sylvia could speak English and German. She lived in a two-room flat in Prague with a loft bedroom, filled with prints by photographer friends and drawings by painter friends. Some of the photographs featured her cats, others featured women in various nude poses. In recent years, intrigued by the snippets her parents had told her about her Jewish background, Sylvia had turned her apartment into a kind of Jewish salon, where friends met to talk about what it meant to be Jewish, even though some of them had only recently discovered their Jewishness. For years, many parents had hidden their children's religious identity from them, for fear it would make life too difficult in a country that prohibited religious expression and attacked Israel at every opportunity. Sylvia's mother had been jailed back in the 1950s for being an Israeli spy, simply because she had been born a Jew. After the Russians invaded Czechoslovakia in 1968, Sylvia's older brother left the country and never returned. Another brother left in 1978, after living as a dissident for ten years following the Soviet invasion. Sylvia's family had had enough run-ins with the Communist authorities already; the last thing they needed was to draw further attention to the fact that they were Jewish.

But over the past ten years, throughout the 1980s, Sylvia had found herself increasingly drawn to her Jewish roots. Amid the artwork by friends, the cats that slunk around the house, leaping from countertop to table to chairs, Sylvia had scattered menorahs and pictures of Jerusalem. It was only appropriate that she lived in Prague, the cultural capital of the Czech province of Bohemia. Her apartment gave special meaning to the term Bohemian.

Like most Czechs, Sylvia Wittmann led a private life and a public life. She had worked as a desk clerk at a hotel, checking people in and seeing to their bags. More recently she had gotten a job as a guide with a Communist-approved tour agency, shepherding groups of Bulgarians, Russians, and other Eastern Bloc "comrades" around Prague's cultural sights. In private, Sylvia mocked and taunted the Communists, disdaining their stupidity with the insouciance of many Czechs who had spent their entire lives under Communism. It was a common attitude among the young. After the Prague Spring in 1968, when Czechoslovakia's Communists tried to create "Socialism with a human face" by lifting censorship and promising political reform, the Soviets had invaded and brought the country's Communist leaders to the Soviet Union in chains. The new Communist leadership, hand-picked by Moscow, turned Czechoslovakia upside down. The worst opportunists had been recruited into the Communist Party, where their loyalty was rewarded with important jobs and larger apartments.

Czechoslovakia's best and brightest, refusing to knuckle under, were tossed into the most menial of jobs. Prague's bishops, journalists, intellectuals, artists, and dissidents became coal stokers, milk deliverymen, garbage collectors.

In autumn 1989, Sylvia traveled to Brussels to visit her brother who had been forced to flee Prague after the Soviet tanks invaded. Sylvia remembered those weeks vividly—the interrupted radio broadcasts, the tanks rumbling down Prague's streets, the young people hurling themselves at the armored vehicles in fury, her father driving a volunteer ambulance to help the wounded. Prague had never been the same afterward.

From Brussels, Sylvia and her brother went to Paris to meet friends of his, Czech dissidents who had also fled the country in

1968. They huddled around the television when the news about the Berlin Wall burst across the screen. They talked excitedly about what it might mean for Czechoslovakia. "Oh, the Czechs," said one of the exiles dismissively. "The Czechs won't do anything." They had lived under the Russian boot for too long, the dissidents reasoned. Unlike the Poles, Czechs had food on the shelves, and many had built small country houses. The Czechs had made their peace with their compromises. The spirit of 1968 and the Prague Spring was over. Czechs would not rise from their long torpor.

The exiled dissidents were wrong. Two weeks after the fall of the Berlin Wall, more than a thousand students gathered in Prague. It was supposed to be an official march to commemorate the murder of two Communist heroes by the Nazis during World War II. But the demonstration quickly spun out of control. As dusk turned to darkness, the students veered away from the park where the demonstration was supposed to end and headed for the center of town. Police moved in to cut them off. Like a ghost, Alexander Dubček, who headed the Prague Spring before he was toppled by the Russian invasion, appeared at the fringes of the crowd. He was swiftly arrested. As the students massed on the main street leading to Wenceslas Square, they began singing "We Shall Overcome" and chanting "Resign! Resign!" to the Communist authorities. They lit candles and placed them at the feet of armed riot police. They held their keys aloft, jangling them, saying these were the "final bells" of the Communist regime. "Ask not for whom the bell tolls!" a Czech woman shouted into the night. "It tolls for you!" The police charged. They beat the students relentlessly. But the next day, the students were back. The day after that, they were joined by secretaries, factory workers, and retired clerks. Within three days, more than one hundred thousand people were packed cheek by jowl in the vast rectangular plaza of Wenceslas Square, chanting "Resign! Resign!" and calling the names of Communist leaders with long-drawn-out chants, like baseball fans mocking rival players at Yankee Stadium. Then, as dusk turned to darkness again, a low, gravelly voice wafted over the square—the voice of playwright and dissident Vaclav Havel, calling for the peaceful overthrow of the Communists.

Sylvia Wittmann boarded the overnight train to Prague. Once there, she headed straight for Wenceslas Square. Dusk was falling, and yet again the square was a sea of people, packed so tight it seemed as if all Prague was there in the chill November air. They jangled keys, chanted "Resign! Resign!" and called for Vaclav Havel to appear again.

Then people began to raise their hands. They are taking an oath, thought Sylvia, some kind of Christian oath. Not this! she thought. Not, after forty years of Communism, a religious dictatorship. Her family had known enough of both kinds, the stupid Communists and the stupid anti-Semites.

"Why aren't you putting up your fingers?" a man next to Sylvia asked, his arm aloft.

"I am not a Christian," Sylvia said. "I will not make a Christian sign."

"It is not a Christian sign," the man shouted, over the roar of the crowd. "It is the V for victory."

Wittmann thrust her hand up into the air. First one, then a stream of tears ran down her face. After twenty-one years, spring had returned to Prague.

# Part I

Liberation

Within a few weeks of November 9, 1989, Germany and Eastern Europe were transformed. Communist governments fell with stunning speed. Bearded dissidents and former political prisoners were thrust into top government jobs. Many of these countries symbolically shed their Communist pasts. They put eagles back on their flags and restored the traditional national anthems. Many old Communists moved swiftly to revise their images. Communist factory bosses reappeared as entrepreneurs. People who had been informers declared they had always supported democracy—and they hoped their secret police files would be sealed forever. Some Communists dropped from sight entirely, hoping to avoid retribution and prison sentences from the new democratic governments. For many Jews, however, the fall of the Berlin Wall meant the opportunity not to bury the past but to expose it. They wanted to tell the world what had happened to them under the Communists. For forty-five years, many of these Jews had led double lives. They had worshiped in secret, seen their friends persecuted, been cut off from relatives overseas. Many had hidden their Jewish background entirely.

Now they felt liberated, free at last to tell their stories. They wanted people to understand the world that had shaped them and the choices they had made. The Germans had a phrase for this: "You must understand my biography." No one knew on the night of November 9, 1989, what the future held—not the Nachamas of West Berlin, the Communist Gysis of East Berlin, the searching Barbara Asendrych in Poland, the dissident Rabbi Tamas Raj in Hungary, the Wittmanns of Czechoslovakia. Their journeys had begun more than four decades earlier, in the hope-filled spring of 1945. World War II had ended. The Nazis had been defeated. And the Jews of Germany and Eastern Europe believed, for a moment, that they were free.

As the war ended, they came staggering out, stunned by what they had endured. They embraced the soldiers who had freed them, unaware of—or not caring about—the political beliefs that would soon reshape their lives.

"It is not fashionable to say it now," a Jewish survivor said to me in Hungary. "But the Soviets liberated me." He paused and repeated himself, as if carefully underlining every word: "The Soviets liberated me."

# Chapter Two

# Erna's Son

The mansion sat on the edge of the Schlachtensee, a large lake on the outskirts of Berlin. It lay untouched by the war, its fourteen rooms still as grandly furnished when the bombs were silenced as they had been when Hitler had stormed to power twelve years earlier. The mansion itself was surrounded by a ten-foot-high wall that was in turn surrounded by woods that shielded the house from the prying eyes of neighbors. It was the perfect spot to escape the hustle of Berlin. During World War II it was the perfect place to hide if you were a Jew.

Klaus Gysi, a Jew and a Communist, had hidden here for almost five years, enduring the suspicious stares of the Germans who came and went, wondering why a seemingly healthy young man was not at the front, fighting for Germany. In many ways Gysi fit the German stereotype of a Jew. Even as a young man his dark hair tended to baldness. The round spectacles he wore accentuated the intelligence that gleamed from his eyes. Yet what Nazi scientists would have labeled a distinctly "non-Aryan" face had, miraculously, not attracted much attention. After being bombarded year after year with the grossest stereotypes and carica-tures of Jews in newspapers, books, and movie newsreels—noses that looked like beaks, sharp teeth, scraggly hair, rapacious eyes— the Germans who passed through the house at Schlachtensee or saw Klaus Gysi on the street, or in the mountains when he and his fiancée went hiking, never concluded that Gysi was Jewish. If they had suspicions, they kept them to themselves.

His moment of triumph came in May 1945. For months, the Allies had pounded the city with bombs, reducing block after block to rubble as Russian troops closed in. Many Germans feared what the Russians would do to them in revenge for the brutal Nazi invasion of the Soviet Union. Klaus Gysi did not fear the Russians. One spring day, he spotted a lone man in a Russian officer's uniform striding down the street. Quickly Klaus fetched his fiancée, Irene, who was part Jewish and who had hidden him all these years in the mansion she shared with her parents. Irene had been born in Saint Petersburg. Her family had made its fortune building factories in Russia. Hurrying through the gates of her family's compound, she greeted the officer in her broken Russian. Then she stopped and ran inside the grand house. She reemerged waving a book—a book by Karl Marx, banned by the Nazis, that she and Klaus had kept hidden for years. Like her fiancé, Irene was a Communist. The book was like a passport guaranteeing safe passage; the Russian officer decided that the people standing before him, Klaus Gysi and the woman who would soon become his wife, were allies, not enemies. The three stepped inside the mansion and ate and drank together. Soon the stillness of the lake and the quiet of the woods shook with the rumble of tanks, trucks, armored personnel carriers, and wave after wave of troops. The officer had been an advance scout. Now the full Russian army of occupation was arriving. The war was over. The German army had vanished, nowhere to be seen. Klaus Gysi was astounded. He had never believed he would survive. More than two thousand Jews had survived in hiding in Berlin, the center of the Third Reich. But Klaus Gysi's achievement was even more miraculous. He had survived though he was both a Jew and a Communist, the two greatest devils in Hitler's pantheon.

Klaus Gysi was born in 1912 in a working-class neighborhood of Berlin known as Neukölln—an area so filled with laborers and the ethos of class struggle that after World War II, though located in West Berlin, the main street was named Karl Marx Strasse. In

Communist-controlled East Germany, it was fashionable, indeed politically essential, after World War II, to come from a workers' background. Communist Party leaders boasted of the manual labor they had done. Intellectuals were viewed with suspicion. The address of Klaus Gysi's family was politically impeccable. But Klaus Gysi's family was far from working class. The Gysis were, in fact, one of the oldest and most cosmopolitan families in Berlin.

The Gysis had first come to Berlin in 1770, from Switzerland. For generations, they were physicians; Klaus's father practiced at the prestigious Charité Hospital, near the center of the city. Young Klaus, short and owl-faced, with his gift for languages and his interest in economics and literature, was the first Gysi in generations who did not want to be a doctor.

Klaus's mother, Erna, came from a well-established and well-to-do Jewish family from southern Germany. The Frank family's roots stretched back to the fifteenth or sixteenth century. The Franks had made their fortune in manufacturing. Like many German Jews of their lineage and wealth, they considered themselves more German than Jewish. Their religion was Jewish, but their identity was German. With their solid Germanic name, they were indistinguishable from their prosperous neighbors.

Before Erna was born, the Franks had moved to Berlin. There, Erna's mother had married into the Potolowski family, Jewish immigrants from Poland who had opened two glove shops in the fashionable Friedrich Strasse, amid elegant cafés and shops in the heart of Berlin. Erna had the fine features of the Franks. She was a German beauty with dark hair and an intelligent face. Her grace extended all the way to her hands. By the time she was twenty, all Berlin could admire those hands. On billboards dotted above the city, Erna's family put pictures of their daughter's slim hands modeling the wares of the Potolowski glove shops.

But Erna's delicate hands gave no hint of the steely side of her nature. Sharp-tongued and fierce in her convictions, she fought for the right to abortion and for women's rights. She rejected political convention and embraced a radicalism that shocked her contemporaries. Politically, she was more Potolowski than Frank—heir to the turbulent Jewish embrace of Socialism and

Communism that grew in Poland and Eastern Europe rather than to the safe bourgeois values of the established German Jewish families. Her political choices placed her in the center of the storm that engulfed Germany in the years after World War I, when the Nazis began their climb to power. Faced with growing political and economic chaos—rampant inflation, high unemployment, street battles between Left and Right—many German Jews sought safety in the middle. They supported parties like the Social Democrats, who were far more liberal than the Nazis but less radical than the Communists. Not Erna. For her, radical times called for radical solutions. Though it was highly unusual for a woman—especially a married woman, and one with children—to plunge into politics, Erna stormed ahead. In the political hothouse of Berlin in the 1920s, Erna Gysi embraced Communism—a decision that would forever mark her son Klaus.

The Jewish romance with Socialism began in the ghettos and villages of Poland and Russia in the late nineteenth century. In Russia especially, those years saw growing religious discrimination and violence. Jews were forced to live in what the Russians called the Pale of Settlement, a crowded swath of territory whose borders remained fixed even as the number of its inhabitants increased from 1.6 million to 4 million. Jews were forced to serve in the czar's army for twenty-five years; some were conscripted as young as twelve and forced to convert to Christianity. Jews living in the Pale of Settlement typically worked fourteen to sixteen hours a day six days a week under brutal conditions in textile, tobacco, or food-processing factories. They were paid less than their Christian neighbors, and their health deteriorated faster. Hovering in the foreground was the constant threat of pogroms— mob rampages often incited and sanctioned by the government. In the late 1890s, the Russian secret police wrote and began distributing "The Protocols of the Elders of Zion," an anti-Semitic tirade that claimed to transcribe "secret" plans by Jewish leaders to subjugate Christians and dominate the world. The "Protocols" became a pretext for further pogroms and attacks.

Beset by this barrage of unrelenting poverty, violence, and anti-

Semitic propaganda, many Jews fled Russia. Between 1881 and 1914, two million left, most for the United States. Many of those who remained became—understandably—politically radicalized. They turned to the two new radical philosophies pulsating through Russia, Poland, and the rest of Eastern Europe: Zionism and Socialism. The Zionists dreamed of a Jewish paradise in Palestine; the Socialists dreamed of a workers' paradise in their native lands.

Over the next fifty years, millions of Russian and Eastern European Jews embraced Zionism as an ideology, a movement that culminated in the founding of the State of Israel in 1948. But no less stunning was the fervor with which many Jews embraced Socialism and its more radical successor, Communism. Their fervor was matched by the success with which they scaled up the Communist ranks.

In the 1920s, just a few years after the Communist revolution in Russia, Vladimir Lenin observed with approval that Jews "with their stubbornness and fanaticism make excellent revolutionaries. . . . The eminent, universally progressive traits of the Jewish culture—its internationalism and its heedfulness to the progressive movements of the epoch—have manifested themselves distinctly." He went on to note that "The percentage of Jews in democratic and proletarian movements [i.e., Communism] is everywhere higher than the percentage of Jews in the population generally."

On the eve of the Russian Revolution, Jews held six of twenty-one spots on the Bolshevik Central Committee, which masterminded the Communist takeover—even though Jews made up just 2 percent of Russia's population. Among the top Jewish Communists was Lenin's closest collaborator, Leon Trotsky—born Lev Bronstein, a Jewish man with a traditionally Jewish name. By the time the smoke had cleared from the Russian Revolution in 1917, Jews in the new, Communist-ruled Soviet Union had reached the apex of influence. The new president of the Soviet Union was Jewish. So was the leader of Saint Petersburg, Russia's second-largest city. So was the head of the Comintern, which oversaw Communist activity worldwide. All of these Jews had long before severed their ties to organized Judaism and the Jewish community.

But their presence in the Communist hierarchy and their continued fascination with Communism would reverberate—with often catastrophic consequences—for generations.

Joining the Russian Revolution was for many Jews the "admission ticket" for access to power in the new Soviet Union. Even though Jews made up just 2 percent of the Russian population, they accounted for 5 percent of the membership in the Russian Communist Party, 12 percent of state employees in Moscow, 20 percent of all state employees in the Ukraine. By 1921, Jews actually constituted a majority of the small Politburo that ruled the Soviet Union.

Despite the heavy presence of Jews in top Communist positions, and notwithstanding the attraction of Communism and Socialism to many younger Jews, Russian Jews generally shied away from the Communists as they swept to power. The Communists' atheism offended Jewish religious beliefs. Their economic policy threatened Jewish livelihoods, especially for merchants, traders, and shopkeepers. Many Jews also feared the upheaval created by the revolution. History had taught that popular uprisings, no matter how they began, often turned against the Jews. Indeed, many Jews worried that so many of the prominent Communists in the Soviet Union were identifiably Jewish. When the Communists became unpopular, they assumed, the Jewish Communists would be blamed, and all Jews would suffer. The Chief Rabbi of Moscow took aside Leon Trotsky, born Lev Bronstein. "The Trotskys make the revolutions," the rabbi warned. "But the Bronsteins pay the bills." The comment was prophetic.

In Germany too, the rise of Socialism and Communism was marked from the start by the prominence of Jews. Among the Jewish population as a whole, direct support for the Communists was small. But Jews who joined the Communist Party rose quickly. The eleven-person central committee of the German Communist Party included four Jews: Rosa Luxemburg, Leo Jogiches, Paul Levi, and August Thalheimer. When Communists in Bavaria—one of the most conservative and anti-Semitic areas of Germany—decided to seize the local government in 1919, following Germany's surrender in World War I, they chose as their leader Kurt Eisner, a bearded, free-spirited Jewish theater critic. Jewish citizens of Bavaria immediately begged him to resign in favor of a non-Jew. Eisner wrote back to them dismissively, declaring that any question of his background belonged to "an age that has now been overcome." He was wrong. Eisner's coup collapsed, and he was assassinated. Another group of Jewish leftists and intellectuals seized power and declared Bavaria a "Soviet Republic." This was too much even for the liberal government in Berlin, which joined forces with conservatives to send troops to Munich to crush the rebellion. The short-lived Communist experiment in Bavaria slipped into history. But it left a vivid image of the role of Jews in trying to set up a Communist state. One person upon whom it would make a lasting impression was living in Munich at the time of the failed, Jewish-led Communist rebellions: Adolf Hitler.

The years after World War I in Germany constituted a time that seemed to cry out for hard choices. Germany had been traumatized by its defeat. In the wake of a disintegrating economy and political chaos, the country was becoming more and more polarized. The Nazi Party, founded by Hitler, was winning more and more support. So were the Communists. The political middle, in which many Jews sought refuge, was not holding.

Erna Gysi was initially attracted to the Communists by their support of women's rights, especially the right to choose abortion, which was then illegal in Germany. Her enthusiasm grew until, by the 1920s, she had become one of their most loyal followers. Family lore claimed that she joined the Communist Party soon after it was founded in 1923. Others said she was just a sympathizer, though a devoted one. What is sure is that in 1928 she enrolled her sixteen-year-old son, Klaus Gysi, in the Communist Youth League. At an age when most boys are still groping through their political beliefs and social awkwardness, Klaus, with the aid of his mother, had set upon the political path that would determine the rest of his life.

Klaus Gysi may have joined the Communist Party under the influence and guidance of his mother, but his commitment grew from the turmoil he saw enveloping Germany. Klaus stood out at school. In his working-class neighborhood, he was one of the few students from a "better" family. His father was a doctor; his mother came from a family of prosperous shop owners. Most of Klaus's classmates were the sons and daughters of workers and laborers. As inflation rocketed in Germany and unemployment swelled past six million, worker demonstrations became a feature of everyday life. Just before he formally joined the Communist Party, Klaus stood at the window of his family's apartment and watched a workers' demonstration. Perhaps two hundred men marched by, carrying placards that protested the closure of their factory. Klaus sympathized. All his friends were working-class kids, for whom getting a job was essential to survival.

Klaus studied the scene outside the window. Suddenly a truck full of armed police arrived. There was a fight, then a shot rang out. The protestors scattered, leaving a dead worker sprawled on the street. Some tried to go back and help the man, but the police chased them away. Most of the police then boarded the truck and drove off.

Looking down at the body lying in the street, Klaus thought to himself: Anything, whatever it is, is better than this—better than murdering workers just because they want jobs.

Klaus's father supported the boy's decision to become a Communist. Though not a Communist himself, Hermann Gysi sympathized with the left. That was why he had set up his medical practice in Berlin's working-class neighborhood of Neukölln, even though he could afford far better. He wanted to help the poor. He was the kind of man about whom neighborhood people said, "Look, he is a real Communist." But the passion for Communism and the Communist view of the future came from Erna. She was firm in her belief that Communism would not only solve Germany's economic problems but eliminate the age-old problem of anti-Semitism as well. Erna was not just a Communist but a Jewish Communist. Though she was a political radical in a party that dismissed religion as the "opiate of the masses," she knew the world was more complex than that dismissive slogan. Her mother—Klaus's grandmother—still went to synagogue regularly, often taking Klaus along. Erna often regaled her son with tales of prominent leftists and Communist heroes who were Jewish, like the well-known left-wing German writer Kurt Tucholsky. She reminded him that Karl Marx himself had been born a Jew. As the Nazis stirred up racial hate in the 1920s and 1930s and other German parties were reluctant to defend Jews, the Communist Party took a firm stand that one's religious background was irrelevant, an anachronism. To Erna and Jewish Communists like her, Communism appealed as an ideology that was good for German workers, good for a just society—and good for Germany's radicalized, secular, assimilated Jews.

For a young man growing up in Germany in the 1920s and 1930s—a young man like Klaus Gysi—Communism was not the leaden, oppressive system of gray-suited leaders with sagging jowls that it became in later years. The Communist he knew best—his mother—was a glamorous woman whose hands graced billboards and who filled her home with books and an ever-changing salon of artists and writers debating the issues of the day. At one of the first Communist Party meetings Klaus attended, he would recall years later, Albert Einstein played the violin. Amid collapsing monarchies and rising Fascism, Communism had spread like wildfire across Russia and seemed on the verge of an almost invincible sweep across Europe. The trauma of World War I and the chaos of the Great Depression, which struck Europe earlier and more severely than it struck America, drove people to search for new answers, new sources of "community" to replace the system that had led Germany and Europe into war and now threatened it with economic collapse. This disaffection turned many young intellectuals to the radical Right—to Nazism, which promised a sense of collective purpose based on a shared "Aryan" past and a renewed sense of German identity. Jewish intellectuals seeking new answers to Germany's problems could find no home in the burgeoning Nazi movement or other such right-wing groups. The left-of-center parties, like the Social Democrats, retained the loyalty of most Jews, but some saw, correctly, that these parties and the democratic middle were helpless before the rise of Nazism. Zionism grew in popularity, with supporters believing that Jews now could be safe only if they established a Jewish homeland in Palestine. Then there was Communism, a visionary Communism that was not just an economic system but a new definition of community—an egalitarian culture that would unite all men regardless of their origin. This was the faith that Klaus and Erna Gysi embraced. They were looking for utopia and found it in the Communist future.

It was easy, amid such yearning, to overlook the contempt Marx had for his fellow Jews, whose faith, he wrote, "is repugnant to me." Although baptized when he was six, Marx remained haunted by his Jewish background and scorned Jews, whose main characteristics, he believed, were selfishness, haggling, and an inordinate love of money—the anti-Semitic stereotypes of his day. Lenin welcomed Jews as Communist revolutionaries, but he, too, scorned Judaism, just as he scorned all religion. "Whoever, directly or indirectly, puts forward the slogan of a Jewish 'national culture' is, whatever his good intentions may be, an enemy of the proletariat," Lenin warned. In the theology of Communism, there was no greater evil than being an "enemy of the proletariat."

The seeds of anti-Semitism that would later blossom under Communism were already sown. But Klaus Gysi, like many other young Jewish Communists, was blind to this. When he formally joined the Communist Party as an adult, he considered his political agenda very simple: create a Germany with a political and economic system as progressive and as just as possible; do away with unemployment; redistribute wealth; give every German equal access to education and culture. For a bright, quick-witted nineteen-year-old with a love for books and literature, such changes might have seemed simple; in fact they were revolutionary. Klaus Gysi and many young Jews like him were progressive by inclination and upbringing. They were eager to catch a ride on the crest of history. Communism was their first intellectual love. And like many first loves, it would be hard to give up.

Erna never tried to hide her Jewish background. She had raised her sons to be comfortable and familiar with the rituals of the synagogue. As a child, Klaus had gone to synagogue with his mother and grandmother. But as he grew, his relationship with Judaism became ambivalent and contradictory—much as it was for many German Jews in Berlin in the years before Hitler came to power.

For centuries, to be Jewish meant carrying a heavy burden in Germany and the rest of Europe, especially Eastern Europe. Unlike Protestants or Catholics, Jews faced limits imposed on them by law and by custom. The ghettos that had once walled in Jews in cities across Europe had disappeared. But to varying degrees in various places, Jews were always victims of discrimination. Even in the most liberal countries—and Germany, before the rise of Hitler, was considered progressive in its treatment of Jews—Jews were barred from some professions and social circles. They could not teach at certain universities or join many clubs. In more repressive countries, like Romania, Jews were denied citizenship altogether before World War I. The degree to which a Jew identified himself as "Jewish" often determined how successful he would be in the broader society. The less one identified as a Jew, and the more one tried to assimilate, the better one's chances for success.

By the 1920s, Judaism in Europe resembled a large, sprawling country. Some Jews chose to live in the interior, in the heartland, embracing Jewish learning and traditions. They knew this meant isolating themselves from the world beyond their borders, since the "outside" world scorned pious Jews and pious Jews responded by scorning the outside world. Other Jews chose to live closer to the borders, their ties to Judaism weakening as they tried to assimilate. They were drawn to the promise of the world that lay beyond. Starting in the 1880s, a new Jewish movement in Berlin reflected this yearning. Known as Liberal or Reform Judaism, it attracted many middle-class and well-to-do German Jews. It later crossed the Atlantic and became a pillar of American Jewish life as well. The Reform Jews modernized traditional Jewish ritual until it resembled rituals in Catholic and Protestant churches. The layout of synagogues changed. Instead of putting the rabbi at the center, surrounded by benches of the faithful, the Reform Jews put the rabbi at the front of the synagogue on a pulpit, with rows of benches facing him—like a minister in a Protestant church or a Catholic priest. Music and songs were introduced. By the 1920s, the first women were speaking from the pulpits of Reform Jewish synagogues in Berlin. Jewish Communists like Rosa Luxemburg went even further, envisioning a future where differences between Jews and Christians would disappear. They believed that anti-Semitism was caused by the segregation of Jews into ghettos. Rapid assimilation, they reasoned, was the answer to anti-Semitism.

By the time Klaus was born, the Gysis were already living at the far border of Judaism. They considered themselves Germans first. They went to synagogue rarely. Klaus's father was not even Jewish, though he shared a deep appreciation of Jewish life. The family joked that Hermann knew more about Judaism than many of their Jewish relatives. He would visit his in-laws and joke, "Where's the mezuzah?"—the small rectangular icon that religious Jews often nailed to the front doorpost of their homes. The Gysis, of course, would never have something so obviously religious and old-fashioned as a mezuzah at their door. The Gysis' Jewishness manifested itself not in their faith but in their intellectual outlook. They were an intellectual and cosmopolitan family. They epitomized the Jewish tradition of challenging the status quo and being open to new ideas. It was taken as a matter of course that their two sons— Klaus and his younger brother, Gerd—would go to France to study, maybe even to America. The shelves of books and the wide-ranging discussions of literature and culture dazzled friends who visited. The openness to new ideas in the Gysi house was striking in part because it contrasted so sharply with the Germany that was emerging outside their door. In a Germany that was becoming more embittered and inward-looking, the Gysis looked outward. In a country that would soon burn books, the Gysis treasured them. In a nation that in a few years would use definitions of race and religion to select who should live and who should die, the Gysis carried their religion with insouciance, as if it were something that made them a little more interesting, a little more exotic. When young Klaus Gysi was asked in grammar school to fill out a form that asked his religion, he wrote, with a flourish: "Dissident."

In the Berlin of the 1920s and 1930s, a politically radical and ambitious young man like Klaus Gysi could well have seen two possible roads open to him. He could embrace Judaism and accept a kind of second-class citizenship—be hemmed in by the traditions and rules of Jewish life and looked down upon by his fellow Germans. That was far too small a ghetto for Klaus Gysi. Or he could ape his mother's relatives, the Franks, and become a well-to-do, assimilated German Jew, hoping that with money and finer clothes, he could win the acceptance of German society. But that meant embracing capitalism and the economic inequalities that were leaving workers dead in the street. And it would mean breaking with his mother, who had made her political choice clear.

That left Communism. To be a Communist meant being more than just a Jew. It meant joining a group of comrades to fight for justice. It was, in its way, a different kind of assimilation—shedding the narrow identity of Jew for the broader and more exciting one of Communist. It meant crossing the border.

Soon after joining the Communist Party, Klaus left his parents' apartment for Paris, to study economics at the Sorbonne. In keeping with his upbringing and the expectations of his parents, he learned French and acquired a greater appreciation of wine and of art.

When Klaus returned to Berlin in 1933, everything had changed. The Nazis had risen to power, elected on a wave of disenchantment and the conservatives' mistaken belief that they could control Hitler. Hitler's anti-Semitic ravings and his belief in a worldwide Jewish conspiracy against Germany had turned him into a figure of ridicule among most left-leaning Berliners like the Gysis. Indeed, in the national election that brought the Nazis to power, Berlin had voted against Hitler; the Communists had won millions of votes in Berlin, earning the city the sobriquet "Red Berlin." But Berlin's feelings notwithstanding, all Germany was now under Hitler's aegis, and a ragtag group of anti-Semites controlled the most powerful country in Europe.

After a brief stay in Berlin, Klaus had intended to go to the United States to continue his studies. But his brother had developed leukemia, and Klaus did not want to leave his family. He enrolled at Friedrich Wilhelm University in the center of Berlin. The country's most prestigious university was located on the tree-lined Unter den Linden, a few blocks from the Kaiser's old palace, which anchored one end of the boulevard. Hitler's new Reichs-chancellery now anchored the other. The first day of classes, Klaus walked through the iron gateway and was handed his student iden-tification card. A yellow stripe was slashed across it. Alongside Klaus's name and picture were the words: "NOT a Member of the German Student Organization." The countrywide German Student Organization included only "Aryan" students. The yellow stripe and the cumbersome jargon carried a simple message: Klaus was a Jew.

Barely a few months in power, the Nazis had already begun sin-gling out Jews for discrimination. Klaus was unable to take it all seriously. The Nazis would fall soon, he believed. The insou-ciance he had displayed years earlier in listing his religion at grammar school persisted.

It continued when, soon after, he met the woman who would become his wife. Irene Lessing's family was even more distin-guished than the Gysis were. The Lessings had made their for-tune in Saint Petersburg, where the family inhabited a sixty-room mansion filled with fine art and furniture. After they moved to Germany, their business interests mushroomed until they included factories across the country. Irene's sister-in-law, Doris Lessing, would go on to become a world-famous novelist.

The two students, Irene and Klaus, met soon after registration at the university.

"Would you like to have coffee?" Klaus asked Irene.

They headed off to the Schlosskonditerei at the busy intersec-tion of Friedrich Strasse and Unter den Linden—a restaurant famous for its rich German cream pastries and the fine vantage point it gave for watching passersby. Irene, too, had received a student card with a yellow stripe; her grandfather was Jewish. Explaining to Klaus, who feigned ignorance, what it meant to carry such a card, she described the Nuremberg Laws that the Nazis had just passed, limiting the rights of Jews. Exasperated at Klaus's silence, she put her card on the table. Klaus then took out his yellow-striped card and placed it on top of hers.

"After that," Irene recalled later, "you either separate forever or you get married." Irene even had to pay for the coffee; Klaus hadn't enough money with him.

Few women, then or later, ever separated from Klaus Gysi. Pictures from the 1930s show a young man always elegantly turned out, with hair combed back carefully and full, sensual lips. His face combined the sensitivity of an artist or a writer with a touch of dandyism. He exuded a magnetic intelligence and charm that made him a formidable ladies' man. The two fell in love. But Irene had plans to go to London, to study at the London School of Economics, and then to South Africa, where her uncle was in business. They resolved to part but remain in touch. After Irene had been away for three years, Klaus wrote to her: "Since you are gone, autumn has come to Germany." Irene at last packed her bags and returned to Berlin to marry Klaus Gysi.

But it was 1936, and the latest anti-Jewish laws passed by the Nazis prevented Klaus and Irene from marrying. A "quarter" Jew like Irene could not debase the Aryan race further by marrying a "half Jew" like Klaus. Soon the family faced another, more serious crisis, stemming from the tightening Nazi noose around Germany's Jews. Erna Gysi and her husband decided to divorce. To the Gysi family, looking back after decades, the circumstances of the divorce remained unclear. Some traced it to the fact that Erna married when she was just nineteen. She had met Hermann when she was a high school student and he was studying medicine at the university. Beautiful and intelligent, she was drawn to artists and writers, as well as to radical politics. (Soon after Hermann and Erna divorced, she became romantically involved with a writer friend of Klaus's whom she had met when the boys were still in high school.) But for a non-Jewish man to divorce his Jewish wife in Berlin in 1937 carried political overtones. The Nazis were encouraging such divorces; many non-Jews saw that they would have no future under Hitler and the Nazis if they remained married to their Jewish spouses.

Whatever the motivation, Erna was in danger in Nazi Germany. Both a Jew and a Communist, she now lacked the protection of marriage to an "Aryan." She fled to France, where she took a job as a cook with a Protestant family. As the Nazis tightened their racial laws, both Klaus and Irene, as "half" and "quarter" Jews, were prevented from returning to the university. One morning, Klaus Gysi woke up in his father's house to the sound of hundreds of people whistling. He looked out the window where years before he had seen police shoot at workers in a demonstration. Again, workers were filling the street, this time bicycling to work and whistling—the traditional German sign of disapproval. Klaus turned on the Nazi-controlled radio and found out what had happened. The night before, in what the announcer called a "spontaneous" uprising of German citizens, the Nazis had smashed the windows of Jewish shops and burned synagogues across Germany. It was November 9, 1938. Kristallnacht.

Of the more than half-million Jews who lived in Germany when Hitler came to power, 300,000 had already emigrated. But there were still more than 200,000 Jews left. Klaus thought immediately about his grandparents' glove shop on Friedrich Strasse. It surely must have been attacked. As he bicycled across Berlin that morning after Kristallnacht and saw the smoke rising from synagogues, he thought: If the synagogues are burning, then Germany will burn too.

The next summer, Klaus and Irene went to France to visit Erna. Erna pleaded with her son not to return to Germany. It was too dangerous, she said. Klaus would not hear of it. He believed the Communist Party needed him there.

Then the Germans made the decision for them. That fall of 1939, Germany invaded Poland, then France. Irene and Klaus were detained in France as enemy aliens. Their Communist Party sympathies and anti-Nazi politics did not matter. They were taken to separate labor camps near Toulouse, where they were forced to work until a friendly French guard reunited them and helped them to escape. At Toulouse they reconnected with the Communist Party. They had no papers, no documents that would allow them to escape to other parts of Europe. The Communists could not help them. Too many German Communists already in France were better known to the advancing German forces and needed to be sent abroad to safety. There was no alternative: Klaus and Irene would return to Berlin.

"This is madness!" declared Irene. She feared more for Klaus than for herself. She was but one-quarter Jewish, and while she sympathized with the Communists, she had never joined the party; she had some protection. But Klaus, with his Jewish mother, was considered a Jew. And he was a full party member. He was running a double risk. It was suicidal to return.

Klaus insisted that he faced danger not because he was Jewish but because he was a Communist. This was in keeping with the way he viewed his politics and his background. His politics he could choose; his religious background he could not. To be a Jew meant to be a victim; to be a Communist meant to be a fighter, a man who resisted, a hero.

Klaus and Irene crossed the border and made their way back to Berlin. They moved into Irene's family's house near the Schlacht-ensee, in the western part of Berlin. It offered Klaus some protec-tion. The lake lay on one side, some elevated train tracks on the other. There were few prying neighbors.

For the next five years Klaus and Irene lived a life of deception. At first the Communists, in disarray, wanted nothing to do with Irene and Klaus, who lacked proper papers and money. Gradually, a Communist underground formed, the Rote Kapelle, and finally Klaus and Irene found jobs that allowed them to be of use to the underground movement. They were hired to write industrial histo-ries of German factories. Because they were freelancers, no one asked for their papers. Questioned as to why he was not in the army, Klaus would present fake medical excuses drawn up by his father, who, having remarried, still lived in Berlin. Klaus traveled the country, visiting factories that were involved in the war effort— passing on tidbits to the Communists along the way. At one point he discovered the building that controlled electricity for the entire city of Cologne, information that could be useful if the resistance decided to undertake a campaign of sabotage. Klaus worked with the Communist underground to print newspapers and leaflets. He kept in touch with anti-Nazi intellectuals and scientists. But the Communist resistance movement in Germany—like all the resis-tance in Germany—was pitifully small and ineffective.

Klaus saw the noose tightening around the Jews in Berlin. The yellow stripe across his student identification card had been just the beginning. When war was declared in 1939, Jews were denied ration cards. They were stripped of their homes and their jobs. Klaus's father tried to help by getting them coupons for food. But the Nazis were arresting more and more Jews, shipping them off to unspecified destinations "in the east." Then, in 1943, the final roundup of the Jews in Berlin began.

The notice was delivered to apartments and houses across Berlin. Pack all you can carry in one suitcase, it said. Be prepared to leave in twenty-four hours. You are to be "resettled." Nothing was said of concentration camps or gas chambers or crematoriums. Irene and Klaus suspected that what awaited these Jews was death. Klaus learned that several of his Jewish relatives had received deportation notices. He had been spared because the Nazis had no record of his whereabouts. Klaus and Irene scrambled to come up with medical excuses to spare his relatives—they were too old, too sick to travel. When nothing would dissuade the Nazis, Klaus and Irene went clandestinely to help family members pack.

They climbed the stairs to the apartment of one of Klaus's aunts. In happier times, the family had gathered there to while away the entire afternoon in the German tradition over coffee and cake and conversation. "I'm so sorry I have no cake for you," Klaus's aunt said as she opened the door. Jews were forbidden to buy cakes. "I made some sweet almonds." It was terrible, Irene thought. These aunts and uncles didn't know where they were going; and Klaus and Irene, suspecting what would happen, did not want to frighten them further. What choice did they have? It was impossible to hide them in Berlin. As for the Schlachtensee house, Klaus's presence there was stirring enough suspicion.

The Nazis shipped Klaus's aunt and more than a dozen other relatives south, to Theresienstadt in Czechoslovakia, a model concentration camp set up by the Nazis to deceive the Red Cross into believing that Jews were being treated well. Soon after Klaus's relatives left, a friend in Berlin received a postcard from Klaus's aunt. He passed it on to Klaus. Written in her neat hand, it said she had arrived in Theresienstadt and was doing well. It asked the family to send food. The Nazis routinely coerced such postcards from

Jews to mask the reality of the death camps. By the time Klaus read the postcard from his aunt in Berlin, he learned many years later, she had already been shipped to Auschwitz and gassed.

Within a few months of the final roundup of Berlin's Jews, the tide of the war turned. Klaus and Irene followed the progress of the Allied advance on a clandestine radio, listening to the BBC— the D-day invasion, the liberation of France, the advance into Germany itself. As the bombing of Berlin increased, they awaited the city's liberation, which—for them—occurred when a solitary Soviet officer came walking down their leafy street.

The Soviet troops that liberated Berlin liberated Klaus as well. For the first time in five years, he could walk the streets without fear. When Klaus Gysi said that you had to understand his biography, he meant his years under the Nazis, from 1933, when he was twenty-one, until 1945, when he turned thirty-three. Klaus had joined the Communist Party as a teenager, seen his country turned into a Nazi state in his twenties, and spent his early thirties living underground in Berlin, seeing his country reduced to ruin and his relatives dragged away to their deaths. So many had suffered. So many had died! Whatever combination of teenage idealism and Erna's influence that first turned him into a Communist at sixteen solidified into firm conviction after twelve years of life under the Nazis. At thirty-three, Klaus Gysi was a committed Communist, and nothing in the next fifty years would separate him from his convictions.

Around him, the city lay lifeless. But the Soviet occupation forces were determined to move swiftly. The Cold War, the battle between two systems, had already begun. As Soviet cultural officers followed fast on the heels of Soviet troops, they decided to reopen the Deutsches Theater, Berlin's most famous playhouse. They announced it would put on a production of *Nathan the Wise*, by Gotthold Ephraim Lessing. Written in 1779, the play was revered by liberal Germans as one of the most eloquent pleas for tolerance and against anti-Semitism ever written by a German. It told the story of a noble, wise, and generous Jew who treated others fairly and raised an adopted Christian as his own daughter, even after his entire family had been massacred by Christians. When the play was first performed, Irene's family had changed its last name to honor the German playwright. Its favorable portrayal of Jews caused the Nazis to ban the play. But now, in liberated Berlin, the Deutsches Theater was staging a revival.

Irene and Klaus set out for the theater from their house. The western part of Berlin, in which the Schlachtensee villa lay, was now being occupied by American troops; the Deutsches Theater was in the center of the city, under Soviet control. The journey took five hours. Irene and Klaus took the elevated train over the segment of the city where it still functioned. An American army officer in a jeep gave them a lift part of the way. Then they walked, picking their way through the rubble, past the shrapnel-ridden Branden- burg Gate, which still straddled Unter den Linden, past the ruins of Hitler's headquarters and the bunker where he had spent his last, demented days, past the shell of the Schlosskonditorei coffeehouse, where twelve years earlier—a lifetime ago—two fresh-faced stu- dents had met for coffee and gazed at their college identification cards with the ominous yellow stripe. Weary, Klaus and Irene settled into their seats inside the theater. Nearby lay one of Berlin's oldest Jewish neighborhoods, now shattered and ominously quiet: there were no Jews left there. Onstage, Nathan the Wise spoke his famous plea for tolerance to a Christian anti-Semite:

> We must be friends, we must. Despise my race
> as much as you please. We did not choose
> our races for ourselves. Do you and I
> make up our races? What is race?
> Are Jews and Christians Christians and Jews
> rather than men? Oh, how good if I've found in you
> one more for whom it is enough to be
> a man!

Klaus, who always insisted he ran the greater risk returning to Germany under the Nazis because he was a Communist, not a Jew, had lost nineteen Jewish relatives to the concentration camps. All those who had been transported to Theresienstadt had died. The postcard from his aunt was the last memory he carried of them. But here, onstage, was eloquent testimony to the future he and Irene envisioned, a future that Communism promised. Klaus Gysi could be a *man*, not just a Jew. Klaus and Irene watched the play and wiped away tears. The war was over. They had survived.

Klaus and Irene could now do something the Nazis had forbidden: They could get married. Klaus made his way to the city clerk's office and asked if they were registering marriages.

"Yes; why not?" said the official. Above his head, on the wall in the room where Klaus and Irene would be married in a civil ceremony, was a framed quotation from Adolf Hitler. Klaus said they would wait until it had been taken down.

A few months later, on the day of the wedding, a clatter of vehicles made their way up the drive at Schlachtensee. The subways and trains were still not running. Klaus's father arrived in a Polish horse cart with his sister and his second wife. Others came by bicycle, pedaling for hours to cross the city. Friends nearby had managed to get an old horse, which they turned into horsemeat goulash for a wedding feast.

Klaus and Irene were already known to the Russians as loyal Communists, thanks to their service to the party underground during the war. The Russians placed a sign saying "Do Not Loot"—in Russian—on the front of the grand house in Schlachtensee, to keep rapacious Soviet soldiers away.

But under the agreement drawn up by the Allies, the villa on the lake now lay in American-controlled territory. From the start, Irene and Klaus had no love for the American occupiers. The Americans, Irene liked to tell people, were not polite to them like the Russians. The first American soldiers who came by, she said, stuffed silverware into their pockets. Then came other soldiers— merchants in civilian life, Irene guessed. These had an eye for quality; they took only what was valuable. The airborne units were the worst, she insisted. Irene parroted Nazi propaganda that the Americans had opened their prisons for anyone who would parachute over Germany. It was the start of an unpleasant relationship between Klaus and Irene and the Americans.

Because the Americans controlled the western sector of Berlin, they appointed the German "mayors" of each neighborhood. But the Russians retained the right to select deputy mayors. They chose Klaus Gysi as deputy mayor of his neighborhood, the Zehlendorf district. He could speak well and was a staunch Communist who had proved his loyalty during the war. Irene Gysi now joined the Communist Party. Deputy Mayor Gysi's most important job was to oversee the local distribution of food in a city where food shortages were rampant. Klaus ran a lottery for what few chickens there were, and for goats that could produce milk. This supremely urbane man, educated at the Sorbonne and at Germany's most renowned university, speaker of English and French as well as German, now mucked around with chickens and goats. There were benefits; he could bring home an occasional fowl for supper. Irene was given a job at the old Luftwaffe headquarters in the heart of Berlin, where she helped distribute scarce products. She, too, had dividends: she brought home silk stockings.

The Communists soon had bigger plans for Klaus. Even before the Nazis formally surrendered, Communist Party organizers had arrived in Berlin on trains carrying the conquering Red Army. They had blueprints for the reorganization and takeover of every aspect of life: from the economy to culture. The Soviets considered culture an important battleground. Stalin had put cultural activities in the Soviet Union completely under Communist control. He himself read film scripts before they were produced, penciling in changes. Even as the victors were celebrating Hitler's defeat, it was clear that the Soviet Union and the Western Allies—the United States, Britain, and France—were edging toward friction over who would dominate Germany and Eastern Europe. The Soviets sensed early on that culture could be an important weapon in winning over the loyalty of Germans in the Soviet zone of occupation—the eastern part of Germany, stretching between the Elbe River and the Polish and Czech borders. This, after all, was the land of Schiller and Goethe. In the aftermath of the horror and devastation of Hitler's war, emphasizing German culture was a way to reassure Germans—and for Germans to reassure themselves—that the German Communists represented the other, better Germany, which had been blotted out by the rise of Hitler. It was the Soviets who decided the Germans should put on *Nathan the Wise*, to emphasize the "good" German tradition even as the ashes and rubble of Nazism lay around them. Writers and artists had fled to England, America, and the Soviet Union. Many of them sympathized with the Left and with Communism. The German Communists were eager to have these writers and artists return to Germany and settle in the Soviet zone. It would bolster their case that the future of a peaceful, civilized Germany lay in a Germany under Communism.

Many of the Soviet cultural officers put in charge of retooling German culture to Communist specifications were Jewish—a fact they themselves did not emphasize but that other Jewish Communists, like Klaus Gysi, quickly noticed. They had been chosen because, like Gysi, they were well educated, were familiar with literature, and spoke foreign languages. The East German official picked to oversee culture was not Jewish. He was Johannes R. Becher, who had spent the war in exile in Moscow and whose thinking reflected the reality of Communist intentions rather than the propaganda. Becher favored swift adoption of a hard line that would make artists and writers, like everyone in a Communist state, follow the dictates of the Communist Party. But the Communist hierarchy in the Soviet-occupied zone of East Germany rejected Becher's plans in favor of a policy designed to attract German writers and artists who had suffered under the Nazis. They did not have to be loyal Communists, just "anti-Fascists." To oversee the return of these left-wing writers and supervise culture in general, the Communists established the Kulturbund—the Cultural Association for the Democratic Renewal of Germany. Becher was named president, Klaus Gysi his deputy.

Gysi relished his new role. He believed that Communism provided a better atmosphere for culture than the ruthless capitalism of the West, with its slavish devotion to a market economy. The man who had grown up around books was now surrounded by some of Germany's greatest writers. Gysi became one of the four founders of the Aufbau publishing house, which produced books by German writers who had been banned by the Nazis, such as

Thomas and Heinrich Mann, and Russian writers like Maxim Gorky. He became editor of *Aufbau* magazine, which published new German writers.

Gysi's scrapbook soon filled with pictures of a smiling young Klaus shaking hands with the playwright Bertolt Brecht and other German writers returning from exile to be wined, dined, and feted. Gysi opened cultural events and literary symposiums. He helped returning writers and artists to find apartments and guided them through the cumbersome Communist bureaucracy. His position allowed Klaus to indulge his love of literature and culture, but also to hone his political skills. By 1946, Klaus had lost the dandyish look of his youth. He now carried the confident air of a young man on the rise.

Many of the writers who returned to the Communist-controlled zone of Germany were like Gysi. They were Jewish—the novelists Stefan Heym, Stephan Hermlin, Anna Seghers, and Arnold Zweig—and most of them did not consider their Judaism part of their primary identity. None became a member of one of the Jewish communities that were reestablished in the Communist-dominated parts of Germany. They were part of an intellectual middle- and upper-middle-class Jewish stratum that in the 1920s discovered a vision for the future in Communist theory. They saw their concerns and warnings confirmed by the rise of Nazism after 1933 and the devastations of World War II. Now, with the war over, they thought they could put their ideals into practice. They sought a world in which intellectuals were treasured and listened to by the government. This could be a new Germany, rejecting the destructiveness and discrimination of the Nazis, rejecting such old-fashioned labels as "Jew," which had served only to divide people. In the new Communist state, old identities and divisions would disappear, as people treated each other as true equals.

Consciously or not, these Jewish Communist writers and cultural officials represented an extension of the great German Jewish cultural symbiosis that had blossomed in the late nineteenth and early twentieth centuries. Germany's Jews before the rise of Hitler had tried to integrate "through the stage door of culture," in the phrase of one historian. Successful German Jews had become patrons of the arts. They flocked to the theaters and opera houses—because they loved the arts but also because sitting in the audience gave Jews a sense of social acceptance. The participation of Jews in German culture before World War II had produced an outpouring of literature, music, and ideas unparalleled since the Italian Renaissance. Poets, painters, composers, philosophers, scholars, critics, hurled themselves into a frenzy of new creative movements: Expressionism, Dadaism, and other isms that flared into the public's sight. In the new Communist-controlled East Germany, surrounded by the ashes of Nazism, Klaus Gysi and the artists and writers he mingled with hoped to re-create a new cultural renaissance—this one bolstered by Socialism and idealism. Like the Jewish intellectuals and artists a generation earlier, these Jewish Communist intellectuals believed their identities as Jews would disappear—this time into a glorious "brotherhood" of Communists.

And yet, despite their fervent beliefs and lofty rhetoric, many of the Jewish leftists and Communists who returned to the Communist sector of Germany after the war lived in a kind of ghetto. Many had fled the Nazis and spent the war in London or the United States. The Gysis' friends included Jewish refugees returned from France, Great Britain, and the United States. Though they always insisted they were more Communist than Jewish, they shared a common bond of returning to a country that had annihilated their people and, often, their families. The children of Jewish Communists immediately felt different upon returning to Germany after the war. They were children without grandparents, without aunts and uncles. Even in his dealings with Soviets overseeing German cultural life, Gysi sensed a close, unacknowledged bond with those who were Jewish. He felt they could trust each other.

The Jewish Communists who returned to Germany tended to be more cosmopolitan and educated than many of their comrades. Their time spent in exile in the West had exposed them to more culture, more intellectual life, and more freedom. By contrast, German Communists who had spent the war in Moscow—most of whom were not Jewish—were coarser and tougher. They had lived for years under the brutality and unpredictability of Stalin. They had seen the darker side of Communism and were willing, even eager, to impose it on Germany. Most of the top Communists installed in Soviet-occupied Germany right after the war came from this latter group. Stalin trusted them. He had spared them the purges that sent so many other Communists to their deaths.

Like the well-to-do German Jews of the 1920s who imagined anti-Semitism had vanished because they were free to sit in the boxes at the opera house, the Communist Jews of the late 1940s believed anti-Semitism had vanished because they were able to sit at the cultural meetings of the Communist Party. Both groups of Jews were wrong. A fatal mistake in perception, it would have enormous consequences for the Jewish Communists, including Klaus and Irene Gysi.

The Soviets and Americans had barely completed their occupation of Berlin when postwar tensions began to develop within the city and throughout Eastern Europe. The Soviets were moving to tighten the Communist grip on the countries they occupied. In 1946, the Soviets officially recognized the German Communist Party in the Russian-controlled eastern half of Germany and called for elections. The Americans refused to recognize the Communist Party in the western zone. In 1947, the Americans introduced a new currency, the deutsche mark, in the western zone; the Soviets introduced a new currency, the ostmark (or east mark), into the eastern zone. The western sector of Berlin remained an island surrounded by the Soviet zone of occupation. In June of 1948, the Soviets imposed an economic blockade around West Berlin, determined to force the American, British, and French out so they could unify the city under Soviet authority. For almost a year the Americans conducted an airlift, which brought in supplies. More than anything else, the blockade and airlift changed the feelings of West Berliners. They were no longer the conquered and the Americans the victors. America and West Berlin were now united, resisting a new enemy: the Communist East.

Klaus Gysi was still living in American-controlled West Berlin, commuting to work every day at the Kulturbund in the Soviet-controlled eastern zone. The Americans watched Klaus closely. Several times the American occupation force made Klaus and Irene move, as they requisitioned first the mansion in Schlachtensee and then other houses for soldiers and American personnel. Gysi's coworkers at the Kulturbund began to sing a little chant: "During the week we work so hard / On the weekend we move Mr. Gysi!"

Then, in 1948, the Americans banned the Kulturbund as a Communist organization. Klaus was in danger of being arrested. He and Irene packed up and moved to the Soviet Zone. The spiritual journey Klaus had embarked on as a sixteen-year-old when his mother enrolled him in the Communist Youth League was now reinforced by a physical journey. Klaus and Irene bid farewell to Irene's mother, who had hidden Klaus during the war years. They traveled across American-controlled West Berlin, through the checkpoints manned by Soviet soldiers, and into East Berlin.

As a rising Communist star, Klaus Gysi won choice accommodations: a three-story, seven-room house in a leafy neighborhood on the outskirts of the city. An entire Russian army regiment had vacated the house a few months earlier. The original owner had fled to Frankfurt, in West Germany. The house had a large backyard, perfect for children, and a park and trees behind the yard.

When Klaus and Irene had begun living together in 1937, Irene swore that she would never have children while the Nazis were in power. She would never bring a child into Hitler's dark and murderous Germany. In 1945, soon after the Nazis were defeated, she became pregnant and gave birth to a daughter, Gabriele. Three years later, in 1948, just as she and Klaus were preparing to move, she gave birth to a son, Gregor.

The Gysis quickly filled the house with bookcases and prints and original works signed by artist friends. The art reflected their myriad interests and far-flung connections. Along the stairway leading to their bedroom, Klaus and Irene hung sketches of New York City bought by Irene's father; in the entry hall, a signed and inscribed sketch by Bertolt Brecht's wife, the actress Helene Weigel.

What had once been one country had now become two: East Germany and West Germany. East Germany was allied with and dependent on the Soviet Union, West Germany on the United States. One would soon emerge as the leading power in Eastern Europe, the other as the leader in Western Europe. The Berlin Wall had not yet been erected, but already Germany was divided. Klaus Gysi had made his choice, completing a path that fate and his family had set him upon twenty years earlier. At thirty-six, he faced the future with ambitious eyes.

# Chapter Three

# The Singer from Auschwitz

The death march from the concentration camp was brutal. As the Russians closed in on Berlin, the German concentration camp guards at Sachsenhausen, just a few miles outside the city, roused their prisoners and assembled them for another march. Six months earlier, when the Russians closed in on Auschwitz, in Poland, the Nazis had packed the surviving prisoners into trains and cattle cars and shipped them here, hoping for more time to murder them more systematically. Now the guards gathered the ailing prisoners and began another forced march south, deeper into Germany.

Estrongo Nachama had survived the journey from Auschwitz. He had been a prisoner of the Nazis for three years now. When he had been seized by the Nazis in Salonika, Greece, he was a strikingly handsome young man, barrel-chested and with dark, almost black eyes. He was engaged to be married. His father traded grain, and Estrongo was being groomed to take over the family business. But then the Germans came and he was sent to Auschwitz, where he was separated from his family. The years that followed had shrunk him physically and battered his spirit. To be a strong young Jew meant surviving while thousands around him collapsed and died. In Sachsenhausen, Nachama was forced to work in the crematoriums, pushing corpses into the ovens, one after another, as the heat from the flames turned the crematorium blockhouse into an oven itself. After three days of nonstop work, Nachama collapsed from exhaustion. The Nazi guards dragged him away, displayed him in an open square, and flogged him—twenty-five lashes. Assigned to another work detail, Nachama marched five miles every morning to dig a ditch to fend off the approaching Russians. Along the way, he and a friend one day passed a dog kennel run by the feared Nazi SS. Nachama lured the dogs away so that his friend could dart in and grab the dogs' food. Nachama had to live too.

Nachama had always possessed a beautiful voice, a rich tenor that could hold quavering notes poised between joy and sorrow. In Auschwitz, the guards demanded that Nachama sing for them— Greek folk tunes, German marching songs. Nachama stood in front of the guards in his striped uniform, pulled deep breaths from his chest, and sang. The Nazis applauded, nodded approvingly, and tossed the hungry Jew crusts of bread. Nachama gnawed them eagerly. The Nazis dubbed him the "Singer from Auschwitz." Shipped from camp to camp, his reputation followed him. He sang for scraps of bread even as he grew thinner and weaker and the Jews around suffered and died.

Now Sachsenhausen was to be abandoned. Twelve thousand prisoners began the march, but within a few days, hundreds had collapsed from hunger and exhaustion. The Germans left them to die by the side of the road. As the arrival of the Soviet soldiers grew imminent, the German guards began shooting the Jews, twenty or thirty at a time. After a few days, the Germans literally ran into Russian soldiers. They were encircled. The last remaining prisoners—only twenty-five hundred of them—were freed. Nachama, the young man from Greece, the "Singer from Auschwitz" who had once had a burly chest and a powerful voice, had survived. It was May 4, 1945, Nachama's birthday. He was twenty-seven years old. He weighed sixty-five pounds.

Nachama planned immediately to go back to Greece, to find out the fate of his family and to rebuild. But ten days after he was liberated, he became sick with typhus and entered a hospital in the Soviet-controlled zone of Berlin. As, recovering, he walked around the hospital, he met a man wearing a Star of David around his neck. Nachama showed him the concentration camp number stenciled on his arm: 116155. Unlike Klaus and Irene Gysi, who a few miles away were fleeing their Judaism for the embrace of Communism, Estrongo Nachama wanted to reembrace Judaism and Jewish life. He wanted to find a synagogue, so he could pray. The man sent Nachama to the office of the Jewish community in Berlin. In Germany, as throughout Europe, each city had its own official "Jewish community," which coordinated activities and dispensed money. The Berlin Jewish office was trying to oversee what remained of the city's once vibrant Jewish presence. Nachama showed up in a Soviet army greatcoat, lent to him by a Russian soldier. The coat hung loosely, its broad shoulders exaggerating the withered frame of the man inside. Nachama was from a pious family. He stepped inside the building. "Where is the synagogue?" he asked. The officials gazed at the gaunt man before them and sent him to the one functioning synagogue left in Berlin, the Pestalozzi Strasse synagogue, in the British-controlled part of the city.

Berlin sagged under the weight of the bombs and the final battles. The Tiergarten, the large wooded park in the city's center, was barren. Desperate residents had cut down the trees to heat their homes. Food was scarce. Estrongo Nachama trudged through the rubble, just as Klaus and Irene had walked from their refuge near the lake to the first postwar performance of *Nathan the Wise*. Nachama's destination was different from Klaus Gysi's, as his journey through Germany and the Second World War had been far different. Nachama was searching for the place where he could begin to make sense of the horrors that had consumed him over the past four years. Klaus Gysi and Estrongo Nachama had both had their lives forever changed by Nazism. But in the aftermath of the war, they were heading, literally as well as politically, in opposite directions—the Gysis to the east of Berlin, to their hoped-for Communist utopia; Nachama to the west of Berlin, toward what he hoped would be the rebirth of Jewish life.

When Nachama finally made it to the small synagogue on Pestalozzi Strasse, in a formerly fashionable neighborhood that had been about 25 percent Jewish, he found a building desecrated and left in shambles. The Nazis had used the main sanctuary as a stable. The few Jews who came to services sat on salvaged beer garden stools in a small room. Three days after the war ended, the synagogue had begun services again; soon there was a bar mitzvah. But it was a deceptive show of normalcy. Two thousand Jews had spent the war hidden in Berlin. Others, like Nachama, now joined them as the concentration camps were liberated. Tattered and worn, they emerged like ghosts in a city that had once epitomized the achievements and glory of European Jewry.

Nachama began attending services at the synagogue as often as his strength allowed. The old cantor often had difficulty singing, and Nachama, who had briefly studied to be a cantor back in Greece, began to assist him. He sang solos at Sabbath services. Sometimes he sang with harmonium accompaniment. After a few weeks, the board of the synagogue asked Nachama to become their full-time cantor. He refused. He still intended to go back to Greece. But it became apparent that the old cantor was failing. Nachama agreed to serve as the synagogue's temporary cantor. When he regained his health, he would leave for Greece to pick up the pieces of his life.

As Nachama grew stronger, he began to radiate a strength and warmth and confidence that were desperately needed by Berlin's shattered Jewish community. Unlike Nachama, the Jews in Berlin—refugees or Jews who had hidden—mostly turned their backs on the synagogue. They had lost not only their homes and their families but their faith. Nachama began visiting people's homes, speaking to them in the simple German he was beginning to learn. "There is no God," one Jewish survivor told him. "The Nazis burned us. There can be no God." Nachama listened and pleaded. "Look, I've got a good voice," he said. "Why don't you just come and listen. You'll like it." First twenty came to the small synagogue. Then thirty. Then fifty. The crowd swelled, until the room where Nachama sang at services became too small. Nachama helped put some benches in the main synagogue, stripped by the Nazis, and then went in search of fuel. In his broken German, he appealed to a Berlin city official for coal. "I'm Cantor Nachama.

Please, our synagogue is too small. We want to reopen the big one. Give us coal."

"There is no coal," the man replied. "But there is wood."

So every Thursday, before Friday-evening services, Nachama pushed a handcart along the streets from the synagogue to the city offices and picked up five crates of firewood. He then pushed the wood back to Pestalozzi Strasse, so the small band of Jews gathered to pray would not be driven off by the cold.

Soon the old ways that had been buried under so many years of fear returned. Estrongo Nachama, many concluded, needed a wife. One evening he was invited to have dinner with a German Jewish couple who had hidden in Berlin throughout the entire war. They wanted him to meet Lilli Schlochauer, a young woman from a prominent Berlin family who herself had survived the war in hiding. Nachama considered himself a Greek Jew; he did not feel he belonged in Berlin. The Nazis had dumped him here when they ran into the Soviet army. Lilli, by contrast, was part of Berlin's prewar Jewish aristocracy. She was beautiful, with blond hair and creamy skin, and the story she told Estrongo, at that dinner and in the many dinners that would follow, was of the glorious rise and shattering fall of Berlin's prosperous Jews.

Jews first arrived in Berlin in the seventeenth century, but the true growth of the Jewish community did not begin until two centuries later. As Berlin blossomed from a provincial backwater to a European metropolis, Jews flocked to the city, drawn by its rapid industrialization, its trade activities, and—ironic in light of what would come to pass—its reputation for tolerance. In 1848, there were 8,000 Jews in Berlin. By 1880, there were 40,000. They ranked among the city's leaders in industry, banking, law, medicine, commerce, and the arts. By 1920, the number of Berlin Jews had swollen to 175,000—4 percent of the total population. They created a political, cultural, and religious ferment that rippled out from the Jewish community and transformed the city. Berlin's Jews constituted a community that could produce Communists like Klaus Gysi but also capitalists, like the Jewish merchants who owned the great department stores that lined the

Kurfürstendamm, and scientific geniuses like Albert Einstein. At Berlin's great universities, one-quarter of the medical and law students were Jewish—and one-third of the graduate students in philosophy. On the eve of Hitler's ascension to power, three-quarters of the directors who worked in Berlin's thriving theaters were Jewish, as were the leading editors, reporters, and critics of the city's best newspaper, the *Berliner Tageblatt*. Berlin had by far the largest number of Jews in Germany; no other German city had more than 30,000. The Jews were the reason Berlin became, financially and culturally, one of the richest cities in Europe, rivaling London and Paris.

No place better reflected the growth and changing stature of Berlin's Jewish community than the Jewish cemetery. The first cemetery, tucked on a small street within sight of the grand Unter den Linden boulevard, was built in 1646; it took almost two hundred years to fill. When the Berlin Jewish community founded a new cemetery in 1820, they expected there would be enough space for more than a century's worth of burials. They were wrong. In less than sixty years, it was filled to capacity. For its next cemetery, the Jewish community purchased a vast wooded field on the edge of the city, in a suburb called Weissensee. With a set of elegant wrought-iron gates at the entrance, a domed hall surrounded by porticoed walkways, well-tended lanes stretching out for acres under tall elm trees, the new cemetery was one of the largest and grandest serving any faith in all of Europe. Along the prominent first row lay the most illustrious and most successful of Berlin's Jews—rabbis and scholars and the businessmen who could afford a prestigious position to remind those who came after them just what their family had achieved.

It was in this first row that Lilli Schlochauer's parents bought their family plot.

The Schlochauer family moved to Berlin from Poland in the 1800s and started importing and exporting women's underwear on Oberwall Strasse, which would be the traditional center of the Jewish ready-made clothing industry in the 1920s. From this business, Lilli's father, Siegfried, and his brother, Hermann, expanded to manufacturing underwear. They invested in other factories in

Berlin and as far away as the Black Forest. They moved into a grand apartment in one of the city's best neighborhoods.

In religious terms, Lilli's family were liberals—what became known in the United States as Reform Jews. Reform Judaism had got its start in Berlin in the late nineteenth century, when Jews began achieving greater success in German, and especially Berlin, society. It reflected the desire of Jews like the Schlochauers to leave behind the old ways and traditions of the Polish villages and join the cosmopolitan vibrancy of Berlin—to be both Jewish and German. The family went to synagogue twice a week. They prayed in both German and Hebrew and listened to choral music, just like their Protestant and Catholic neighbors. From thick black prayer books they read traditional Jewish prayers but also a new prayer that asked for God's blessing on the "ruler of the land," the Kaiser. When World War I broke out in 1914, Lilian's father and uncle enlisted to fight for their country. The family proudly displayed photographs that showed them, looking stern and serious of purpose, in their German army uniforms.

By 1922, the year Lilli was born, Jews made up the business and cultural spine of Berlin—much as they would in New York forty and fifty years later. Of the forty German Nobel Prize winners before 1933, eleven were Jews. One hundred thousand German Jews fought for Germany in World War I; twelve thousand died. As a girl, walking with her mother along the Kurfürstendamm, Berlin's premier shopping street, Lilli patronized the three grandest stores in Germany: the KaDeWe, Wertheim's, and Israel's. All were owned by prosperous Jewish families. The newspapers her family read, the books they bought and discussed—not only on Jewish topics but on literature and the events of the day—were often edited by Jews, and Jews ran many of Germany's most prominent newspapers and publishing houses. The Jews of Berlin had long since broken out of the ghetto and become part of the German mainstream. They shaped German culture as much as they were shaped by it.

And yet, for all the success of Jews in Berlin, a persistent resentment and anti-Semitism smoldered beneath the surface. Lilli's family chose to ignore it. It did not impinge on their daily lives. But it was a whiff of the inferno that would soon engulf them all.

Like Christians in most countries, Germans had grown up with the anti-Semitic teachings of their churches: that the Jews had rejected Jesus and betrayed him, that Jews were an outcast people condemned to wander the earth. The stereotypes passed down through centuries of folktales had hardened into prejudice: Jews were miserly and insular, untrustworthy and far too shrewd in business. To this prejudice, which existed in all of Europe, was added the particular anti-Semitism of Martin Luther and Protestantism.

The success of Jews in science and culture, in business and the arts, the very tangible contributions they were making to turn Germany into a stronger state, did nothing to alleviate these prejudices. If anything, they exacerbated them. For every achievement of the Jews, there was a strong German counterreaction, a resentment of the new world that Jews—especially German Jews—were shaping. It is impossible, for example, to conceive of science in the twentieth century without Einstein—or finance without the Rothschilds or culture without Gustav Mahler or psychology without Sigmund Freud. Yet it was precisely this rapid and disorienting change that many Germans found so objectionable. As the biographer of one of the great Jewish banking families, the Warburgs, wrote: the Jews "symbolized a modernity that many Germans found profoundly threatening and preferred to regard as a foreign graft, an alien presence and not an organic development of their own society. . . . It was when Jews emerged from the ghetto—when they shed their beards and badges and became indistinguishable from other Germans—that the anti-Semitic movement first emerged."

The Russian Revolution and the abortive Communist revolution in Bavaria added a new page to the anti-Semitic catechism. For decades, the Jews had been viewed suspiciously as manipulators of capitalism, the new economic system that was building cities and upending traditional European hierarchies. The Rothschilds, the powerful Jewish banking family, were the new "masters of the age," anti-Semites raged. Now Jews were seen as the force behind the great Socialist conspiracy as well. The very successes that exhilarated Klaus Gysi terrified middle-class Germans, including many German Jews.

The German Right, growing in power after Germany's defeat in World War I and the economic chaos that followed, did not restrict its hatred of Jews to Communists. The German Right hated Jewish Social Democrats and Liberals as well. A right-wing poster in 1919 pictured, under the headline "Variety of Cohens," leading Jewish politicians in parties of every political persuasion.

Hitler, who had lived through the Bavarian uprising, tapped into these tendencies—traditional anti-Semitism, resentment of Jewish success, fear of change, fear of Communism—to concoct his powerful anti-Semitic cocktail. The image of the Jew as devil was central to Hitler's message, the simple and diabolic explanation for why Germany had lost the war, why so many Germans were unemployed, why the economy was in chaos. "The Jews," the Nazis declared, "are our misfortune." Jews, especially Jews in Berlin, were stunned by Hitler's election. To answer anti-Semitic attacks, the German Jewish War Veterans Association, to which Lilian's father and uncle belonged, listed the 10,623 Jewish soldiers who had given their lives for Germany during World War I. But that didn't matter to the Nazis, who considered the Jews to be Germany's greatest threat. They planned to combat that threat.

Lilli's father viewed the election of Hitler as an act of temporary political insanity, one that would pass once Germans saw what a charlatan Hitler was. Siegfried did not fear for his safety—he was, after all, a German patriot; he had fought for the Kaiser in the war. Still, it was wise to be prudent. His brother and business partner, Hermann, had just married a non-Jewish woman. Soon after Hitler came to power, but before he could pass the first anti-Jewish laws, the family quickly transferred its business holdings to her name. With an Aryan as the legal owner, the family believed nothing would happen to their property. And as for young Lilli . . . well, Lilli was blond. She didn't look Jewish at all.

By 1934, the Nazis in Berlin had begun compiling information about where Jews lived—taking a secret census of Jewish children in every neighborhood. Lilli entered the Charlottenburg Lyceum, a public high school. But soon all Jewish children were forced to attend Jewish schools. Then the Jewish schools were abolished as well. Jews were ordered to wear a yellow Star of David. Lilian's family began making plans to emigrate. The Nazis demanded a huge fee for potential "unpaid taxes"—in effect, a ransom—before exit visas were granted. The family turned over the money. Then, in 1937, Lilli's mother became ill and died, delaying their departure.

The family's plans for emigration accelerated again after Kristallnacht. The Nazis set fire to virtually every synagogue in Berlin that night of November 9, 1938, including the big synagogue where Lilian and her parents went to services on Friday nights and Saturday mornings. Six weeks later, on December 22, Lilian's father and her uncle received notification that they, like all Jewish men, were to change their first name to Israel. All adult Jewish women were to take the name Sarah. It was part of the continuing Nazi plan to single out Jews—to lump them all together and dehumanize them in the minds of other Germans. All around them, Jews were fleeing the country. Lilian's family prepared to leave for La Paz, Bolivia.

It all became too much to bear. Lilian's father committed suicide. Siegfried had seen his synagogue, his values, his entire world, destroyed. He realized now that this was not a brief episode in German history. The Germany he had known had been snuffed out.

The family buried Siegfried in the family plot at Weissensee, in the prestigious first row, next to the rabbis and the scientists and the other captains of industry. By tradition, suicides were not allowed burial in a Jewish cemetery. But the Weissensee cemetery was making exceptions. By 1939, suicide had become one of the leading causes of death for Jews in Berlin.

Lilian's uncle Hermann, now the family patriarch, announced that he would not desert his brother's grave. It was a stunning reversal. Perhaps Hermann still retained some optimism that life would get better for the Jews in Germany. Certainly he could not conceive of the death camps. Whatever his rationale, the members of the other branches of the family had no patience for it. They swiftly headed off to La Paz, and safety. The orphaned

Lilli was part of her uncle's family now. She stayed. She was seventeen.

Life quickly deteriorated. The Nazis forced the Shlochauers to move out of their spacious apartment and share a flat with two other Jewish families. Soon the Nazis began rounding up Berlin's Jews and sending them to concentration camps. Lilian was marched to the Jewish old age home near the vibrant cultural center of the city, a few blocks from Berlin's famous Museum Island and the former palace of the Kaiser. Her non-Jewish aunt, Henriette, got her out before she could be deported, but she was then pressed into forced labor at a Siemens factory. A Jewish friend of Lilian's at the factory received a deportation order and gave Lilian a necklace to keep safe for when she returned. The girl never came back.

Berlin was becoming too dangerous. With Henriette's help, Lilli went underground. She was given a fake identification card that said she was a clerk for the Luftwaffe, the German air force. Her blond hair helped. She moved from house to house. Early one morning, when she saw two men standing at the front door of the house where she was hiding, she threw on her coat and jumped out of the second-story window to the garden below. Across the way stood a large mansion that had once belonged to a Jewish acquaintance of Lilli's family but was now occupied by the SS. The door was open. A Nazi officer with a gun stopped her. "Do me a favor," she said, out of breath. "My husband just got back from the front, and I was in bed with my lover." The officer looked at her. "Anybody can say that," he barked. Lilian opened her coat, to reveal only her underwear. The officer, stunned, admitted Lilian. She had barely escaped.

The last Jews were deported from Berlin in 1943, in the roundups that sent Klaus Gysi's aunt and other relatives to Theresienstadt and then Auschwitz. Life underground became even more dangerous. In late 1944, Lilli's aunt came to her. "Lilli, you have to get out of Berlin for a few weeks," she said. With a non-Jewish friend, Lilli boarded a sleeper to Vienna. A fur coat heightened the image that she was just another rich Berlin girl off on a vacation. The train was patrolled by Nazi and military police. They looked at Lilli's fake identification as a Luftwaffe clerk. The military police came by to check again.

"In what capacity are you traveling?" she was asked.

"That you will have to ask our Führer in Wilhelmstrasse," Lilli responded haughtily. Wilhemstrasse was the address of Hitler's headquarters in Berlin. "Only he can tell you." Lilli's bluff worked. The police let her continue on her way.

In Vienna, Lilli and her friend stayed at the Grand Hotel. It was New Year's Eve. Lilli went down to the lobby for a cup of tea. There were SS officers and German army officers everywhere. An army officer made his way through the crowd and sat beside her.

"I've seen you here before. You are staying with your girlfriend, aren't you?" the officer asked the twenty-two-year-old Lilli. "Is she around too? I'd like to invite the two of you to our party." Giddy after her successful ruse on the train, filled with the invincible confidence of youth, Lilli agreed to go with the young officer. She dressed and met her escort, making excuses for her friend, who had no intention of spending New Year's Eve with a bunch of Nazis. Lilli's officer took her to a huge banquet hall filled with Nazis in dress uniforms. She was the only woman there. A lavish dinner was served—better food than Lilli had seen in years of hiding and living off stolen food coupons. But she could not eat much. The sea of medals and uniforms unnerved even someone who had become as adept at deception as she. Midnight approached. Champagne was passed. Lilli planned her secret, unspoken toast: "Let them perish with this." Then her escort stood and began a toast praising Hitler and his accomplishments. Abruptly he turned to Lilian: "Look at this young lady who is celebrating with us today," he announced proudly. "She'll give a toast to our beloved Führer now." Lilli began to shake. "Look, look, how emotional she is," the officer declared. "She's trembling." Lilli—trembling from fear—quickly touched glasses with the officer, took a sip of champagne, and excused herself to the ladies' room. She left the hall and headed back to the hotel. She stayed in her room until she received word that the crisis in Berlin had passed and it was safe to return.

As the war turned against Germany and the Russians advanced

on Berlin, Lilli and her uncle and aunt, who were in hiding as well, listened to the BBC broadcasts from London. The Russians had entered the city! The Schlochauers were in the cellar of their old apartment building when they came face-to-face with their liberators. A group of Russian soldiers burst in, shouting, *"Uri! Uri!"* "Watches! Watches!" Lilli's uncle Hermann ran up to the second-floor apartment they had occupied and found a Russian officer and his men setting up headquarters. The Russian spoke German. Hermann told him of the group of Jews hiding in the cellar. The Russian looked at Hermann quizzically. "You are Jewish?" he barked in German. "Say something in Yiddish!" Hermann obliged, and the soldier embraced him in a hug. *"Tovarish! Tovarish!"* he exclaimed. "Comrade! Comrade!" The Russian soldier was Jewish too.

The war was over. The synagogue Lilli and her family had attended had been destroyed. So, like Estrongo Nachama, Lilian Schlochauer made her way to the synagogue on Pestalozzi Strasse. When Lilli told other Jews who had been in hiding during the war that she planned to visit the synagogue, some looked at her in anger and astonishment, just as they had at Estrongo Nachama. "Synagogue?" they said. "Where is God? Where was he?" But Lilian had not lost her faith. She was at ease with God and her Judaism. And so she found herself at dinner one evening with this handsome Greek Jew with his soulful eyes and dramatic dark eyebrows.

It was not love at first sight. Estrongo was *"ein Jüngelchen,"* Lilli declared to her friends afterward—a far from impressive young man. He was still gaunt from his years in the camps and his bout with typhus. But the two young survivors talked. It was a time for possibilities again—for Germany, for Jews, for a young man and a young woman.

The course of their love followed a winding road. Nothing came of that first meeting at dinner. Over the next few years, Estrongo and Lilli fell into other relationships. Each was married, then divorced. Lilli had a son, whom she named Andreas. In the small world of Berlin's Jews, and the smaller world of the Pestalozzi Strasse synagogue, they remained in touch, and in 1950 they moved in together. Soon, they married and Estrongo adopted Andreas, who was still a baby. Lilian and Estrongo were a family now, and Andreas grew up with Estrongo as the only father he ever knew.

Estrongo still talked of Berlin as a temporary home. He sang at synagogue every Friday night and Saturday morning. But he continued to await word on the fate of his family in Greece. He expected the worst after so many years. But in the turmoil of displaced persons camps and the massive efforts under way to document the fate of Europe's Jews, there was still a glimmer of hope that someone besides Nachama might have survived.

He began to study voice, spurred on by an opera performer who had heard Estrongo's rich tenor in the synagogue. In 1951, his teacher invited him to sing at a rehearsal at the Staatsoper, the State Opera House. It would be Nachama's first step in a career as a professional opera singer.

A week before the rehearsal, a letter arrived from the American Joint Distribution Committee, which oversaw the repatriation of Europe's Jews and the grim accounting of the Jewish victims of the Germans. The letter carried the stark official news. Nachama's family was dead—his mother, his father, his brothers and sisters. There was no one left. Lilian and Andreas were all his family now.

This crushing information altered Nachama's life forever. He informed his voice teacher that he would not be attending the rehearsal. He would not become an opera singer. He would remain a cantor. On this Friday night, and every Friday and Saturday thereafter, he would sing the Kaddish, the Jewish prayer for the dead, for his murdered family.

Berlin had changed dramatically by 1950. The Cold War had settled in. The city was now divided. Politics swirled around Nachama—the standoff between the Americans and the Soviets, the Berlin airlift—but he paid it little attention. He had been liberated by the Soviets, but he had no desire to be ruled by them. Lilian's distaste for East Germany had as much to do with lifestyle as with ideology. East Germany called itself the land of "workers and peasants." It had no room for the middle-class comforts and culture that Lilli had grown up with and that she hoped to provide for her son. And it was clear that even now, the outlook for Jews in East Germany was bleak. The Communists mocked religion. There could be no future for a cantor over there.

But was the future of Jews in West Germany any more promising? The once proud Jewish community of Berlin had been reduced to a handful of survivors and refugees. The cantor of the synagogue was a Greek. The new head of the Jewish community was a refugee from Prussia, now part of Poland, and a concentration camp survivor. The Weissensee cemetery, the final resting place of Lilli's father and generations of Berlin Jews, was now under Communist control in the east. The few Jews who chose to remain in West Germany lived with the daily knowledge that a few years earlier, their neighbors had willingly boycotted Jewish shops, enthusiastically cheered Hitler, and turned their heads away as the police rounded up Jews for the concentration camps. No wonder many German Jews, survivors of the war, refused ever to set foot in Germany—East or West—again. They left for Israel or for the United States, turning their backs on the homeland that had turned against them.

Estrongo and Lilli remained. Like a piece of driftwood tossed ashore by stormy seas, Nachama had landed in a place far from home. He had never intended to stay in Berlin. But it was as much his home as anyplace now. Increasingly, what Nachama cared about were his Jews—as he had begun to think of them. There was the small congregation at the synagogue on Pestalozzi Strasse, but also the Jews "over there," in East Germany. In 1948, Nachama was asked by a West Berlin radio station to broadcast Friday-evening Sabbath services for Jews too old or too sick after the war to leave their houses. Nachama agreed. He did it for the Jews, so they could feel the Sabbath coming into their homes. But he also did it because he felt he had to remind the Germans who listened what it was like to be Jewish. He could not allow the Jewish life that had once thrived in Berlin to disappear completely. The shows were so popular, among both Germans and Jews, that soon the East Berlin radio station, run by the Soviets, asked him to broadcast services from its studio as well.

So every week, Nachama packed up his music sheets and traveled back and forth through the checkpoints to the two radio stations. Backed by an East German choir in East Berlin and a West German choir in West Berlin, Nachama sang the traditional Hebrew prayers and songs that greeted the Sabbath. His rich tenor shimmered through the airwaves into both Berlins, a haunting reminder of a Jewish life that had once flourished but was now gone.

# Chapter Four

# Statue of Liberty

"Gary Cooper. John Wayne. Bette Davis." Years later, walking down the steps from her daughter's apartment and down the darkened streets of nighttime Prague, Alena Wittmann could recite the names of the film stars of her youth. She'd hear a snatch of the Andrews Sisters on the radio or in a restaurant, and her face would liven as she moved her head brightly to the music. Alena Wittmann had lived her entire life in Czechoslovakia, but it was not now the Czechoslovakia she had known as a child. She lived with the memories of what had happened to her during the war and, even worse, what happened to her after the Communists took over. With her elegant bearing and gentle manner, Alena seemed to have come from another time. To understand her meant first understanding the special world of Czechoslovakia's Jews before World War II.

It was a world of books and music and trips to the opera. Like the Jews of Berlin, those of Czechoslovakia were among the most cultivated and assimilated in Europe. Let the Polish Jews, with their broad-brimmed hats and side curls, live in their shtetls, speaking Yiddish and praying. Let the Russian Jews entertain their Socialist and Communist ideas. The Jews of Czechoslovakia were different—more genteel, more cultured, certainly more accepted by their countrymen and women. In the house in Pilsen where Alena grew up in the 1930s, everyone played an instrument. While still a girl, Alena learned both the violin and the piano. She traveled frequently to the opera to hear her grandmother perform. The house itself was full of books. Bookshelves lined the walls in the living room, the hallways, the bedrooms. Though they lived in Czechoslovakia, Alena's family often spoke German at home. German was the language of learning and books and the arts, the sign of a cultured, well-to-do family. The great Prague literary figures, like Franz Kafka, wrote in German. The audience that supported them—buying their books, discussing their works in salons, boarding the train to see the opera in Vienna—spoke German as well. Like Alena's family, that audience was Jewish. They made up a cosmopolitan middle class that prided itself on its learning and its successful assimilation.

The money in Alena's family originated in a successful tailoring business that one of her grandfathers had established. The descendants branched out into other forms of commerce and prospered. Some of Alena's cousins were so well off they traveled to Switzerland for ski vacations. Alena's family was not quite that rich, but every summer they rented a house by the seaside, the very model of a successful bourgeois Czech family in the 1920s and 1930s.

Indeed, so patriotic were Alena's parents that in 1921, swept up in the birth of Czechoslovakia after World War I, they joined the newly established Czech Hussite Church, even though they were Jewish. Named after the Czech national hero Jan Hus, the Hussite Church symbolized the hopes of the new nation. Alena's parents didn't view their move as a major departure. They did not go to a synagogue or participate in Jewish rituals. Judaism for them had become an ethnic identity. Joining the Hussite Church was more a political conversion than a religious one. Alena's parents worshiped Tomáš Masaryk, who had relentlessly lobbied Woodrow Wilson and the United States to create the tiny country of Czechoslovakia after Germany's defeat in the war. Before becoming the Czech equivalent of George Washington, Masaryk had defended a Jewish factory owner, Leopold Hilsner, who was falsely accused of killing a young Christian girl in a ritual slaying. The arrest originated in and reinforced the long-standing Christian myth that Jews killed Christian children for sausage meat or to use their blood at the Passover seder. Many Jews feared that Czechs might instigate a wave of pogroms. Then Masaryk intervened and led liberals to combat anti-Semitic lies and to fight for Hilsner's freedom. The Hilsner case inspired heated debates in parliament. It became Czechoslovakia's Dreyfus affair—but unlike the outcome of that case, the anti-Semites in Czechoslovakia lost. Masaryk remained a friend of the Jews and even visited Palestine. He donated money to support Hebrew education in Eastern Europe. And when he died, Jews in Palestine named a kibbutz in his honor.

With such a friend of the Jews as president of his country, Alena's father had no trouble deciding to join the Hussite Church. He changed the family name from Smulowitz to Schmula. He joined a nationalist singing group and a Czech sports club whose membership included Protestants, Catholics, and Jews. There were Jewish sports clubs, and Socialist sports clubs, but Schmula wanted nothing to do with them. He was a Czech—a patriot now in everything from religion to soccer.

All of this meant little when the Nazis came. Hitler had clamored for more and more territory, annexing first Austria and then, with the acquiescence of Great Britain and the other European powers, Czechoslovakia. Alena was twelve when the Nazis marched into Czechoslovakia in 1938. She was fifteen when they occupied Pilsen and began rounding up everyone born of Jewish parents. Because Alena had been baptized and had officially converted to Protestantism, she was spared immediate deportation to the death camps. Instead she and her mother were assigned as slave laborers in a ceramics factory. It was grueling to work in front of the ovens from seven-thirty in the morning to eleven-thirty at night. But Alena knew that if she showed the slightest sign of weakness, her reprieve would be over and she would be sent to even more horrible places, like Jewish friends, so many of them, who had simply vanished. Desperate for food, she and her mother at one point killed a dog and ate its meat. But when the war ended and she returned to Pilsen, she realized that she had been spared the worst. All of her Jewish neighbors, all of her

Jewish school friends, had been killed. Her father survived in hiding. His impetuous decision to embrace nationalism by enrolling the family in the Czech Protestant Church had saved his daughter's life.

The Russian army liberated and occupied most of Czechoslovakia. But Pilsen was in the western part of the country, and it was the Americans who liberated the Schmulas from their labor camp and occupied their home town. A coalition government of Communist and traditional democratic Czech parties took power in Prague. The President of the country was Edvard Beneš, who had served with Tomáš Masaryk before the war; the foreign minister was Jan Masaryk, Tomáš's son.

The country was poor and depleted, but Alena's family was full of hope. They began rebuilding and reopening some of their businesses in Pilsen—a photography studio, then a photography laboratory, and a factory that made steel for automobiles.

Alena, approaching twenty, was tall and slim, with a handsome face and a soft, warm smile. She cherished the occupying American soldiers for their rough good looks and the swing music that blasted from their radios and record players. She stood in line to see the American movies that now played at movie theaters. Gary Cooper. John Wayne. She could recite the names of her favorite movie stars by heart. Alena had listened to the underground radio during the war and dreamed about the American soldiers coming to liberate her. Now here they were, walking by and visiting her house almost every day. Alena's family felt blessed that their town was occupied by Americans, who were so different from the Russian soldiers. Alena visited Russian-occupied Prague and was shocked at the young soldiers' behavior. Starved of material goods at home, every Russian had a collection of watches he had stolen. They were stealing bicycles. In every shop they entered, they just pointed to the things they wanted. After they gathered up their pile of goods, they turned and left. No "good-bye," no "thank you"; no money was exchanged. The Russians just quietly looted Prague. In Pilsen, the American soldiers paid for what they bought. The Russians in Prague often lay, drunk, in the dirt in the streets. American soldiers' uniforms were always ironed. Once, soon after the war ended, a Russian officer visiting Pilsen came into the family photography shop, wanting photos to be developed immediately. Impossible, Alena told him; the lab was located elsewhere. He took out his pistol and aimed it at Alena. Suddenly two American soldiers came through the door. Just like in the movies! They politely, but firmly, asked the Russian to leave. On his way out, the Russian soldier slammed the door so hard the display windows shattered.

Alena took out her finest dresses and joined the Czechoslovak-American Friendship Society. Their symbol was a small Statue of Liberty pin. Alena pinned the Statue of Liberty on her dress and walked proudly around town. Now she could be free again, and flirt.

In Prague, too, life seemed to be returning to normal, to the democracy and freedom Czechoslovakia had enjoyed before the Nazis invaded. The Communists, backed by the occupying Russians, were a powerful force, but they seemed content—for now—to govern the country in cooperation with the democrats.

Alena decided to look for work in Prague. She soon found a job at the agricultural ministry, in a department that was returning land confiscated by the Nazis to its original owners. Communists in the ministry kept approaching her, urging her to join the party. She listened but said nothing. One brought her an application form and urged her to fill it out. "Thank you," Alena said. After the man left, she stuffed the application into a drawer. When the Communist recruiter returned, Alena lied. "Actually, I lost it," she said. He brought her another form. Into the drawer it went.

Already it was clear to Alena what kind of people these Communists were. A few were idealistic, serious people. The majority were nasty and aggressive. They hated everything that came from the West, especially Western music and movies. They glorified everything that came from the East, from Russia. Anyone who failed to glorify Russia was suspect. For Alena, the suggestion that she join the party was a joke. But she couldn't just throw the application at them and say so. The Communists, though not yet in full control of the country, were very powerful. Alena could lose her job. So she kept stuffing the application forms into her drawer. Of course she would not join the Communists.

Then in February 1948, backed by the Soviets, the Communists staged a coup. They purged most of the non-Communist ministers. When President Beneš tried to maintain a democratic coalition government, they convened "action committees" at factories and seized control of the country from below, driving out non-Communist leaders in factories, offices, and the press. The Communist military leaders kept the army neutral. President Beneš capitulated and appointed an all-Communist cabinet. Jan Masaryk, who represented the last link with the democratic Czechoslovakia founded by his father, was discovered dead in the courtyard beneath the windows of his office, having either leaped or been pushed. The West, bound by the agreement in Yalta that ceded Czechoslovakia, Hungary, Romania, and Poland to the Soviet sphere of influence, did nothing. In May 1948, only Communist-approved candidates were allowed to run for office. A Communist dictatorship was established.

The Iron Curtain descending on Czechoslovakia not only wiped out private enterprise; it began to blot out much of the popular culture as well. By 1950, the Communists had banned Western music—jazz, jitterbug, boogie-woogie. Alena went to dances back in Pilsen, but young people there were allowed to dance only the polka. Women had to dress as modest, asexual "Socialists" and behave accordingly. Communist officials chaperoned all the dances. As soon as they saw couples pick up the pace and drift into a contemporary dance, they would stop the music. One day, as she walked along the street in Pilsen, Alena noticed some women looking at her. A fat woman with a scarf tied around her hair approached. "Look at this monster—she has makeup and painted fingernails," the woman shouted. "Take it off!" Others joined in. "You painted bourgeois!" "You painted whore!" A Socialist woman was supposed to hide her hair under a scarf, they insisted. Alena hurried on, shaken.

But she would not be cowed. She still walked the streets with her small Statue of Liberty pinned to her dress. Then one day a Communist woman came up to Alena on the street and ripped it off.

The Communist nightmare engulfing Czechoslovakia had begun.

# Chapter Five

# Homecoming

There was no question, everyone agreed: The Raj boys, Tamas and Ferenc, would go to a Jewish school. The war had ended in the spring, and now, in the winter of 1945–46, Hebrew schools were reopening all across Budapest. The rabbinical seminary had reopened as well, ordaining nineteen new rabbis. Religious congregations were organized again in all the city's neighborhoods and in a number of small towns. Jewish sports clubs were springing up again—for soccer, general athletics, and fencing.

Budapest's activity and hope contrasted sharply with the devastation among the Jewish communities in Berlin, Prague, and Warsaw. The Holocaust had passed through Hungary like a hurricane that holds a city in its grip and then suddenly departs, miraculously leaving the center of town still standing. More than 450,000 Hungarian Jews had been killed by the Nazis, almost two-thirds of Hungary's Jewish population. But the miracle was that 160,000 had survived, almost all of them in Budapest. The Hungarians, who allied themselves with the Nazis, had passed a handful of anti-Jewish laws, such as limiting the number of Jews who could go to universities. But they resisted German demands that they ship Jews to the death camps. Even into the 1940s, a large number of Jews in Budapest were able to continue in their jobs and keep their property. Indeed, in an Eastern Europe consumed by virulent anti-Semitism, the relative mildness of Hungary's strictures made Hungary look attractive. Jews in Poland, Germany, and Romania began to look to Hungary as a haven; some tried to flee there. In 1944, enraged with Hungary's foot-dragging, Hitler sent German troops to occupy the country and Adolf Eichmann to supervise the deportation of its Jews. "The Jews are parasites undeserving of any forbearance," Hitler declared. "They must be dealt with like tubercular germs."

Eichmann worked with maniacal efficiency, herding Jews into ghettos, diverting trains from Germany's beleaguered war effort to ship Jews to Auschwitz. When the advance of the Allies stopped the rail transports, thousands of Budapest Jews were marched to the banks of the Danube, which winds gracefully through the center of the city. The Jews were shot on the riverbank and thrown in. The river ran with blood.

The resistance of the Hungarian government to Hitler's demands saved many of Budapest's Jews. So did the heroic efforts of Raoul Wallenberg, the Swedish diplomat, who appealed to the Germans' well-known obsession with official documents. He mass-produced Swedish identity papers, complete with official-looking stamps and seals, and distributed them to hundreds of Jews as the Nazis raced to round them up. The papers "officially" offered the doomed Jews the protection of the neutral Swedish government. Wallenberg worked tirelessly. He crammed the identity papers through cracks in the cattle cars crowded with Jews as the trains were about to depart and ran around to the front, demanding the Nazis open the cars because there were "Swedish citizens" inside. The Nazi guards complied, studied the documents, and let the Jews go. The ruse worked. Wallenberg shepherded Jews to houses in Budapest—Wallenberg Houses—slapped Swedish flags on the outside, and declared everyone inside protected by the Swedish government. By war's end, Wallenberg had saved thousands of Jews. As the Soviet army entered Budapest to liberate the city from the Nazis, Wallenberg headed down one of the main roads to greet them. In a chilling precursor to the Cold War, Wallenberg was suspected of being an American agent and taken prisoner by the Russians. He was never seen again.

\*　　\*　　\*

The Rajs were among the Jewish families saved by Wallenberg. They had stayed in their apartment in the Jewish quarter of Budapest as one family after another was plucked away. Soon after World War II began and Hungary joined the side of the Nazis, Sandor Raj, a lawyer, had been conscripted by the Hungarian army, along with other Jewish men, in a forced-labor battalion. Sandor's father died of starvation. His mother and his father-in-law were seized and taken to a farm outside Budapest to dig antitank traps against the expected Soviet advance. Left at home were Sandor's children—little Tamas, four, and his two-year-old brother, Ferenc—their mother, Margit, and her seventy-eight-year-old grandmother, Mutti.

The Rajs were observant Jews. They kept a kosher home and worshiped regularly at temple. Sandor's first cousin was a rabbi at one of Budapest's temples. Unlike the Gysis, who shed their Judaism as an old-fashioned garment, the Rajs wrapped themselves in Jewish life, finding in it both comfort and the moral and spiritual guidance they needed.

A streak of stubbornness poured into the Rajs from both their mother's and father's side. Margit's father, Vilmos, was a wonderful man with a glorious singing voice but no money—a poor marriage prospect. But Matilda, Margit's mother, fell in love and overruled her family's objections. She married this poor man and built her family with him. Before the war, before the Hungarian Fascists carted him away to work digging ditches against the Soviet advance, Vilmos ran a small shop selling cigarettes and clothing. He left the running of the family to his strong-willed wife.

Those two family traits—spirituality and obstinacy—served the family well as they remained in their apartment overlooking Budapest's main avenue, Joseph Boulevard, in 1944. They prayed and waited, wondering who would arrive first, the advancing Red Army or the German Wehrmacht, with its orders to speed the liquidation of the Jews. Little Tamas was the first to hear the noise. Motorcycles! Tamas's mother picked up her son so he could look out the window. Motorcycles swept down the boulevard, each of them carrying a Nazi soldier. Hungary was under German occupation.

Behind them, the Rajs' young maid peered out the window as well. "What a good thing the Germans are coming!" she exclaimed. "At last they'll take the Jews away." Tamas's mother put the child down and went out of the room with the maid. She paid the maid her wages, plus a few weeks extra, and sent her on her way. The Rajs would not be needing her services anymore.

The Rajs lived in Budapest's oldest Jewish neighborhood. The Nazis quickly walled it in—a ghetto. From another house, one of Tamas's aunts disguised herself as a refugee from Romania and snuck out of the ghetto walls. She obtained some of the treasured Wallenberg documents—papers declaring that the holders were under Swedish protection and could not be arrested or deported. Quickly the family assembled all the belongings that could be loaded into a large, hand-pulled cart. Tamas looked after his younger brother, Ferenc, changed his diapers, and helped with the packing. Pile after pile was heaped onto the cart: clothes, cooking pots, feather comforters. Amid the comforters, Tamas's great-grandmother buried the family Torah scroll—two feet long, nestled in a blue velvet cover embroidered with her name. It was the most precious possession of all.

The makeshift caravan made its way through the streets of Budapest to 49 Holan Street, a gray-stone apartment building facing the Danube, with a Swedish flag. The Rajs shared a cramped basement space with a Jewish composer and his family. The Wallenberg documents did not guarantee protection. Sometimes, the Nazis respected them; but at other times, they or their Hungarian allies, the Arrow Cross, shot Jews on the spot and tossed their bodies into the Danube.

Wallenberg's documents saved the Rajs. The war ended. The Red Army liberated Budapest. But Sandor Raj did not return. The Soviets had seized him, along with a squadron of Hungarian soldiers, and were holding him as a prisoner of war. The Rajs pressed for more information, but there was none. Sandor was in a prisoner-of-war camp somewhere in the Soviet Union—that was all.

The Rajs moved back to their apartment. Again a hand cart was piled high with their possessions, including the family Torah.

Perched atop it all sat Mutti, Tamas's great-grandmother, the family matriarch.

The occupying Soviet soldiers filled Budapest. Food was scarce. People spent hours scrounging for bread and other necessities. The streets outside the Rajs' window were in ruins. One morning, Grandpa Vilmoś took little Ferenc for a walk. A Soviet soldier approached them. *"Shma Yisroel . . . ,"* he said, beginning the best-known prayer in the Jewish religion. Startled, Vilmos completed the prayer automatically: *"Adonai elohenu, adonai echad"*—Hear, O Israel, the Lord our God, the Lord is One. It was the prayer that Jews had recited for centuries and that many Jews had mumbled, under their breath, as they were taken to the gas chambers. The Soviet soldier burst into a smile. He asked for the address of the Raj apartment. Within a few hours, he arrived with a parcel of food—a Soviet Jew helping Hungarian Jews.

With Sandor away, Tamas's grandparents oversaw the house. They were eager to enroll Tamas in a Jewish school as soon as possible, to resume life interrupted by the war. The family began attending synagogue again; Tamas's mother, Margit, began teaching religious classes at the temple. When a Jewish school reopened across the street, Margit bundled her son up and took him. He was promptly sent back home. Tamas was only five. No matter how eager his family was to immerse their son in Jewish life, they had to wait until he was six, the minimum age to start school.

For the 160,000 Jews who survived in Hungary, life continued to improve. Soviet troops occupied the country, but as in Czechoslovakia, there was a coalition government, pledged to full democracy. Synagogues were reopened. Soup kitchens were set up to feed survivors of the ghetto. The new government urged Jews to reenter economic life and help rebuild the country. Before the war, Hungary's Jews—especially those of the middle class, who constituted 20 percent of Budapest's population—had played a key role in the economy. As industrialization began to spread across Europe in the mid-nineteenth century, Hungary's aristocratic elite, which drew its power and wealth from its vast landholdings, recognized that Hungary had to build up its trade and industry if it was to move forward and avoid domination by neighboring countries. The aristocrats would not dirty their hands by engaging in trade or finance or building new companies; the peasants and workers lacked the necessary education and skills. Almost by default, the industrialization of Hungary was left to the Jews. Hungary granted the Jews complete political freedom in 1867 and recognized Judaism as a legal religion in 1896. From that moment on, Jews became increasingly active in politics, industry, science, and culture. The Jews built railroads and factories, providing employment for thousands of peasants. They cemented their alliance with the aristocrats by enlisting noblemen to sit on their boards of directors and allowing them to become important—and well-rewarded—stockholders. Hungary's Jews prospered. By 1920, half of Hungary's lawyers were Jewish, along with two-thirds of its doctors, 35 percent of its journalists, 27 percent of its professors, and 24 percent of its actors. Sixty percent of the people who owned shops in Hungary were Jewish.

Now the government urged the Jews to reopen their stores. People needed to buy clothing and food and cigarettes. Even the Communists encouraged the Jews to get back into business. Grandpa Vilmos decided to reopen the small shop in which he sold cigarettes and fabrics. His sister-in-law reopened her wholesale fabric shop. Within a few months, Budapest was bustling. A *New York Times* correspondent reported:

> That commerce is alive is largely due to the Jews. . . . The majority are loyal Hungarians who desire to remain in their country and help reconstruct it. . . . These are the hopeful citizens of Hungary. It is impossible not to admire their courage, energy and patriotism as they clear a little space among the ruins and begin over again. "I see here," said a keen American observer of the prostrate lands of Eastern Europe, "that what this part of the world needs to get going is to resurrect the Jews."

Budapest did not have to resurrect the Jews. Before World War II, it had been one of many Eastern European cities with robust Jewish populations. Now, amid the ashes of the Holocaust, the Jews of Budapest constituted the largest Jewish community left on the European continent.

Though the war had been over for more than a year, there was still no word of Sandor. Frustrated and angry, Margit Raj sought a personal audience with Matyas Rakosi, the Jewish head of the Hungarian Communist Party. If anyone in Budapest could help her find her husband, surely Rakosi could. Rakosi had influence with the Soviets. He could bring her husband back. Margit arrived at the Communist leader's office with her two boys in tow. She appealed to Rakosi directly. "The boys miss their father," she told him. And then she made a fatal mistake. Rakosi should help bring Sandor home because he was Jewish—just like Rakosi. Rakosi threw her out of his office. No one spoke of his religion like that, especially not someone from a family of bourgeois shopkeepers!

The mood in Hungary was beginning to change. The Communists prepared to seize power; the Jews were to be one of their first targets—no matter that the leader of the Hungarian Communists was himself a Jew. Hungary's Jews, like Jews in most places, had always fared better in the cities than in the countryside. Small towns and villages had always been more suspicious of Jews and more susceptible to anti-Semitic canards like the "blood-libel"— the myth that Jews killed Christian children and used their blood to make matzoh at Passover. In 1946, a wave of rumors swept the Hungarian countryside: Christian children were being kidnapped and ground into sausages. A Jewish doctor was accused of poisoning Christian children in the guise of vaccinating them. A teacher warned her Hungarian students to stay away from Jews, who would cut off their heads. Mobs in several towns attacked returning Jews and burned synagogues. The wave of anti-Semitism culminated in a massacre in the town of Kunmadaras, in which three Jews were killed.

The real motive for the resurgence of anti-Semitism was not religious but economic. Jews liberated from the concentration camps were returning to their villages to reclaim their homes; the Hungarians who had moved in when the Jews were deported did not want to give them back. "We are hated because we returned from the dead," a Jewish doctor declared. "They thought of us as dead. They buried us. They were quite satisfied that there were no more Jews, and no more Jewish problem. Our return was a painful surprise for them. They look upon us as ghosts, and no one loves ghosts." When a Jewish woman at the Kunmadaras massacre pleaded with the mob to stop, attackers shouted: "Did you have to come back? Why didn't you stay in Germany in the concentration camps?"

Under the new coalition government, the Communists controlled the police. But the police did nothing to stop the pogroms. In Kunmadaras, evidence mounted that the police chief had incited the attacks against Jews. The Communists, still jockeying for power, fanned the flames of anti-Semitism higher as proof that Fascism still existed in Hungary—and only the Communists would be strong enough to stamp it out. At the same time, they used popular distrust of Jews to attack capitalism and boost their support among farmers and townspeople. Jews in the countryside were accused of being black marketeers. As Hungary's economy began to deteriorate and inflation spun out of control, Rakosi gave an inflammatory speech demanding that black marketeers be hanged. Ten days later, the Communists organized a demonstration against them. It swiftly turned into an anti-Jewish pogrom. Two more Jews were killed. After several organizers of the pogrom were arrested, the mob marched on the local police station and beat a Jewish police captain to death. Asked to halt the violence, Rakosi responded, "My hands are tied. I am responsible only for 17 percent of the policies of this government"—a reference to the 17 percent of the vote the Communists received in the election.

Rakosi's hands were not tied for long. New elections were scheduled for the summer of 1947. A few months before election day, Sandor Raj reappeared. He had been freed by the Soviets, along with thousands of other Hungarian prisoners of war. It was a joyous homecoming, but for his in-laws, wife, and children, joy soon turned to puzzlement. Sandor Raj, who had been raised as an Orthodox Jew, for whom a seat was being held at his family's Orthodox synagogue, said he no longer considered himself an observant Jew. His faith, he told his children, had been lost during his years as a prisoner of war. He also announced that he was now a member of the Communist Party. He had joined before leaving the Soviet Union, as a condition of his release, and had agreed to vote for the Communists in the upcoming elections. He did not believe in Communism, but a Jewish prisoner of war in 1947 had few options.

Sandor Raj was a formidable man, who considered his word around the house to be law. There was no discussion, at least in front of the children, of the morality of his decision or of what other options the family had. Sandor did not object to keeping a kosher home or having the boys accompany their grandfather to the Orthodox synagogue a few blocks away. The boys continued to attend the Jewish school down the street.

That summer Raj voted for the Communist Party. The Communists increased their share of the vote to 22 percent, far less than the majority they had hoped for. Backed by the occupying Red Army, the Communists proceeded to coerce and intimidate the other parties, and finally they took control of the parliament. They immediately nationalized banks and heavy industry. They seized the newspapers, the radio stations, and the police. Within months, their control was complete, and Hungary became a Communist dictatorship.

Hungary's Jews held their breath, and waited. In two of the rooms in the Raj apartment overlooking Joseph Boulevard, Sandor Raj had reestablished his law practice. Every morning, the boys said good-bye to him on their way to school, where they learned Hebrew and Jewish history along with Hungarian history. In the afternoons, classes met in the school basement, where Zionist songs about building the new State of Israel and Israeli folk dances like the hora were learned. The Rajs considered themselves lucky: Of their immediate family, almost everyone had survived the war. The relative whose death cast the longest shadow was Denes Friedman—Sandor's cousin—who had been a rabbi at one of Budapest's synagogues. Friedman had perished in Auschwitz. As Tamas started his Jewish education, he began to think that he, too, might become a rabbi, like his uncle.

It was a naive hope. One winter afternoon soon after the

Communists seized power, Tamas's teacher walked into the afternoon class, picked up a piece of chalk, and on the blackboard wrote the name of a Communist partisan fighter who had battled the Nazis during the war. There was no hora taught that afternoon, no Israeli folk songs. Tamas, who was eight, went home and told his father what had happened. "We are not learning the hora anymore," he said. "We are learning about the partisans. What does that mean?" Sandor peered over his newspaper. "Probably your school has been nationalized," he responded. "That's what it means."

The next morning, Tamas and Ferenc went to school as usual. They attended the same classes, with the same teachers. But there was no more Hebrew and no more talk of Jewish history. Instead the teachers extolled the great accomplishments of Comrade Joseph Stalin, the leader of the Soviet Union. Overnight, the boys' school had ceased being a Jewish school. It was now a Communist school.

# Chapter Six

# "The Jews Live in the Houses, the Poles Live in the Streets"

As the Nazi occupation of Poland entered its third year, Leokadia Burzynska decided to visit her lover's family in the small town of Zelechow, a speck of a village on a flat plain thirty miles northwest of Warsaw. At seventeen, Leokadia was a strikingly beautiful young woman with blond hair. Her mother and grandmother, back in Warsaw, were simple people enduring the German occupation. Like many Poles, they were devout Catholics, the mother's faith the family's driving force. They had moved to Warsaw from the countryside. They could barely read. When Leokadia left Warsaw, she had printed a note in big capital letters so her mother could make it out: She was going away to visit and would be back in a while.

Leokadia left Warsaw not to flee the Germans but to flee the disapproving glances of family and friends. She had been having an affair with an older man—Bruno, who lived near her family's one-room apartment. Bruno had a wife and children, but the two were in love, and their increasingly public affair had scandalized the neighborhood. Bruno made plans to go to the tiny village of Zelechow to visit his mother, and Leokadia went with him.

The first thing that struck any visitor upon entering the town was the white-brick church on top of a small hill at the town's entrance. It dwarfed the rest of the buildings, its regal dome and towers rising high into the sky. Zelechow had been founded in the fourteenth century, and the church had been there from its earliest days, shaping the life of the town as Catholicism shaped Poland. When the original modest church, made of wood, burned down in 1692, work began on a grander building. The cornerstone was laid by the local feudal lord. The new church took thirty-six years to complete, and when it was finished, it was one of the wonders of the region. A century and a half later, in 1889, the church expanded again, blossoming into the formidable, neo-Baroque structure that dominated Zelechow physically just as Catholicism dominated Zelechow's residents spiritually and often politically. Here, it proclaimed to visitors, was a typical Polish village—market square, neat single-story houses, the Catholic Church visible from anywhere in town.

But things were not what they seemed in Zelechow. Past the church, across the market square, stood another building: a grand red-brick synagogue, set in beautifully landscaped grounds behind an iron fence. Inside it was seating for several hundred families. The Jews had begun coming to Zelechow later than their Polish neighbors—they first arrived in the sixteenth century, invited by local feudal lords to set up trade. But their numbers swelled, and by 1889 there were almost five thousand Jews in Zelechow, 70 percent of the population. Zelechow was more a Jewish town than a Polish one. One reason the Catholic Church decided to build so imposingly in a tiny town was to match the grandeur of Zelechow's synagogue across the way.

The Jewish community of Zelechow was a thriving, prosperous version of the shtetls, or Jewish villages, that were scattered across Poland and were home to its three million Jews. Indeed, one of the town's native sons immortalized the town in the well-known Yiddish novella "A Shtetl," which was based on the rhythms of Zelechow's daily life. The town had a rabbinical seminary and several religious schools, Jewish theaters and lecture series, and thriving Jewish businesses. Under the leadership of several Jewish industrialists, the Jews of Zelechow began manufacturing shoes and soon became known for their high-quality footwear. They employed many of the local Poles and prospered. Though many Jews in Poland lived in poverty, in Zelechow the Jews lived well. By the end of the nineteenth century, Jews not only made up 70 percent of the town; they made up by far the richest 70 percent. Zelechow was the kind of town, the Poles liked to say, where the Jews lived in the houses and the Poles lived in the streets.

And the Poles resented it. In the 1920s, when Polish Catholic nationalism reached its height, soldiers marched into Zelechow and terrorized the Jewish population. Five soldiers burst into one Jew's home and threatened to cut off his beard. They relented only when a Jewish officer intervened. Other Polish soldiers disrupted Jewish lectures and theatrical performances. The spasm of nationalism passed in Zelechow, but the uneasiness of Jews remained. They began to watch their Polish neighbors more warily.

In its divided population, its bursts of anti-Semitism, its rival houses of worship—the church on one side of the market square, the synagogue on the other—Zelechow symbolized the intimacy and the divisions, the cooperation and the simmering resentments, that ran through the history of Poles and Jews.

Poland sat on the perimeter of Europe, more backward than countries farther to the West. In the thirteenth century, the Polish prince Boleslaw the Pious was the first ruler in Europe actually to invite Jews to settle in his country. Poland needed settlers to fill its rapidly expanding empire. Following a series of massacres in 1348 by Christians who blamed the Jews for spreading the Black Death, Jews streamed in from Bohemia (later part of Czechoslovakia), Austria, Germany, and even Turkey, hoping to find a haven from the persecution they encountered elsewhere. The Jews who came were often more educated than the Poles, knowledgeable in trade, and with a network of family connections in other parts of Europe. They were people who could help Poland develop and modernize. By 1490, there were 30,000 Jews in Poland. By the mid-seventeenth century, that number had increased tenfold to 300,000. By 1800, the number had doubled and nearly doubled again. Of the 2.9 million Jews in the world, almost 1 million of them lived in Poland. By 1936, there were more Jews in Poland than in any other country—

almost 3.5 million, 8 percent of Poland's population. In big cities like Warsaw, Jews made up 25 percent of the population.

The Jews of Poland spoke their own language—87 percent spoke either Hebrew or Yiddish, not Polish. They read 30 Yiddish-language daily newspapers, 132 weeklies, and 224 other publications—monthlies, quarterlies, special literary magazines. Poland's Jews produced more works of traditional Jewish scholarship every year in the 1930s than in any decade of the seventeenth or eighteenth century. They maintained 826 banks, with capital of more than $2 million—a formidable sum in those days. They supported an extensive network of schools and hospitals. At a time when people still died of famine and untreated diseases in Europe, a Jew in Poland hardly ever died of starvation or lack of medical care. Jewish hospitals provided a home for highly skilled Jewish doctors who could not get jobs in Polish hospitals. They served as centers of medical research—the fruits of which were shared with all of Poland.

From food to prayer books, Polish Jews reshaped Jewish life and set the standard that would follow their descendants to America. The bialy, which American Jews ate in New York and Los Angeles, originated in Bialystok in Poland. The story of *Fiddler on the Roof*, which millions all over the world saw on stage and screen, was based on the stories of a Polish village written by a Polish Jew, Shalom Aleichem. People often joked that after 1948, Poland was the only country with two prime ministers; from that year until 1992, every prime minister of Israel had been born in Poland.

But the Poles never accepted the Jews. When Poles and Jews talked of each other, they spoke not of Polish Christians and Polish Jews but of the "Jewish Nation" and the "Polish Nation"—as if they were two separate peoples coexisting uneasily on the same land. Polish Catholics grew up with the anti-Semitic images of Jews that were common in churches across Eastern Europe. As Jews began to succeed in trade and business—as in Zelechow—Poles found new reasons to hate them. "The money was indeed the thing that killed the Jews," a Pole wrote after a massacre of Jews in 1348. "If they had been poor and if the feudal lords had not been in debt to them, they would have not have been burned." Polish peasants resented Jewish traders and peddlers, who, they believed, were always ready to cheat them. To be called a "Jew" became a Polish insult. "Jewish honesty," in Polish, meant dishonesty; "Jewish courage," cowardice.

As the economic situation in Poland deteriorated in the 1920s and 1930s, hatred of the Jews grew dramatically. Even before the Nazis invaded, Poland's government launched a boycott against Jewish-owned businesses—a boycott endorsed by the cardinal of Warsaw. It was against this background that the Nazis invaded Poland in 1939 and began to round up the country's Jews.

The Nazis marched into Zelechow on September 14, 1940, a few days before the Jewish holiday of Rosh Hashanah, celebrating the New Year. The next day, they burned the great synagogue on the market square. Within a few weeks, the Nazis established a ghetto in Zelechow and began to round up the town's Jews and herd them inside. By the end of 1940, all 5,500 Jews in Zelechow had been put into the ghetto; by 1941, over 2,000 Jews from other towns had joined them.

Immediately, the Nazis began doling out Jewish-owned houses in town to the Poles. The Poles gladly took them; there is no record of someone refusing a house because it belonged to a Jew. In Zelechow, it was now the Poles who lived in the houses while, a few blocks away, the Jews, crammed into tenements, their synagogue destroyed, lived in the streets.

It was around this time—late 1942 or early 1943—that Leokadia came to Zelechow with Bruno. They visited friends who had moved into the houses of the Jews—handsome wood-frame houses with trapezoidal roof lines, which filled the streets just behind the church, a few blocks from the market square and the rubble-strewn site where the great synagogue had stood. In Zelechow, Bruno began introducing Leokadia as his wife. They took up residence in the town, and in a while the reason for their hurried departure from Warsaw became clear: the two were seen strolling down the streets with a new baby. They named her Basia, the Polish version of Barbara.

From a few blocks away, Jewish children snuck out of the

ghetto and darted over to their former streets to play with the Polish children. They tickled the baby and cooed to her. Inside the ghetto, Jews were dying of hunger and disease. But Leokadia and her friends averted their eyes, and they slept at night in the Jewish homes, surrounded by the pretty objects the previous owners had been forced to abandon.

Zelechow, Leokadia soon decided, was no place to raise a child. The Germans treated the Jews horribly, but they had scarcely better plans for the Poles. Poland, in the Nazi plan, was to become a country of slave laborers, all serving Germany. Leokadia was not yet twenty. Caring for the baby was a burden. It would be better, and safer, to return to her family's home, where her mother could help her. Leokadia headed back to Warsaw with her new baby. Bruno returned to his wife and family.

A few weeks after Leokadia left, the Nazis liquidated the Jewish ghetto in Zelechow. They rounded up all the men, women, and children, loaded them into trucks and cattle cars, and shipped them to the death camp at Treblinka. The night before the Germans came, with rumors of the deportations sweeping the terrified ghetto, several Jewish leaders hurried across the dark market square and knocked on the door of the rectory, across the street from the church. When the priest answered, they asked him to hold the documents of their community—the birth and death records and the most important papers—in safekeeping. They would be back to retrieve them when they could. The priest agreed, and he hid them in the rafters of the rectory for safekeeping. The next day, the deportations to Treblinka began. A few hundred Jews managed to flee, but as they begged for help from people in the countryside around Zelechow, many were turned in to the Nazis by local farmers.

Over time, the priest died and the hidden papers were forgotten. Forty years later, the Church decided to build a new brick rectory. As the workmen clambered through the old wood building, preparing to tear it down, they discovered the documents of the Jewish ghetto up in the rafters. No one had ever returned to Zelechow to collect them.

The annihilation of the Jews in Zelechow was repeated in cities and towns across Poland. Three million of Poland's three and a half million Jews were killed by the Nazis in death camps built on Polish soil, often near Polish villages and with Poles looking on. As the Russians liberated the country, the few Jews who had survived began to return to their villages and towns. Most were alone: husbands without wives, wives without husbands, parents without children, children without parents. Their first impulse was to "go home" to see what remained.

Nothing remained. Immediate family and distant relatives alike were gone, all dead. Every remnant of hundreds of years of Jewish life was obliterated. The Nazis had leveled synagogues, destroyed Jewish schools, ripped up tombstones from Jewish graves. The Jewish nation—so vibrant and colorful, so rich in culture and tradition—had disappeared. It was as if Denmark or Spain had suddenly been wiped off the map.

Like the Hungarians who had taken possession of Jewish homes, many Poles looked askance at the returning Jews, as if they were unexpected and unwelcome ghosts. "Still alive?" their neighbors asked. "Didn't the Nazis kill you?" The Nazis had doled out Jewish homes, shops, possessions, to Poles as they cleared out the Jews from city after city, village after village. Now Poles and the returning Jews fought over houses and stores, over furniture, heirloom china, even portraits of Jewish ancestors hanging on the walls. "We Jews of Poland have never been coddled by our neighbors, and we knew they did not love us," a woman said at the time. "But never until the years of horror did we realize how deep is their hatred."

In Zelechow, returning Jews were met with anger and knives. Those trying to reclaim their houses were turned away. One Pole slashed the throat of a man he found wandering in his old backyard. The Poles in Zelechow embraced the Communist Party, believing that the Communists would not force them to return their houses to the Jews. A wave of pogroms engulfed Poland, climaxing in Kielce, where more than forty Jews were killed. In 1946, the year after the war, 1,400 Jews were killed by Poles in pogroms. By the end of 1947, 100,000 Jews had fled Poland for the West, and only 50,000 remained.

Life in Zelechow adjusted to new rhythms. The town that had once been 70 percent Jewish now had no Jews. The church still stood guard at the entrance to the town. The Jewish homes that had all been taken over by Poles remained in Polish hands. A friend of Leokadia's and Bruno's, little Barbara's godmother, moved into a green timbered house once owned by Jews just down the street that ran behind the church.

By 1947, there were no signs that Jews had ever lived in Zelechow. The cemetery became overgrown. While they occupied the town, the Nazis had turned a school for rabbis into the headquarters for the SS. The pathway leading to the front door was paved with gravestones ransacked from the Jewish cemetery. The Nazis left; the gravestones stayed. The building became a village office. The gravestones lay mute, weathering beneath the heat of the summer sun, the weight of the winter snow, and the shuffling shoes of Poles going about their daily lives.

Back in Warsaw, Leokadia arrived at her mother's apartment with her baby. She did not speak of her affair with Bruno, the neighbor. She said she had fallen in love in Zelechow, that the baby's father had left to join the Polish underground. She believed he was dead and she was now a widow—a widow with an infant to support.

Of course, her mother welcomed her back. Leokadia and baby Barbara moved in with Leokadia's mother and grandmother—all four in a one-room apartment. Together, they waited for the war to end. The images of the suffering Jews slipped from Leokadia's mind. The Poles were obsessed with their own suffering. By the time World War II ended in 1945, half of all Poles had been killed, wounded, or imprisoned during the war. Six million Poles had died—half of them Jews. A survey of Warsaw after the war reported that 96 percent of the buildings had been damaged. For a time, the government even considered relocating across the river to the less devastated part of the city. As the Soviet army advanced on Warsaw, the Nazis had systematically blown up every building in the city. It was like Sherman's march. The Nazis blew up structures that had stood for four hundred years in the picturesque Old Town. Explosions pierced the night, building by building, block by block, up and down the city's streets. Soviet soldiers, ostensibly the army of liberation, sat on the banks of the Vistula and watched. The Russians wanted to liberate a prostrate Poland, not one that could threaten the Soviet Union or demand independence. A few months later, when the Soviets erected a memorial to the Red Army liberation of Warsaw, the Poles mockingly dubbed it "Monument to the Sleeping Soldiers."

The Russians swiftly invested the Polish Communists with power and began treating Poland like a colony. They stripped factories and farms of whatever machinery they had left. Horses and cattle were scarce. Food shortages were rampant; the Russians had taken much of the seed and shipped it back to Russia.

The apartment that Leokadia shared with her family was damaged. The windows had been blown out by artillery barrages. The floorboards had been pulled up and burned for heat. Next to a small balcony was a huge hole in the wall from an artillery shell. Only a few cars eased their way through the rubble-strewn streets. A horse cart stationed near the apartment was the only transportation. Bread lines stretched for a mile. Leokadia waited for hours to get enough food for all her family.

The ghosts of Jews were everywhere. Near the center of the city lay the ruins of the Warsaw ghetto, liquidated by the Nazis in 1943. Leokadia's mother had heard the explosions and seen the pillars of smoke. Leokadia's family were now told they could move from their war-damaged apartment into one of the few buildings left standing in the ghetto—a five-story stone structure, with a marble arch framing the entrance. The apartment block, built around a courtyard, had been one of the last holdouts of the Jewish resistance. Leokadia counted herself lucky; as in Zelechow, Jewish misfortune became Polish fortune.

As the Allies defeated the Nazis, the full scope of the Holocaust became known. But as the Communists seized power in Poland and across Eastern Europe, it began to strike many people—including, no doubt, Leokadia—that for all their lamentation and suffering, Jews seemed to wield more power than ever before.

The newly installed head of the Communist Party in Poland

was Polish, but no one believed he held the real power. That lay instead with what Poles dubbed the "troika"—Hilary Minc, who oversaw the economy, Jakob Berman, who oversaw ideology, and Roman Zambrowski, who controlled the party bureaucracy. All were Jews.

In Romania, where the Communists had also seized power soon after the war, the most powerful person in the government was Anna Pauker, the daughter of a rabbi. Officially, Pauker served as Romania's foreign minister; in reality, she controlled the country.

In Hungary, where Jews had long been prominent in the Communist movement and in the revolution of 1919, the four most powerful people were Jews: Matyias Rakosi, leader of the Communist Party; Peter Gabor, chief of the secret police; Joseph Revai, head of the economy; and Mihaly Farkas, boss of culture. By the late 1940s, seven of the thirteen members of the Hungarian Politburo, the body that controlled Hungarian life, were Jewish.

In Czechoslovakia, the head of the Communist Party and dictator of the country was Rudolf Slansky—born Rudolf Saltzmann, the son of Jewish shopkeepers who ran a small store in a town near where Alena Wittmann and her parents vacationed in the countryside. His most feared aide, the head of Czechoslovakia's secret police, was Jewish as well.

On and on it went. In Poland, Jews were threaded throughout the new Communist bureaucracy. Many showed up in the darkest corners—with the secret police.

None of these Communists identified themselves as Jews. Certainly they were as hostile to religion or dissent as any Christian Communists—as Rakosi showed by angrily evicting Margit Raj from his office when she came to plead for Sandor's release from a Russian prisoner-of-war camp. Someone once asked Rakosi, who had served in the 1919 Communist revolutionary government in Hungary, why the Communists selected a non-Jew to be president then when there were so many Jews in other positions. "We needed someone to sign the death warrants on Saturday"—the Jewish Sabbath—Rakosi explained with a grin.

These Communists were different from the Jews who had flirted with Socialism in Russia and Poland and even those who had joined the Communist Party before World War II in a burst of idealism. They were hardened, opportunistic Communists, who had spent the war years in Moscow learning to fear Stalin and his brutal purges but also, sadly, learning his methods. They were not above using anti-Semitism to whip up popular anger and support for the Communists.

What explains the sudden prominence of Jews in Communist Eastern Europe after 1945? Jews had been prominent in left-wing movements as far back as the nineteenth century. Whether in the United States, Europe, or the Soviet Union, Jews flocked to left-wing movements for the world they promised, free of prejudice and discrimination. In Eastern Europe, left-wing parties offered Jews the only avenue of political emancipation. They welcomed Jews without the anti-Semitic nationalism that infected other political movements.

But Stalin, who masterminded the Communist takeover of Eastern Europe, had always been anti-Semitic. When he began his rise in power in the 1920s, Stalin had stirred up prejudice against his Jewish opponents, including Leon Trotsky. Stalin detested the high percentage of Jews in the Russian Communist Party, hated their prominence. In 1939, Hitler told intimates that "Stalin made no secret before Ribbentrop that he was waiting only for the moment of maturation of a sufficiently large indigenous intelligentsia to make short shrift of the Jews."

For Stalin, a paranoid who saw enemies everywhere, Jews were always a suspect minority. They often had ties to the West. They had a long religious tradition and a sense of community—even those who did not consider themselves religious—which seemed to pose a threat to the absolute power of the Communist Party. It had not escaped Stalin's notice that Russian Jewish soldiers had embraced foreign Jews in the liberated death camps and had mingled with the Jewish troops of other armies. He worried the Jews would bring the virus of Western ideas into the Soviet Union.

Unlike Hitler, however, Stalin did not allow his anti-Semitism to stop him from using Jews when it served his purposes. Hitler was a man whose hatreds overwhelmed his cunning. So powerful was his hatred of Jews that he allowed Eichmann to divert trains crucial to Germany's defense to deliver yet more Jews to the gas chambers. Stalin was a calculating and ruthless strategist, happy to exploit Jews to further his aims.

In the years preceding World War II, Stalin had grown suspicious of the loyalty of the Communist Parties of Poland, Czechoslovakia, Hungary, and Romania. Members swore loyalty to Stalin, but they had strong nationalistic streaks that would prevent them, Stalin believed, from becoming subservient to Soviet wishes. So Stalin had the nationalist leaders of these parties killed. The leadership of the Polish Communist Party, for example, was wiped out in a purge Stalin ordered before the war. After victory, Stalin replaced many of these nationalists with selected Jewish Communists, confident that they would owe their primary allegiance to him.

It was a brilliant move. The trauma of the Holocaust—the destruction of their families and communities—ensured that Jewish Communists, no matter how unimportant they considered their Jewish background, would be fanatically "anti-Fascist" and determined to root out any vestiges of the old systems. Many would be consumed with revenge. Being Jewish also immunized these Communists from local nationalism, which Stalin saw as the greatest threat to Communist domination. Nationalist feelings, whether under Pilsudski in Poland or Admiral Horthy in Hungary, always came wrapped in a parcel lined with anti-Semitism. Jews would battle against nationalism. Best of all, from Stalin's point of view, Jewish Communists were unlikely to develop a following of their own, given the resentment that ran throughout Eastern Europe. While Communists might not consider their Jewish background very important, the people they ruled would. When the time came, as well it might, to purge these Jewish Communists, who would object?

To be sure, most Jews who survived the war in Eastern Europe feared Communism. As soon as they were released from the concentration camps or emerged from hiding, many headed for Palestine, where they would help found the State of Israel. As Communism grew stronger, large numbers of Jews went to the West. Many of those who stayed behind did so because they were too old, or because the ties of tradition bound them tightly to their country, or because they had no place to go.

But some Jews remained because, like Klaus Gysi, they were Communists or leftists who believed Communism offered hope for the future. The scope of Stalin's evils—the purges, the massive oppression—were not yet evident in the years immediately following the war; it would be more than another decade before the Soviets, in 1956, themselves acknowledged Stalin's crimes. Some Jews who remained in Eastern Europe believed that Communism, even Communist totalitarianism, was the best defense against the rampant anti-Semitism that had resurfaced in Poland and Hungary. Jews had no love for the nationalist or Christian parties that vied with the Communists for power. They feared a return to the kind of nationalism that had consumed Germany and Eastern Europe in the 1930s. As pogroms had swept across Poland, and later began in Hungary, many Jews came to believe that their personal safety depended on the Communists' coming to power.

But there were also Jews who, as in any group, were ambitious and opportunistic. Stalin's purges in the 1930s had decimated the Communist Parties of Eastern Europe. As the Communists assumed power after World War II, they needed loyal party members to fill key positions in the government. Political reliability was more important than age or experience. The years right after the war were a boom time for Jewish Communists. Jews and other loyal Communists, some only in their twenties, were placed in key positions throughout the country. Jews specialized in foreign trade and foreign affairs because they were the only trustworthy people who spoke foreign languages; they took key jobs in newspapers and radio because of their high education levels and urban, cosmopolitan backgrounds.

And in what became the most disquieting legacy of this period, they flocked to the secret police. In Czechoslovakia and Hungary, Jews headed the feared bureaus. Jews were woven throughout the security forces in all of Eastern Europe, as interrogators, officials, police chiefs. At a time when the greatest enemies of Communism were considered former fascists and nationalists, who was more trustworthy to root them out than Jews? Who else understood the dangers so clearly?

But there was another motive at work as well. In Poland, a Jewish man, a newspaper editor, told me how he had been seized by the Nazis as a teenager but escaped with several other Jews during transport to Auschwitz. After wandering in the forest for several hours, they came upon a unit of the Polish underground, which was fighting the Germans. They offered to join but were turned away. The Poles wanted nothing to do with the Jews. Eventually, the teenager managed to find his way over to the Russian front, where he joined a unit of Polish Jewish Communists who fought the Nazis and helped liberate Poland. When he returned to his hometown in search of his family, he learned they had been wiped out by the Germans. The Poles seemed happy they were gone. Indeed, every Jew in his town had been killed; the Poles had moved into their houses. At this point the Communists asked him if he wanted to become a member of the secret police. He agreed.

When I asked him why he had joined the secret police, the man uttered a single word: "Revenge."

Especially in places like Poland, the annihilation of the Jews and the pogroms that erupted after the war confirmed for many Jewish Communists that these societies were so infiltrated with Fascism that extreme measures were required to extirpate it. The collaboration of Poles in the crimes against the Jews astounded and infuriated these Communists. Their reactions were, of course, understandable in young men returning home to find everything they knew and loved wiped out. But instead of sympathy, the Communists handed many of these angry young Jews guns and truncheons, urging them to root out the enemies of Communism—in essence to do the Communists' dirty work.

It is important to remember that despite the presence of top Jewish officials in all these countries, most high-ranking Communists—most Communists—were not Jewish. But the Jews were visible—out of all proportion to their tiny numbers in the general population—especially in countries that had always kept a wary eye on Jews in the past. What made the Jewish presence worse, in the eyes of many Eastern Europeans, was that the Jews were doing the bidding of the Russians. They were not only outsiders; they were acting as puppets for the Russian colonizers.

Stalin thrust Jews into positions of power because he saw a way to harness their idealism, their loyalty, and their ambition, using them toward his own ends. The mistake Jewish Communists made was to take the bait. They believed they were joining "Comrade Stalin" in a grand new enterprise—to wipe out Fascism and anti-Semitism. In fact, Stalin held the Jews in contempt. When they were no longer useful, they were expendable

# Part II

"What Hitler Did Not Finish, We Will Complete"

The years following the war were marked by a deep sadness as the Jews of Eastern Europe stitched together the remnants of their lives and mourned their dead. But there was also hope. Synagogues were reopened. Free elections were held. There would be a future.

Within a few years, however, shadows were cast upon their expectations. Whatever slim hopes for freedom these countries had nurtured after World War II were snuffed out as Communists, backed by the Soviets, seized power and the United States and the West refused to intervene. The Soviet liberators had become Soviet occupiers; the Communists had seized power and established one-party states. In a speech at Westminster College in Fulton, Missouri, Winston Churchill declared in 1946 that from the tip of the Baltic to the tip of the Adriatic Sea, "an Iron Curtain has descended upon the Continent." It was a curtain that Klaus Gysi had chosen to live behind in East Germany. But the Iron Curtain imprisoned the Rajs of Hungary, young Alena Schmula of Czechoslovakia, even Leokadia and her new baby Barbara in Poland.

What the Nazis began, the Communists now strove to complete.

# Chapter Seven

# Foul Compromises

The trip from West Berlin to East Berlin did not take long—a few miles by car through the checkpoints manned by American guards on one side, Soviet guards on the other. But it was like traveling to a different world. By 1948, the battle lines of the Cold War were already drawn. West Germany had allied itself firmly with the Americans. The Marshall Plan was financing the economic redevelopment that would rebuild West Germany, bringing it undreamed-of prosperity. Barely three years after their defeat, the West Germans were a bulwark of the West and democracy, standing on the new front line of the Cold War. East Germany was already poorer, strapped for money and stripped of factories and industrial equipment, which had been requisitioned by the Soviet Union. In East Berlin, construction would soon begin on the new Soviet Embassy, a building that dwarfed every other East German government edifice, as if it was the true center of the East German government—which, in effect, it was.

The gap between West Berlin and East Berlin yawned wider. But it was an easy journey for Erna's son Klaus Gysi, the cosmopolitan Communist whose beliefs had been formed as a young man in the tumult of Berlin and steeled during his years of hiding. Soon after Germany's defeat, the Soviets had plucked this charming man who spoke French and English as well as German, who conversed easily about literature and the arts, and made him a deputy mayor in occupied Berlin and then second in command of the organization overseeing all East German culture, the Kulturbund. The Americans had grown suspicious of Klaus's Communist activities. He and Irene decided it was better to move across the border. The Rajs in Hungary, Leokadia in Poland, Alena in Czechoslovakia—none of them had chosen to live under Communism. When the Iron Curtain descended, they simply found themselves behind it. Klaus and Irene Gysi had, by contrast, consciously chosen this life.

The last time Klaus and Irene Gysi crossed borders, back in 1940, when they had slipped from occupied France back into Germany, they had traveled as clandestine lovers. Now they did so as a family. They would raise their children, Gabriele and Gregor, in the Communist future.

Ensconced in his spacious house in East Berlin, Klaus Gysi set about building a juster society—one that had never existed before, certainly not in Germany. He, together with the writers—many of them Jewish—whom he welcomed back, thought they were forging a new intellectual movement, one that would reject the Fascism of the Nazis and the soulless capitalism of the United States and West Germany. Irene began editing books at an East German publishing house. At parties given by Bertolt Brecht, who had returned from exile in the United States to establish a theater company in East Berlin, they mingled with East Germany's cultural elite. Little Gregor, when he turned six, marched proudly in East Germany's May Day parades, his blue kerchief tied around his neck by his mother. Klaus Gysi visited his son's class to speak about culture and building the East German state. A photographer captured Gregor looking at his father with worshipful eyes.

The deepening of the Cold War only confirmed for Klaus that he had made the right choice. It was the United States that prompted the division of Germany, not the Soviet Union. It was the United States that began the Cold War—by forming NATO—not the Soviet Union. It was only a short while before Klaus Gysi's, and his fellow intellectuals', dreams for a burgeoning intellectual and artistic community foundered. East Germany soon abandoned any notion of artistic freedom. The Communists instructed their writers to celebrate Socialism and follow Soviet guidelines on how to write and what to write about. Increasingly, loyalty counted more than talent. In a black-and-white world, gray was being squeezed out. But Klaus went along. From where he stood, all problems still seemed to be the fault of the West, and of the Americans. The Communists had been right about Hitler. They had been the only Germans to oppose him actively. Who was to say they were not right now?

Klaus's ascent continued for five years, until 1953, when the tornado of Stalin's anti-Semitism touched down in Germany.

Stalin had always loathed the Jews. But in May 1948, he had joined the United States as midwife to Israel's birth because he hoped Israel would undermine British influence in the Middle East; England's influence was greatest among the Arab states. Stalin also hoped that Israel, which had been founded largely by Eastern European Jews, most of whom were Socialists, might open a "second front" of Socialism in the Middle East and ally itself with a friendly Soviet Union. When it quickly became clear that Israel would ally itself with the United States and the West, Stalin was enraged. He was further incensed by Golda Meir's jubilant reception as Israel's first ambassador to the Soviet Union. Thousands of Soviet Jews thronged the block around the new Israeli embassy in Moscow and began dancing in the streets. This confirmed Stalin's long-standing suspicion that Jews, even Communist Jews, were unreliable and disloyal.

At the same time, in Yugoslavia, the Communist Marshal Tito was breaking with Stalin and the Soviet Union. Stalin feared that unless he responded quickly and ruthlessly, other countries in Eastern Europe might follow Yugoslavia's lead.

Two streams converged. It was time to solidify Moscow's control over its satellites by eliminating anyone disloyal to Stalin. And it was time to get rid of the Jews. It was time for another Great Purge. The Jews would not be the only target. The new purge would banish all those suspected of disloyalty. The Jews were a useful target, an easy way to stir up a frenzy in countries accus-

tomed to anti-Semitism and pogroms. It might be difficult to persuade people that Communists considered loyal by Stalin until
then had suddenly, in the space of a few months, become traitors
and conspirators. It would be easier to persuade people that the
Jews were to blame—that Jewish Communists had joined in a
great conspiracy that threatened Communist interests and
enticed other Communists to be their dupes. It was a new version
of the anti-Semitic myths that had been floated around Europe for
centuries: The Jews secretly controlled the world; they could
never be trusted.

The purge began in late 1948, with an article in *Pravda* that
attacked Israel, signaling the end of Stalin's support for the new
Jewish state. Jews were attacked as "homeless," "rootless," "tribe-
less vagabonds," as "strangers to the people and the national culture" of the Soviet Union.

Stalin's campaign against the Jews spread with a fury. Soviet
teams were dispatched to satellite countries to begin the purges.
Their first stop was Czechoslovakia, where they were welcomed
by the Jewish head of the Communist Party, Rudolf Slansky. A
ruthless leader, Slansky welcomed the Soviet advisers and helped
them in their hunt for purge victims. Then the Soviets turned on
Slansky and arrested him in 1951, charging him with being a
"Zionist" and a traitor. They ordered the arrest of scores of Jewish
diplomats and Communist Party officials, dragging them into
prison cells and stark interrogation chambers.

In one jail, Arthur London, Czechoslovakia's deputy foreign
minister, a loyal Communist, was berated by the prison warden:
"You and your dirty race—we shall eliminate you! You are all the
same! Not everything Hitler did was bad, because he killed the
Jews and that was a good thing. Too many escaped the gas chambers. What he did not finish, we will complete."

In the fall of 1952, Slansky and thirteen codefendants were put
on trial as "Trotskyite-Titoist-Zionist bourgeois nationalist traitors
and enemies of the Czechoslovak people." Of the fourteen defen-
dants, eleven were Jews. Of the fourteen, eleven were sentenced
to death, including Slansky; three were sentenced to life in prison.

The condemned men were hanged on December 3, 1952. Eight of the eleven hanging from the scaffold were Jews.

A few weeks after Slansky was hanged in Prague, the East German Communist Party issued a sixty-page report on the "lessons" of the Slansky trial. It called Zionism and international Jewish organizations like the Joint Distribution Committee, which gave money to feed and clothe Jews, "agencies of American imperialism." These groups, it said, misused sympathy for Jews to organize espionage and sabotage. Leaders of East Germany's Jewish communities were interrogated and pressed to sign Communist-drafted statements. These statements equated Zionism and Fascism; protested the death sentence for Julius and Ethel Rosenberg, an American Jewish couple sentenced to death for stealing atomic bomb secrets and passing them on to the Soviets; and condemned the campaign to make East Germany pay restitution to Israel for the crimes of the Nazis.

Many Jews in East Germany, including the leaders of all the country's Jewish communities, decided to flee to West Berlin. On January 13, 1953, the first group, twenty-five strong, arrived safely in West Berlin.

Over the winter, the East German Communists stepped up anti-Jewish measures. Police raided the homes of almost all Jews and seized their identity cards. The largely Jewish Union of People Persecuted by Nazis was dissolved. In its place the Communists established a Committee of Anti-Fascist Resistance Fighters, which downplayed the suffering of the Jews under Nazism.

The fight of Jews continued. East Berlin's leading rabbi declared it was no longer safe for Jews to live in East Germany and urged them to leave. He then fled himself, taking with him the most important books from the East Berlin Jewish library. The Jews wanted to leave nothing behind this time.

Klaus Gysi watched, stunned, as his friends and colleagues lost their jobs. This could not be happening here in the new Germany, he thought. He knew about purges in the Soviet Union; who in the Communist Party had not heard of them, of the terror Stalin had spread? But here, in Germany, a new, young country, it was absurd. On January 13, 1953, nine prominent Soviet doctors, six of them Jews, were accused in Moscow of attempting to poison Soviet leaders and generals at the direction of the CIA, British intelligence, and international Jewish organizations. The Gysis were friends of the East German ambassador to the United Nations and of his Russian wife. She took Gysi aside soon after the arrest of the Moscow doctors. "Don't you see what is going on?" she said. "You are such a bright guy normally. This is a preparation for a pogrom. The thing with the doctors. It is like when the czar suspected people of trying to kill him. Only now Stalin is the czar."

Johannes Becher, Gysi's boss at the Kulturbund, called him into his office. Becher, under pressure by the Soviets to dismiss Gysi, sent him out of Berlin on an assignment, to buy him time. But the campaign against Jews was unrelenting. Returning to Berlin, Klaus was visited by the head of the Communist Party Control Commission, in charge of discipline. The Communist Party that Klaus had joined as a teenager, that his mother had supported from its inception, had passed a resolution stripping Klaus Gysi of all his positions—deputy director of the Kulturbund, editor of *Aufbau* magazine, member of the East German parliament, the whole panoply of status he had acquired over the past seven years. "Klaus, you know the situation," the man said. "We didn't draw up the decision ourselves."

Irene was dismissed from her job as well. Klaus insisted, and his family would maintain long afterward, that it had nothing to do with their being Jewish. Irene asserted that they were fired because Stalin was suspicious of Communists who had emigrated to the West during the Nazi period instead of to Moscow; everyone who had emigrated to the West was a spy. Klaus and Irene had been in France, so they lost their jobs.

Klaus believed this would all pass, just as he believed Stalinism would pass. To an outsider, Gysi's life seemed full of options. He spoke English and French as well as German. He was well read, skilled, clearly able to succeed in any number of fields in West Germany or the United States. But where could he go? The

United States was deep in the McCarthy era, with Communists, actual and presumed, arrested or dismissed from their jobs. Klaus had had run-ins with the Americans when he was living in West Berlin, before the city was divided. The Americans kept requisitioning his house. He and Irene had left for the East because the Americans did not trust him. To leave East Germany would mean having to renounce Communism. That he could not do. Stalin's purges, the attacks on Jews—this was not true Communism for Gysi. It was an aberration. It would all come out right in the end, Klaus believed. He was still a Communist. He was still a believer. He had to be patient.

So Klaus kept quiet. He did not defect. He remained loyal. And he was vindicated.

On March 5, 1953, Stalin died. The purges abruptly stopped. By mid-June, the stream of Jewish refugees fleeing East Germany abated. East German policy changed abruptly. Persecution of Jews stopped; the rehabilitation of Jews dismissed from their jobs began. Several Jewish officials and artists who had been purged in the early 1950s returned to their jobs. The Communists began doling out government grants to repair the few synagogues left in East Germany, to maintain Jewish homes for the elderly, to establish a kosher butcher. East German Jews were now awarded pensions as "Victims of Nazism."

Klaus had been out of work for just six months. As the anti-Semitic campaign eased, he was offered a job—not a return to his lofty position as deputy head of the Kulturbund, but a modest job as an editor at a small publisher of schoolbooks. He wrote a history of German literature and bided his time, continuing to develop his contacts within the Communist Party.

Then Klaus got his chance.

In 1956, the Soviets invaded Hungary to crush a nascent rebellion. The Hungarian uprising—the most serious revolt by a Soviet satellite—sent shock waves throughout Eastern Europe, as it exposed to the world how unpopular Communist regimes were becoming with their own people. In 1953, workers in East Berlin had revolted against Communism, seizing the historic Brandenburg Gate, until East German police shot at them and beat them back. East German Communists were nervous about any signs of dissent, especially within the party. When in 1956 they discovered that some top Communist officials were voicing support for the Hungarian uprising, the sympathizers were immediately arrested and a show trial began. One of those arrested was Walter Janka, the editor of East Germany's most important publisher, Aufbau Verlag, which Klaus Gysi had helped found after the war. Janka favored a more liberal spirit in East German culture and politics. What triggered his arrest was a joke that appeared in *Sonntag* magazine, published by Aufbau: In an imaginary East German town, it was discovered that for years the math teacher had been teaching that $2 \times 2 = 9$. To preserve the teacher's authority and power, the staff decided to reveal the truth gradually. The next day, the children were told that $2 \times 2 = 8$; the day after that, $2 \times 2 = 7$. But before the staff could work their way down to the truth, "precociously bad-mannered students" scrawled the forbidden equation on the bathroom walls: $2 \times 2 = 4$.

In East Germany, where direct criticism of the Communist leadership was forbidden, the message was clear: The math teacher was Walter Ulbricht, the head of the East German Communist Party, spouting ideology that no one believed any longer. The other teachers were party officials pushing for gradual reform. The rambunctious students were the East German public—who already knew that the Communists were spouting lies and that the system did not work.

The East German leaders did not find the joke funny. Janka and several of his associates were charged with "counterrevolutionary activities" and "spying." Janka was sentenced to a lengthy prison term.

The Communist Party then offered Janka's job as head of Aufbau—one of the most important jobs in the East German cultural establishment—to Klaus Gysi.

Gysi later claimed that his decision to take the job was straightforward. He regretted the trial of Janka, he said. He was surprised to be offered Janka's job. The more he pondered it, the more he felt that accepting the position was the logical choice. Klaus Gysi had been one of the four original founders of Aufbau in 1945.

Before being purged in 1953, he had been a top editor at one of Aufbau's magazines. Literature and culture had always been his passion. Taking over from the purged Janka was a chance to continue Janka's work, to introduce reforms into the Communist system slowly. Gysi would publish new writers and reissue old works that the Communists had banned. There was some opportunism in taking the job of a man arrested and imprisoned for political crimes, Gysi acknowledged. There was even some cowardliness. But Gysi's main motivation, he insisted, was to rebuild the publishing house.

The truth was more complicated. Janka, in memoirs written after the fall of the Berlin Wall, charged that Gysi had been among the people who denounced him to the secret police. He reprinted copies of files from the East German secret police, the Stasi, showing that Gysi had met with the secret police beginning in 1956. "I never understood why the . . . people mentioned [who informed on me] agreed to be a party to such machinations," Janka wrote. "There were no personal reasons. But perhaps this wasn't necessary. Party cadres will always do what the Communist Party wants them to. And as they did it with some success, they were rewarded well."

Gysi denied these and subsequent charges that he had been an informer for the Stasi, but it is impossible to believe that the Communists would have tapped Gysi for such a sensitive job at a crucial time unless they felt they could be sure of his loyalty—and his willingness to inform on those who were disloyal. His faith had been fortified under the cruelest of circumstances—during Hitler's takeover and five years of living in hiding in Berlin. He had lost his job during the anti-Semitic purges of 1952–3. But unlike many Jews caught up in the purges in East Germany, Hungary, and Czechoslovakia, Gysi had never been imprisoned or forced into a humiliating show trial. Stalinism had been an aberration, Gysi felt, and the atmosphere had improved since Stalin's death. He continued to believe that it was possible to reform the system from within.

What the Communists offered him now was a taste of real power. For the party leadership, Klaus Gysi was the perfect choice to run the country's most prestigious publishing house. He was the perfect middleman—credible to artists but also loyal to the Politburo; sophisticated to a Western audience and able to polish East Germany's image, but prepared to enforce the government's will. He was a teacher prepared to tell students that $2 \times 2$ was 7.

Gysi could have turned down the chance to run Aufbau and slipped into the obscurity of so many others in East Germany, working away at children's books, his talent and skill crushed by the Communist system. But his ambitions, as the leadership understood, were greater. Klaus Gysi yearned for power and the fine things that power could bring. However he rationalized his decision—that he would continue the purged Janka's work, that he would strive to reform the system from within, that even repressive Communism was better than the corrupt capitalism of the West—the reality was that Gysi had made a choice. While others went to prison for their beliefs, Gysi built his career on the rubble of the shattered careers of Communist reformers like Janka, who were imprisoned for challenging the system.

At age forty-four, Gysi had developed a reputation as a womanizer. His charm and humor were a magnet to women. His marriage would soon break up over his incessant affairs. But here, in agreeing to take over East Germany's most prestigious publishing house, it was Klaus Gysi who was being seduced.

Gysi assumed his duties at Aufbau and began the purge the party wanted. Censors were installed at *Sonntag* magazine. When two Soviet authors wrote a German travelogue, *Sonntag* eliminated all the positive references to West Germany. When authors strayed from the fold, Gysi pulled them back in. He began regular contacts with the Stasi, informing them about writers' political reliability. The Stasi gave him the code name "Kurt." Increasingly, Klaus became the public face of the East German publishing industry. He blithely told Western journalists that "only lack of paper and hard currency" prevented the East Germans from publishing James Joyce and that East German customs officers at the western border were confiscating only reactionary "revanchist material" from book shipments.

But true to his word, Gysi also upgraded the artistic reputation and integrity of Aufbau. James Joyce did not make it past the East German censors, but Gysi published translations of several authors who had been banned since the Communists took over. He rehabilitated some banned East German authors. A West German writer who met Klaus Gysi during this time tried to explain the Gysi paradox. Gysi, he speculated, "understood that in culture, you couldn't use the sledgehammer method. He saw that in this field, it is very easy to prevent or ban something but very hard to achieve something positive. He learned that dealing with writers and artists was an unfortunately necessary but cumbersome job requiring a lot of patience. And maybe he learned a rule that is rather unfamiliar to functionaries: respect for the unpredictability of artistic talent."

Writers who dealt with Gysi were divided. Those who supported him tended to share his political view that one had to do the best one could within the system, pushing the limits gradually for fear that too hard a push would provoke a crackdown. Writers critical of the system feared Gysi and tried to avoid him. They saw in him another sellout to the system, who, however charming and sophisticated, enforced the system's rules—wielding an iron hand inside a velvet glove. One of East Germany's best-known writers, who was also Jewish, blamed Gysi for blocking a trip he planned to take to the United States in the early 1960s. For this writer, Stephan Hermlin, Gysi was the worst kind of opportunist, spouting the Communist line though at heart he did not believe it.

It was among Westerners that Gysi became most popular in the late 1950s and early 1960s. In press conferences with Western journalists, Gysi exhibited a charm and sophistication that set him apart from other Communists. The substance was the same, but the style was different. The purges of the 1950s had eliminated many Communists, Jewish and non-Jewish, who had spent time in the West. Gysi's sophistication saved him. He spoke English and French. He was a Sorbonne graduate who read widely. He was a Communist who did not talk like a Communist. "We are so close to the Kremlin that we don't need Kremlinology," Gysi joked to some Westerners visiting an East German book fair in 1964, referring to Western efforts to discern the intention of the Soviets. "We use astronomy here." Gysi did not have to guess what the Russians wanted. He knew, because the Russians told him directly.

Talking to Westerners, Gysi often spoke in a weepy tone, as if he was regretting endlessly "that everything had to turn out like this in Germany," wrote a journalist who met him in the 1950s. Yet at the same time, Gysi faithfully followed the party's wishes. "He is loyal to the party and yet bright, devoted to Moscow and yet flexible," a West German writer declared after meeting him. "He combines toughness with the ability to be kind, if he wants to, and unrelenting consistency with agility and calmness."

In a rigid East German system, Gysi stood out as a man who represented at least a part of the human face of Communism. He was, a West German journalist wrote, "a fanatic you can nonetheless talk to."

To grow up as Klaus Gysi's children was not to grow up as ordinary East Germans. As the Cold War continued, the Communist Bloc presented an image of a gray sameness, with people living in drab apartments and leading constricted lives. The Gysis were different—both because of Klaus's power and because of his background. Typical East German children did not have a father who was a top party official, or parents who were as cultured and as urbane as Irene and Klaus Gysi were. "It is different when you grow up in a home filled with eight thousand books," Klaus Gysi's son, Gregor, once noted.

Gregor was told stories about Judaism and his Jewish background. The Gysis did not follow Jewish traditions or observe Jewish holidays. Gregor and his sister, Gabriele, were raised as good Communist atheists. But references to Jewish life fluttered through the family occasionally, like the melodies of a rare bird. When Klaus Gysi told his children stories, they were often about poor and underprivileged Jews—the politically correct proletarian Jews that a Communist could boast about. For Klaus, Jews were always underprivileged people who had been unjustly persecuted. Early on, Gregor sensed his father's ambivalence about his Jewish background. Klaus's grandmother, who had been gassed at Auschwitz, had married a man who she said was Jewish, but Klaus told Gregor that he had his doubts—suggesting perhaps that Klaus was not quite as Jewish as the Nazis had made him out to be. And in telling the story of his own persecution and years underground during the Nazi period, Klaus always emphasized to his son that he faced the greatest danger because he was a Communist, not a Jew. Irene Gysi, whose grandfather was Jewish, in contrast filled Gregor with stories of Jewish heroes—scientists, composers, writers. "If Jews happen to be intelligent, they'll be particularly intelligent, and if they are stupid, they are very stupid," Irene told her children. Good or bad, in Irene's view, Jews were always special.

But Gregor's biggest exposure to Judaism came from his grandmother, the formidable Erna. After the war's end, Erna, the Communist firebrand, had not returned to Germany. She remained in France, making visits to her son and grandchildren in East Germany. Her family said she stayed in Paris for love; she was waiting for a man who had promised to marry her. But it was hard to ignore the possibility that as the Iron Curtain fell across Eastern Europe and the Communists came to power, Erna saw things that made her uncomfortable with the reality of the dream she had worked so hard for.

Just as she had forever put her mark on Klaus with her passion for Communism, now she put her mark on Gabriele, and especially on Gregor, with her talk about Judaism.

Erna's visits were always an event in the Gysi household. She was a voluble woman of many opinions, and Gregor realized early on that his grandmother and his father saw the world in completely different ways. It was evident to Gregor, even as a boy, and unmistakably clear when he became a teenager, that politics and Communism were the most important things in his parents' lives. With his grandmother, it was her Jewish background that had become most important. Erna now divided the world into Jews and non-Jews. Whenever talk turned to a musician, a composer, a writer, Erna would interrupt to ask, "Is he Jewish?" This offended young Gregor's sense of justice. He had been taught, at

home and at school, that religion did not matter. "I don't understand why you are doing this," he said once to his grandmother.
"What counts is whether somebody is a good composer or vio-
linist, regardless of whether he is a Jew or not." For the first and
only time in her life, Erna shouted at her grandson. "For me, this
was the crucial element of my life!" Gregor's father may have
believed that he had fled the Nazis as a Communist and not as a
Jew. Gregor's grandmother clearly did not see things that way.

At night, upstairs in their bedroom, out of earshot of their parents, Gregor and his sister wondered about all this. What did it
mean to be Jewish? Their grandmother was Jewish. Their father
was half Jewish. Their parents had Jewish friends and relatives.
Do you feel Jewish? Can you see it? Or was Judaism just some
kind of legend or superstition?

In school, and in visits to concentration camps at Buchenwald
and Sachsenhausen, near Berlin, Gregor, like all East German
schoolchildren, was taught an incomplete history of the Holocaust. The central role of anti-Semitism in Hitler's ideology was
pushed aside, along with any talk of the history of the Jews or
their contribution to Germany and German culture. In atheist
East Germany, the history of religion was neglected. The history
of Christianity merited perhaps a page or two in school textbooks,
with emphasis on Martin Luther's "working-class roots" during
the Protestant Reformation. Judaism was not mentioned at all.
The killing of Jews was described and vigorously condemned, but
the main thrust of textbooks continued to be on Hitler's war
against the Communists, the evil capitalists who aided Hitler's
rise to power, the suffering of Communist martyrs.

Moreover, East Germany's Communist press continually
attacked and pummeled Israel. They never attacked the "Jewish
state" or mentioned that Israelis were Jews. Rather, they attacked
"Zionists" and the "U.S.-dependent state of Israel."

As they became teenagers, both Gregor and Gabriele enjoyed
hearing stories about their parents' resistance against Hitler. His
years underground lent Klaus Gysi stature. There was a difference
between "fighters against Fascism" and "victims of Fascism."
While both groups were victims, one group constituted more

passive victims; the others became victims as a result of their activity. Their father had not been one of the "poor Jews" unjustly persecuted. He had fought back. All the concentration camp survivors Gregor met, Jews and non-Jews, were members of the Communist Party. They, like his parents, had made their choice. Being Jewish gave Gregor the privilege to believe that he, too, would have been on the correct side of the trench had he been alive in 1933. As a member of a Jewish family, Gregor told himself, he would not have had the choice to be on the wrong side.

In the end, Gregor and Gabriele concluded that their Jewish background made them feel a little special and a little more confident. But though he had never been silenced, Gregor also sensed that it was wise not to be too open about his Jewish side.

Soon after Gregor's birth, Irene realized that Klaus had begun seeing other women. "Man is always a sinner," he once observed. Irene consoled herself with the thought that Klaus had affairs because Hitler's racial laws, which prevented Jews from marrying or dating non-Jews, had prevented him from sowing his wild oats when he was a young man. Whatever Klaus's reasons, by 1959 Irene had had enough; she ordered him out of the house. Irene and Klaus, divorced, remained friends and strove to minimize the impact of their separation on the children. Klaus saw them every few weeks, but even then his penchant for women interfered. After one visit to Klaus's house, Gabriele and Gregor came home upset. "There was a lady at Daddy's house," Gabriele said. "Our daddy is not our daddy when he is with her." Irene called Klaus and told him: No women when the children were visiting.

As the 1960s dawned, East Germany was considered the most totalitarian of the Communist satellites. In the summer of 1961, worried by the steady stream of refugees fleeing through East Berlin, the Communists hastily erected the Berlin Wall, rolling out barbed wire early one August morning and then replacing the barbed wire with a more permanent concrete wall, a mined no-man's-land, and, on the other side, another wall. It was a wall, someone remarked, built not to keep people out, but to keep people in. Despite the wall, the ferment of the 1960s began to cross the borders from West Germany. East German bands played "beat" music. Television programs and films reported increasingly anarchical attitudes among young East Germans. Intellectuals began agitating for more freedom. When Erna Gysi visited her grandchildren, she brought a rare, forbidden gift: Beatles records.

Even these small bursts of vibrant life in the stultifying air of East Germany turned out to be too much for the East German leadership. The Communists launched a campaign against "decadent Western forms of life." They warned the subversive musicians they could be considered "gangs" and put in prison. The party dismissed the country's minister of culture for allowing too much freedom.

To restore control over East Germany's cultural ferment, the Communist Party once again turned to Klaus Gysi. In 1962, Gysi was named minister of culture, the East German equivalent of a cabinet post but with far more power, since the Communists directly controlled all theaters, radio, television, newspapers, recording studios, and publishers. The appointment was once again a shrewd move. Gysi had always defended the party's cultural hegemony. He had enforced the party line at the rambunctious Aufbau publishing house. He could be counted on to rein in literature, movies, and television. At the same time, he was more sympathetic than most Communists to writers and had proved himself able to deal deftly with the outside world. The West German literary critic Marcel Reich-Ranicki wrote that even East German writers who did not trust Gysi greeted his appointment with relief: "Some optimists even think it is a reason for hope and see it as a piece of good news in the present gloomy situation in East German culture. This Klaus Gysi is surely not a comfortable fellow traveler." Perhaps, optimists speculated, the "good Gysi"— the man who had known Brecht and grown up in a household full of books, who spoke privately of a more open, cosmopolitan Communism, who wanted to reintroduce Germans to Jewish writers and others banned by both the Nazis and the Communists— would triumph over the "bad Gysi," the functionary who enforced the will of the Communist Party and seemed always willing to do the party's bidding.

Klaus Gysi, who two decades earlier had been forced to abandon his house full of books and hide out in Nazi Berlin, who for years, because of his height, had been known as "the Short One," stood in 1962 at the summit of power in East Germany, with a new nickname—"Kulturpapst." Klaus Gysi was now the "Cultural Pope" of East Germany.

While, in public, their father, the new, powerful minister of culture, denounced Western music and the decadent influence of rock and roll, Klaus Gysi's teenage children debated the seminal question of their generation: Are the Beatles or the Rolling Stones better?

Armed with the records provided by his grandmother, Gregor declared his loyalty to John, George, Paul, and Ringo. Throughout the 1950s, Gregor had grown up as a model Communist. Occasionally, before the Berlin Wall was built, Gregor would travel over to West Berlin to visit his grandmother, Irene's mother, who still lived near the big house in Schlachtensee where Klaus and Irene had hidden during the war. Gregor, accompanied by his nanny, always felt uneasy in capitalist West Berlin, as if he had stepped into enemy territory. He would glare up at anti-Communist graffiti scrawled on bridges and feel a surge of anger and pride. He was ready to defend his country against any adversary! When others told him troubling stories of Soviet soldiers raping German women after the war, Gregor went to his father for an explanation. Were such stories true? Did the Soviet soldiers behave so badly?

"In theory, no," responded Klaus, ever the canny diplomat. "In practice, yes."

But even to a young boy, shadows haunted the East German landscape.

On June 17, 1953, when Soviet troops were called in to help stop a revolt by East German workers, five-year-old Gregor was walking past a police station as the gate opened. He peered through and saw a group of civilians standing in silence in rows, their hands tied. They were faced by armed policemen. An old man with snow-white hair in the first row noticed Gregor and looked at him with a strange, sad gaze. Gregor ran away in shock. He was too young to understand the politics of the revolt, and the proof that the Communists would brook no challenge to their authority in East Germany. But the look of that sad old man stayed with him for the rest of his life.

Gregor led a privileged life. Because of his father's position and his mother's work at the Ministry of Culture, he obtained tickets to special screenings of foreign films. He even dubbed the voices of children in the few foreign movies allowed into East Germany. While other teenagers strained to hear the latest rock and roll on the forbidden West German radio stations and the BBC and Voice of America, Klaus played his Beatles records and brought them to school to show off to his friends.

Then, in 1963, when Gregor was fifteen, he was summoned to his school principal's office and told that an official from the feared Stasi had come to the school to ask whether it was true that Gregor was circulating tapes of Western music. Gregor was shocked. Like most schoolchildren and students, he believed the propaganda that the secret police hunted down only spies and saboteurs. He was also hurt. He had always considered himself a passionate defender of Communism.

The secret policeman was wrong, Gregor told the principal. He was not circulating tapes, just sharing records with friends. He did not even own a tape recorder. Gregor was allowed to keep his records. But he had been warned. The Stasi kept its eyes on everyone, even the son of the powerful minister of culture.

Despite these occasional forebodings, Gregor was clearly marked for special things. He was the son of two Communist Party members, one of whom was a cabinet member. His education had taught him that capitalism was doomed. Communism represented the wave of the future. In Great Britain, the first step on the path to success was Oxford or Cambridge. In the United States, it was the Ivy League. In East Germany, the first step for the "vanguard" of the country was to join the Communist Party, which made up a small percentage of the population but from which leaders in every sector were eventually chosen. During his last year in high school, Gregor was approached by his school's vice principal and asked—the unpleasantness about the Beatles records notwithstanding—whether he wanted to receive his Communist Party membership card on graduation day. It would be a fitting occasion to join the party, especially given Gregor's high-profile father. But Gregor demurred. It seemed too artificial and staged. Gregor would join the party not because of his father but because he himself wanted to.

Before beginning college at his father's alma mater, now renamed Humboldt University, in Berlin, Gregor took an internship as a cattle breeder. It was during the few months he spent outside Berlin, in 1966, that Gregor decided the time was right to join the Communist Party. He chose two of his father's friends as sponsors—a publisher and a man who had worked with Klaus Gysi in the Communist underground during the war. It was a distinguished sponsorship, for a young man coming from a distinguished Communist lineage. Gregor was on his way.

Gregor Gysi at eighteen had lived a life defined and circumscribed not only by the division of Berlin and the newly constructed Berlin Wall but also by the friends and social circle of his family. He was, in many ways, like any son or daughter of the American elite in 1966—before the massive anti–Vietnam War protests convulsed the nation, before the riots in America's black ghettos, before Kent State and campus protests. Gregor was exposed to the best his system had to offer and was largely content with what it promised for him and for the future.

As in the United States, that would all change in just a few years' time. By the time the 1960s ended, Gregor Gysi's faith in the East German system would be severely tested, and his own father would become a target for his criticisms.

The Six Day War in the Middle East that erupted in June 1967 struck Eastern Europe like a thunderbolt. Communist propaganda had built up the Arab states, backed by the Soviet Union, as invincible powers, ready to crush the American-backed "puppet" state of Israel. But within six days, the Arabs were laid low and the Soviet Union was humiliated. The Jews had prevailed.

Gregor Gysi knew there was something strange about the copy of *Neues Deutschland,* the official Communist Party newspaper, he had picked up near his school. He was a law student now at Humboldt University. It was the first week of June. The Six Day War was in progress, and Israel was on the verge of a huge victory, destroying the Egyptian air force, expanding its borders, capturing the holy Old City of Jerusalem. And there, on the front page, was an article featuring condemnations of Israel by more than twenty "Jewish citizens" of East Germany. All the people quoted were either intellectuals or Communist Party officials. Many were people Gregor and his family knew. None belonged to the tiny, state-sanctioned Jewish religious community. None attended synagogue. So how, Gregor wondered, did the regime know they were Jewish? Jews in East Germany—unless they had obviously Jewish names—did not discuss their backgrounds except with people they knew well. Many considered their Jewish backgrounds incidental to their new identities as Communists. Others were wary after suffering under the Nazis and, later, under the Communist anti-Semitic campaigns of the early 1950s. The official East German census never asked for one's religion. So how, Gregor wondered, did the editors at *Neues Deutschland* know how to contact Jews to seek out their comments on Israel?

The obvious answer never occurred to Gregor. East Germany's Communists kept a secret list of Jews in 1967, just as they had in 1953. At nineteen, Gregor shared many traits of his father: the rounded face, the dark hair receding to baldness, the quick wit and nimble intelligence. But he also shared his father's blind spot about the Communist regime, the belief that East Germany's Communists would never single out Jews for special persecution.

The denunciation of Israel in *Neues Deutschland* was just the start of East Germany's campaign against Israel. Over the next few months, East Germany produced more virulent anti-Israel propaganda than any other East Bloc country. West Berliners listening to East German radio thought they were hearing articles read from *Der Stürmer*, the Nazi propaganda newspaper.

Gregor had grown up with other Jewish children of high-ranking East German officials. When he began to ask around, he discovered that several of the parents, approached to join in the denunciation, had declined.

Gregor had learned about Israel in school but felt no special ties to the Jewish state. He was troubled by the article in the newspaper, but the incident receded in his mind as his interests were grabbed by an event far more pressing and immediate: the Prague Spring that began seven months after the Six Day War, in January 1968.

Like their contemporaries who thronged college campuses and the streets of major U.S. cities to protest against Lyndon Johnson's escalation of the Vietnam War in 1968, the children of the Communist elite who made up Gregor's friends were becoming increasingly disillusioned with the stultifying bureaucracy of the Communist system and the way it cut them off from new ideas and culture. They were still Communists, and the Prague Spring appealed to many of them precisely because it proposed to reform Communism, not overthrow it. In Czechoslovakia, Alexander Dubček and the Communist leadership were introducing what twenty years later Mikhail Gorbachev would call *glasnost* and *perestroika*. Dubček lifted censorship of the arts, allowing freer expression in newspapers, movies, and music. He promised more responsiveness from the bureaucracy. The children of the Communist elite were especially susceptible to the appeal of these reforms, since they, because of the position of their parents, had gotten at least a taste of what the West had to offer. They believed the "system" was flawed and they wanted change. That was why the Prague Spring struck such a chord throughout Eastern Europe. And it was why the thaw in Czechoslovakia so frightened the Soviet Union. It was Stalin's children and grandchildren who were endorsing reforms, not capitalist spies infiltrating from the West. This was the 1960s, and Prague was their Woodstock.

Gregor was still in law school when the Prague Spring began.

During the summer, many of his friends headed to Prague to breathe in the spirit. Gregor, that summer, married Jutta, a student he had met at the university. The two went off to Bulgaria for their honeymoon—and were still in Bulgaria when they heard that Soviet tanks had rolled into Prague.

The invasion turned Eastern Europe into a near war zone. Trains and plane flights were delayed and rerouted. Gregor and Jutta made it back to East Berlin with difficulty. Arriving, they discovered that many of their friends, sons and daughters of party officials, were trapped in Prague, some of them arrested by the invading Russians. Others had managed to return to Berlin, only to be arrested by the East German police for distributing "slanderous" leaflets denouncing the Soviet invasion. Gregor was acutely aware that had he not been in Bulgaria for his honeymoon, he might well have ended up in prison with his friends.

In the past, being the child of a top Communist official had provided a kind of immunity from persecution in East Germany. Privately, Klaus Gysi had always joked about the party leaders. Gregor had grown up in an atmosphere that was loyal to Communism but critical of its leaders. His family and friends did not bow to the feudal hierarchy. But in the wake of the crushing of the Prague Spring, having a prominent father was a mark of Cain. The Communists were determined to make an example of these privileged children who had supported the Prague rebellion. The son of Klaus Gysi's deputy minister of culture was arrested, as was the daughter of another Central Committee member. Clearly, even a man as powerful as Klaus could no longer protect his son.

In the fall, Gregor returned to the university, full of trepidation. He was head of the law school's chapter of the Young Communist League, the type of position a young man with a prominent father and a bright future in the Communist Party was expected to hold. The campaign to wipe out "counterrevolution" was spreading to the universities. The law school convened student and faculty representatives to pillory ten students whose "counterrevolutionary crime" was to have skipped Russian lessons. They were accused of conspiring to undermine Socialism in East Germany. An announcement was made before the entire student body: As a first stage of punishment, the accuseds' stipends were to be cut off for three months. One of the Humboldt University lecture halls had been transformed into a "tribunal," with the Communist accusers seated on a podium behind a table while students filled the lecture hall seats. The leader of the tribunal opened the meeting for "discussion." No one said anything. Then Gregor, in the audience, was called upon, as head of the Young Communist League, to speak.

Gregor was fed up with the charade. If the ten students were really counterrevolutionaries, he declared, there should not be any discussion. They should be expelled. But if all they had done was skip some classes, why label them counterrevolutionaries? "A thief isn't called a murderer," Gysi declared.

A classmate chimed in, shouting at the leaders of the tribunal: "I get the feeling you want heads to roll."

Abruptly the tables turned. Gregor and his classmate were accused of having a "liberal" attitude. They were defending students whose bad study habits were eroding the future of Socialism in East Germany. In the vaulted lecture hall of the university where Karl Marx and Friedrich Engels had once studied and where his parents had met, Gregor rushed to the microphone at the front of the hall. He looked down and saw a tape recorder behind the rostrum. The entire proceedings were being secretly taped. Gregor tried to defend himself but was interrupted and heckled by students egged on by the leaders of the tribunal. He left the microphone, despondent.

At the next meeting of the Young Communist League, Gregor was accused, as a league leader, of not being active enough in supporting Communist policies at the university and even opposing them. No one came to his defense. Again, he went to the microphone to defend himself. This time he was trembling. His words were met by silence.

The accusations and denunciations went on for months. Gregor was urged to confess his wrongdoings, to engage in the ritual self-criticism expected of Communists who had "misbehaved." He refused to bend. Professors turned a cold shoulder to Gregor; some were openly antagonistic in class. At home, he tried to reassure his wife. This was all crazy; it would pass. Things would return to normal.

Finally, the situation became so serious that Klaus Gysi decided to visit his son. Always quick to sense a shift in the wind, Klaus had joined in the denunciations and crackdowns that followed the Soviet invasion of Czechoslovakia. The supporters of the Prague Spring, Gysi declared in a speech, had entered the "sloping path gliding into counterrevolution." With Soviet troops occupying Czechoslovakia, Klaus hailed the closer cultural cooperation between the Soviet Union and East Germany—widely regarded as a signal that Moscow would now control East German policies even more tightly in the wake of Czechoslovakia's brief attempt to find a "third way" between Communism and capitalism. Klaus denounced East Germany's two best-known dissidents who had supported the Prague Spring, the philosopher and writer Robert Havemann and the folksinger Wolf Biermann. Havemann's crime was to claim to be a loyal Communist while calling for greater democracy and free speech in East Germany. Biermann had a growing following among young East Germans despite being banned from performing since 1963, when he sang his first protest songs against the East German regime. The two dissidents, Gysi declared in a speech, were now "politically and intellectually defeated and isolated." Harassment of both of them increased. Havemann's son was put under arrest. Biermann was placed in an obscure job, and his works were banned not only in East Germany but in other satellite countries as well.

With the Communists singling out children of high-ranking party members for punishment, Klaus Gysi was apprehensive about the campaign against Gregor—it might even imperil Klaus himself.

Klaus implored his son to stop trying to defend himself. "Be self-critical!" he urged. Gregor objected. If anything, he contended, the others owed him an apology for all they were putting him through. Klaus suggested a compromise that would allow both sides to withdraw without losing face: Gregor should admit some guilt—even though it was not true.

Gregor screamed at his father. "I reject this! If you want to spend your life making such fucking compromises, go ahead. But leave me alone."

The tension between them that had been building for years exploded.

"Until 1945, you risked your life. You went back to Hitler's Germany from your safe exile—you were half Jewish!" Gregor shouted. "The party didn't hesitate to sacrifice you! And then they kept pushing you around. But you just cling to them and avoid confrontations, making foul compromises all the time.

"You were courageous under the Nazis, even risking your life. Why now, in East Germany, do you not have the courage to challenge your own party?"

Klaus glared at his son. "You are twenty years old," he shouted. "You should stop being so naive. If you want to change the world, you can't do it by running your head into the wall! But you are clearly too young and too stupid. You understand very little about life."

With that, Klaus left the apartment and stormed into the night. Gregor remained behind, nursing his anger.

# Chapter Eight

# Walls Without, Walls Within

The singer from Auschwitz and the fair-haired beauty from Berlin society had carved out a life for themselves in the new West Germany. They had chosen to stay in Berlin even as the country was divided and the city became an enclave surrounded by East Germany. Estrongo Nachama had been liberated by the Soviets, but he had no desire to be ruled by them.

But as his fame spread in East Germany, he traveled over to East Berlin two or three times a week to sing at funerals or the occasional wedding. He met with the East Berlin rabbi, Martin Riesenburger, who had maintained the Weissensee cemetery, where Lilian's parents were buried, throughout the war. Some denounced Riesenburger as the "Red Rabbi," a tool of the Communists. But Nachama saw him as a man simply trying to sustain Jewish life under difficult circumstances, just as Nachama was trying to rebuild Jewish life in the West. Together, they helped open a kosher butcher shop in East Berlin for the few hundred Jews still living there who wanted dietary meat. They officiated together at funerals. Estrongo made it a point to visit all the major cities of East Germany—Dresden, Leipzig, Erfurt, Halle. He charted the slow disappearance of East Germany's Jews: two hundred left in Leipzig one year; a few years later, just forty. Time was finishing off what Hitler had started.

In 1953, Nachama watched helplessly as Jews fled East Germany during the anti-Semitic campaigns. When pressure on East Germany's Jews eased, Estrongo began crossing the border again. He smuggled in items that the Jews told him they needed: fruit, medicine, razor blades. Occasionally, he would "forget" his prayer book at a funeral or "misplace" a Jewish book. Even as the Cold War grew and border controls between East and West Berlin tightened, Nachama continued his weekly visits. He became a familiar figure to the border guards—his broadcasts made him almost a celebrity—and they would wave him through without even looking at his visa. To the dwindling number of East German Jews, Nachama became a kind of hero, the spirited cantor who would make time for every funeral, every bar mitzvah, every Hanukkah party. Soon after his liberation from the death camp, Nachama met a Jewish tailor who made clothes in a small shop in East Berlin. Nachama paid him to make his first suit to wear at the synagogue. So pleased was he with the work that he continued to patronize him even after the city was divided, bringing cloth from the West to the small tailor shop. Nachama always paid the man in West German currency, a rare commodity. Their friendship blossomed, and the tailor put a picture of Cantor Nachama, regal in his black cantorial robes and box-shaped skullcap, in a place of honor on the wall of his shop.

Stirred by Nachama's weekly radio performances, a Catholic group in the West German city of Aachen approached the cantor in 1948 and asked him to sing at a convention of Christians from across West Germany. They were deferential, apologetic. "Although you were in Auschwitz, would you sing for us in a church?" they asked him. Nachama agreed, and he became the first cantor to sing in a church after 1945.

But reconciliation was not high on West Germany's list of priorities after the war, and by and large, Germans shied away from confronting their role in the Holocaust. Sickened and enraged American soldiers, fresh from their liberation of the Nazi death camps, forced many Germans from towns surrounding the Buchenwald camp to march through it and see what Germany had done. At other camps, American soldiers made Germans dig mass graves for the bodies of Jewish victims. In some parts of Germany, the occupying armies ordered Germans to see the French film *Night and Fog*, which described in detail the machinery of mass murder. Without showing a stamped admission ticket to the film, Germans could not get a ration card.

All this had little effect, however. Most Germans refused to talk about what had happened during the war and what they, or their families, or their friends, had done. A German wrote at the time that as the full horrors of the Holocaust became known, most Germans "seemed to look away, to see nothing. The outcry at the horrors, which was the natural reaction of the whole world, failed to be heard in Germany. Instead, in [surveys] of a cross section of the population, the majority claimed to have suffered too— through bombing; when driven out of their homes by Poles or Russians; or, at the end of the war, when they had so little food. The Germans gave the impression of being eaten up by self-pity, of thinking only of their own sufferings, but they refused to search or ask themselves for the cause of their personal misery."

Americans began a "denazification" program, designed to weed out all Germans who had participated in the Nazis' rise to power and their crimes during the war. Some American officials proposed stripping Germany of all its industry and turning it into an agricultural state so it could never produce armaments again. "The true test of Germany," John McCloy, the U.S. high commissioner for Germany declared, "will be how it treats the Jews."

Within a few years, however, the rising threat of Communism and the growing tensions of the Cold War pushed Germany's reckoning with its Nazi past into the background. The denazification program was weakened; many former Nazis were allowed to slip quietly into retirement or into government jobs. In 1949, one out of every four civil servants in conservative Bavaria was a former member of the Nazi Party. Chancellor Konrad Adenauer of West Germany appointed as a special adviser Hans Globke. Globke had written legal commentaries on Hitler's 1935 Nuremberg Laws, which prevented Klaus and Irene Gysi from marrying because Klaus was categorized as a "half Jew" and Irene as one-quarter

Jewish. Those same laws had led to Lilian Nachama's parents' losing their jobs and home. The Americans had vowed to rewrite Germany's textbooks, but when they did, the Holocaust was barely mentioned. Germany had become America's frontline ally in its standoff with the Soviet Union. The United States needed a strong Germany, not one hobbled by discussions and recriminations about its past.

This does not mean that West Germany in the 1950s and early 1960s was still a Fascist state or in danger of slipping back into Nazism. It had established strong and vital democratic institutions and proved itself a faithful ally to the United States. It had concluded a reparations agreement with Israel that gave the new Jewish state more than $700 million and awarded individuals who had suffered in the Holocaust lifelong pensions. But on a personal and individual level, West Germans had not confronted the Holocaust and their treatment of the Jews. When Germans talked about the past at all, they focused on the glories of the German "resistance"—such as the July 20 plot to kill Hitler— the heroism of the few Germans who had stood up to Hitler, and the stories of Jews who had miraculously survived. They avoided any discussion of the millions of Germans who had participated in the Holocaust in ways large and small, or who had closed their eyes or willed themselves not to see. Many social studies teachers avoided teaching the Holocaust at all in West German high schools. There was not enough classroom time, they claimed, to explain such a controversial topic. It was as if the Holocaust and Jews were unpleasant topics that Germans preferred not to bring up as they busied themselves building their new country. It was only in 1961, after a rash of anti-Semitic graffiti appeared in West Germany, that the government finally made teaching about the Holocaust mandatory in West German high schools. Not until 1965—twenty years after the end of the war—did West Germany finally open the Dachau concentration camp as a memorial.

Aside from official functions and get-togethers with the Christians and their families who had helped Lilli during the war, Estrongo and Lilian kept their distance from most non-Jewish

Germans. It was not antipathy precisely, but coolness and reserve. Every street of Berlin held memories of the life Lilian had lived before the war and the terror of her years in hiding. The Nachamas did not consider the German friends they had as really "German" at all. They were people like Lilian's aunt who had helped her when she was in hiding, or the nice married couple who lived downstairs from their apartment, who were so warm to their son, Andreas. Estrongo and Lilian embodied the paradox of the handful of Jews who chose to remain in Germany after the war. They were no longer German Jews, an integral part of the country as Lilian's parents and grandparents had been. They were Jews in Germany, physically part of the country but in many ways distant. Lilian knew all too well that many of the people she passed daily on the streets would have denounced her and spat at her just a few years earlier. She and Estrongo harbored suspicions of people, especially those who seemed to go out of their way to say how many Jewish friends they had had before the war and how it was possible that they themselves had a Jewish ancestor. The horrors of Nazism often seemed to lie around every street corner and in every casual encounter. There were few Jewish boys and girls for Andreas to play with in West Berlin; the Jewish community was overwhelmingly elderly. So the children of the non-Jewish Germans who had helped Lilian in her years underground became his friends. So did the children of some left-wingers who had settled back in West Berlin because they could not live with the Communist repression in the East. All shared one thing—their parents had opposed Hitler's rise to power. As Andreas grew up, the geography of his mother's life underground during the war even shaped his teenage wanderings. "If you buy records, go here," his mother would tell him as they passed a shop in the center of West Berlin. "The owner helped me in the war. He gave me food." Avoid that shop, she would warn. Those people were Nazi sympathizers. Years before the Berlin Wall, Estrongo and Lilian were building a wall of their own to shield themselves, and Andreas, from the darker side of Germany.

\*　　\*　　\*

The construction of the wall caught both East and West Berliners by surprise. The Nachamas were in Venice on vacation when they spied the news on a restaurant television.

"What's happening in Berlin?" Estrongo shouted as he pushed his chair back and headed for the small television set blaring in the rear of the restaurant.

The words spilling out were in Italian. The pictures were clear: East German soldiers were rolling out barbed wire along the streets that divided East from West Berlin. Communist border guards were preventing East Berliners from crossing over to the West and West Berliners from entering East Berlin.

That Friday, the Nachamas went to a synagogue in Venice for Sabbath services. Estrongo stayed afterward and spoke to the rabbi about becoming a cantor in Venice if he could not go home to Berlin.

The Nachamas returned to West Berlin, however, and they found that surprisingly little had changed. The East German government still renewed Estrongo's visa every six months. They allowed him to pass through the new barbed-wire barricade without incident. His broadcasts were still carried on East German radio.

"The world does not concern the Jews," Estrongo announced to his family. Whatever world-shaking events were taking place in Berlin, he would continue his tending to the spiritual needs of the handful of Jews left in East Berlin and East Germany. Estrongo resumed his weekly visits on the other side of the wall. There was now a shortage of medicine; Estrongo smuggled it across the border, tucking it in his pockets and his briefcase. The guards never searched him. There was little fruit—no oranges, no bananas; he brought those too, crammed into the trunk of his car. The guards never opened it. Estrongo felt a special affection and obligation to the Jews now trapped *nach drüben,* "over there" on the other side of the wall. These were his people, and Estrongo tended them like a mother hen. When Riesenburger, the "Red Rabbi" of East Berlin, died in 1965, Nachama stepped up his visits.

Gradually, the Nachamas, like other Berliners, adjusted to the new rhythms of life in the divided city. Living with the Berlin Wall was easier for Estrongo and Lilian because, unlike many West Germans, they did not have family or sentimental attachments on the other side. Truth be told, Estrongo and Lilian did not dislike the wall that much. They saw it as a punishment for the Germans, for what they had done to the Jews.

As for young Andreas, when it came time to choose which foreign language he would learn in school, the boy chose English over Russian—a ten-year-old's faith that the Americans would not abandon West Berlin, that the Berlin Wall was not a prelude to a Soviet takeover or invasion.

As much as the war had shaped both Estrongo and Lilian, they did not talk much with their son about their experiences. Andreas knew that his father had been in Auschwitz, but Estrongo never spoke about it. When, as a young child, Andreas asked his father about the number tattooed on his forearm, Estrongo said it was a phone number and changed the subject. He never told his son about his final months in Sachsenhausen, the death march, the desperate hunt for food, diverting the dogs so he could eat their food to survive. Such stories were not proper topics for a young boy. Still, eavesdropping on his parents' conversations with friends on Sunday afternoons, listening to his mother as she drove around Berlin, occasionally reminiscing about places where she had hidden or people who had helped her, Andreas learned bits and pieces about the war and what it had meant to the Jews and to his family. But the outside world, the Germans who had committed and tolerated the crimes, remained at a distance.

As he grew older, Andreas understood that there was another society out there, Germans who had lived through the war and not resisted the Nazis or protected Jews, Germans who had supported Hitler and approved what he had done to Jews. The Holocaust was a constant presence in his living room. His father always sang at commemorations of the Holocaust and at the death camps. Many of his parents' friends were survivors of the Nazi camps. Andreas played with the daughter of the head of the Jewish community in Berlin, a man who had survived Auschwitz. The Ger-

mans who always made Andreas uneasy were the ones in their for-
ties or fifties, old enough to have lived through the Nazi period,
who for no apparent reason would begin telling Andreas that they
had a Jewish grandmother or had hidden Jews in their basement.
For Andreas, that ended the conversation. He did not trust such
people. One thing he had learned from being with his parents'
friends was that Germans who truly had a Jewish grandparent or
had hidden Jews did not speak of it. You found out eventually, but
only after you'd known them awhile. Andreas understood about
evil Germans.

But even in the late 1980s, at the age of forty-five, Andreas
Nachama could still say that he had never met someone he could
consider a real Nazi. The wall erected by his parents to protect
him had held up well.

# "Admit You Are a Spy! A Zionist!"

Alena Schmula never lost her affection for the Americans or for their music. Although an angry Communist woman had snatched the Statue of Liberty pin off her lapel and thrown it to the ground, she had not forgotten the golden days when the American soldiers had come to her hometown of Pilsen and liberated her from the Nazi labor camp. Nor did she forget the walls of books that once lined her girlhood home or the trips to the opera where her grandmother sang. She remembered, too, the sweet breath of democracy and freedom the Americans had brought. But as Communism descended on Czechoslovakia, Alena spoke of none of these. She learned to bury her opinions and shield her past. She stopped wearing makeup and stopped invoking the names of the heroic American generals who had defeated the Nazis: Patton and Bradley and Eisenhower.

Unlike Klaus Gysi, who had chosen to live under Communism, or Lilian and Estrongo Nachama, who were fortunate enough to live on the other side when the Cold War began, Alena was trapped when the Iron Curtain descended. Overnight in 1948, the Communists staged a coup in Czechoslovakia and crushed the brief hope of democracy. One by one they turned on their opponents and crushed them—first the democratic politicians, then the unions, then the newspapers and radios. Alena, who worked in Prague, but took the train often to her parents' home in Pilsen, knew the political climate had changed almost immediately. No one talked anymore about a multiparty system and free speech.

In the countryside, the crackdown was worse. New "action committees" confiscated farmers' property, pooled it, and established cooperative farms. Factory workers and office workers, who had no training in farming, were being forced to volunteer their labor in the fields on weekends. Farmers who refused to give up their land or livestock were arrested. In Pilsen, action committees roamed the streets, confiscating shops and closing factories. Alena noticed that foreign cars and those with foreign license plates were disappearing from Prague. Foreigners were being forced to leave.

Within a few months of the Communist takeover, an action committee descended on one of the Schmula family factories, which they had regained after the war. The Communists declared it nationalized and strung a rope across the entrance. Frightened, Alena's parents rushed home, gathered their most valuable items, loaded them on a truck, and drove out of town to stay with relatives. Later that night, they returned home by train to fetch more of their belongings. Their apartment was locked, plastered with "Do Not Enter" signs. Alena's mother ripped off the signs and began banging on the door, ringing the bell. "I am not going to sleep in a hotel," she screamed. "I am going home." A Czech policeman answered. The Communist Party had given the apartment to him and his family, assuming the Schmulas were fleeing the country. The policeman refused to budge. The Schmulas went back to their relatives.

Alena and her parents did not join in the rush to enter the Communist Party. They despised people who joined—they were mentally unstable, they said with scorn, silly, proletarian. The Communists might get the poor and the workers of Czechoslovakia to join, but not the cultured middle class like the Schmulas. At her office in Prague, Alena had blithely tossed away the applications for Communist Party membership. But now the mood had changed. Alena's refusal, and her background—as a Jew, as a member of the "bourgeoisie"—left her more and more vulnerable.

Soon after the war, Alena met Vaclav Wittmann, a Jewish

sculptor who had survived the war under the protection of his Christian stepfather. Alena and Vaclav moved in together back in Pilsen and soon had two boys, Robert and Michael. Vaclav, whose grandmother had been deeply religious, remembered fondly the smells of cooking in her home, the songs she sang, her care in preparing for the Sabbath and the Jewish holidays. Not a religious man himself, he relished the culture, the music, the spirituality of his upbringing. He believed it set him apart from most people. Like his sculpting and the beard he wore, it was part of Vaclav's maverick identity. Alena, by contrast, rarely talked about the fact that her family was Jewish. Being Jewish had got her into enough trouble during the war. Religion had never been important to her; it was only the Nazis who had labeled Alena a Jew. With the trauma of the Holocaust still fresh in her mind and the Communists seizing power in Czechoslovakia, Alena was afraid to identify herself or her children as Jews. She did not even want to tell her children of their background. It was asking for trouble.

In 1951, the worst fears of Czechoslovakia's Jews were realized. As part of Stalin's campaign against the Jews, Rudolf Slansky, the Jewish head of the Communist Party, was arrested, put on trial, and executed along with other prominent Jewish Communists. Government-sponsored anti-Semitism had returned.

The police came for Alena at three in the morning, pounding on the door. Whisking her to the police station, they began asking about her "contacts." Several years earlier, Alena had sent a letter to friends who had emigrated to Israel. When they opened her file at the police station, she saw her letter inside. It had been intercepted.

The police accused her of being a spy and passing on coded information to Israel. They said a woman at the butcher shop had heard her say that Jews should have their own country and that Americans should come and take over Czechoslovakia.

"Am I stupid?" Alena said to the police. "I'd never speak like that at a butcher's. I have children."

The police released her. Then they arrested her again, questioning her for twelve more hours. They released her at night. She was shaking. The next day, she could not eat.

The third time the police took her in, they accused her of lying and of making self-incriminating statements. She was interrogated in relays. Some interrogators were polite, some shouted and threatened. "In Russia, they would beat you up," said one. Alena struggled to control her temper. She would not become hysterical, she told herself. She would not cry.

The police pressed further. They asked her about her ties to a Jewish Communist and member of the secret police who had been arrested with Slansky. Alena said she knew a man by that name, but he was unrelated to the notorious secret policeman. The names were just a coincidence. The accusations continued: Alena was a spy. She was a Zionist. She was working for the Americans.

The noose grew tighter. Alena had a friend in the Czechoslovak army. The interrogators said the soldier was telling her army secrets, which she was passing to people abroad. Alena denied everything. The police were just wrong! The interrogations continued for hours. After every one, Alena was released.

Then, one day early in 1953, the police returned. They searched the apartment and ordered Alena and her husband outside. Flanked by policemen, they were marched to headquarters. Both were under arrest, Alena as a Zionist and a spy, Vaclav for "currency speculation." He had sold some heirloom gold to support the family. Robert, now eight, was in the country, visiting his grandmother. But Michael, who was two, was at home with his parents. Bring him along, the police said. At the jail, a social worker was waiting. She began playing with Michael, talking to him kindly.

"Follow us," one of the policemen ordered.

"What about my baby?" Alena demanded.

"Leave the baby," the man snapped.

The Wittmanns were searched. The police made a careful list of everything they had with them—rings, Alena's earrings. They took Vaclav's tie and shoelaces. The Wittmanns were to be placed in separate jail cells. What about the baby? Alena kept asking, frantic. What about the baby?

The police officer looked at her. He is in good hands, he said. He will be put in an orphanage. He will be there for a long time, as long as it takes you to absorb a Socialist education and become a Socialist person. Only then will he be discharged.

Over her shoulder, as she was being taken to her cell, Alena caught a last glimpse of her son, in his dark-blue woolen coat with its fur-trimmed hood, playing happily with the social worker. In the cold jail cell, Alena collapsed and began to sob. She could not stop crying for days.

Vaclav was released after eighteen days. He asked for his son's return. The Communists refused. Meanwhile, Alena was jailed with a rotating cast of three other women, prostitutes and pick-pockets. A long platform with a thin straw mattress served as a shared bed. An open pot in the corner was used as a toilet. The women were allowed to shower and wash their underwear once a week.

The police had more in store for Alena. They brought her to a room with a parquet floor, a table, and three chairs. Alena knew the floor well. Her jailers had made her scrub it clean, on her hands and knees. The interrogators came in two-hour relays, each time a different man with a different style. The first man was polite, acting as if he were a friend. "I want to help you," he said, leaning across the wooden table. "If you help us, there will not be any problem." Just tell us who your friends are, the man prodded. Tell us if you recognize these names. Then another man came in, angrier. He shouted names at her, names she had never heard. "We know you know these people," he ranted. "We saw you with them. We already know everything!" The worst was the one she quickly labeled "the rude man." He screamed, trying to frighten her. "Admit you are a spy! A Zionist! That you supported the Zionist movement against Socialism!"

Then came "the seducer." He pretended that he was falling in love with Alena, that he wanted only to help her.

On and on it went, week after week, like actors trapped in a play, repeating the same scenes endlessly. The interrogators told Alena that if she did not sign her confession, if she did not admit to the litany of crimes, they would keep her in jail for years. She still refused. "I have nothing in common with this," she repeated again and again, turning away the proffered confession. "I will not learn it. I will not sign it."

The weeks passed, with no word of Michael, or Robert, or Vaclav. Alena was cut off; her situation hopeless. Then, like a miracle, Stalin died. The new Soviet leaders quickly renounced Stalin's purge and blamed it all on his chief of the secret police, Lavrenty Beria, who was executed.

After three months of almost daily interrogations, Alena was released from jail in spring 1953. But she did not get her children back. As a woman arrested for political crimes and "Zionism," Alena was considered an unfit mother; her husband also carried a scarred record for his "currency speculation." Robert, with the Communists' approval, continued to live with Alena's mother. Michael was kept in an old mansion that served as the orphanage for children taken from criminals and "political cases." Alena and Vaclav were allowed only brief visits. They made a point of befriending orphanage workers to ascertain how Michael was doing. Was he happy? What was he eating? Did he cry? A social worker always accompanied Michael during the visits. Alena wrote to the government, seeking the return of her son. She received no reply. After several months of appeals, Alena was allowed to take her son to the park in a stroller. Then she was allowed to take Michael home for an occasional weekend.

When he had been placed in the orphanage, Michael had been chattering happily. He had begun to make simple sentences, like "Daddy works!" Now he would not talk at all in front of adults. His mute face passively absorbed all that went on around him.

Alena feared she would never get her children back. Who knew what damage the orphanage was doing to Michael? Deciding her only chance was to prove that she was loyal to the system and the party, she resolved to be more Communist than the Communists, if that was what it would take to get her children back.

Alena took a job as a metal presser. In a system that prized huge, brawny production, she was working in the most "Socialist" of factories: heavy engineering. Her fingers bled from handling razor-sharp metal sheets. The factory boss set a quota that each worker was to fill every month. Alena filled her first quota in just three days. She worked six days a week, getting to the factory at six-thirty every morning. On Sunday she would visit Michael. Vaclav, too, strove to become a "model worker." He took a job in a quarry—breaking rock that would one day be used to build a huge statue of Joseph Stalin.

Two years passed—two years of work at the metal factory, of bleeding fingers and Sunday visits to her son. Finally, in 1955, two years after Alena was arrested, Michael was returned to his family. He was four years old. Robert was allowed to leave his grandmother's house and move back with his parents as well. Alena quit the factory. Her family was reunited.

Despite the reunion, times were still hard. Not only was Alena marked as a former political prisoner; Vaclav was considered a rebel too. His frustration and anger began to show. He clashed often with the Communist authorities. When Michael and Robert ran into difficulty at school, Vaclav would storm in. "You are a teacher?" he would thunder. "You teach children, yes? I don't know about your pedagogic knowledge, but I think you'd better go to the countryside to milk the cows. That would suit you better." As an artist, Vaclav did not have a job he could lose, like others whom the Communists wanted to punish. But he was prevented from exhibiting publicly and had difficulty making ends meet. He supported himself by doing restoration work and by teaching.

Stalin's death had freed Alena from prison. But her country remained imprisoned behind the Iron Curtain and under Communism. Czechoslovakia, which fifteen years earlier, before the start of World War II, was one of the most advanced countries in Europe, sank deeper into gray poverty and repression. Virtually all private companies were liquidated. Police ransacked apartments to make sure people were not hoarding clothing or food. Women like Alena were forced to work in unskilled and unsafe jobs in factories. Apartments were confiscated, chopped up into smaller units, and redistributed. Members of Alena's father's family who before the war had enjoyed life in a spacious mansion with servants were allotted two rooms for eleven people. When Alena's hometown tried to revolt openly against the draconian policies, the Communists blamed the revolt on Pilsen's "bourgeois" families, including her parents and grandparents. Alena's relatives were ordered to turn their houses over to the state and leave Pilsen within forty-eight hours. They were allocated dwellings on the border with East Germany—houses that had been bombed and ravaged during the war and never repaired. Alena's grandfather was put to work in a car factory; within the year, he was dead of lead poisoning.

When Alena contemplated her own life under Communism, she came to the conclusion that the Communists' impact on her family was even worse than the Nazis'. The Nazis had been evil. But in the context of Alena's own life, the Communists were crueler. Alena had been a teenager when she was sent to a labor camp by the Nazis. Younger, she was more resilient. The two-year separation from her children had been the worst kind of torture. And there was something else: The Nazis were Germans, foreigners whom Czechs had long regarded with suspicion. Alena had never expected the Nazis to be decent people. The Communists were her own countrymen. The Czechs, she had always believed, were open-minded and democratic.

The Wittmanns were increasingly a family out of step with the rest of the country. At home, with her children, Alena did not talk about her three months in prison. She did not talk about being arrested for being a Zionist. She did not talk about being Jewish. Alena buried her Jewish past as deeply as she could. Like the Statue of Liberty pin she had worn on the streets of Pilsen when the Americans liberated the city in 1945, it was a relic of another time.

In 1956, Alena gave birth to her third child, a dark-haired girl she and Vaclav named Sylvia. As did her playmates, Sylvia grew up in a home that lacked any overt signs of religion. Like most Czech children, she celebrated Christmas, happily opening presents. Religion was never discussed. But Sylvia's father avoided certain foods because they were not "kosher." Vaclav never explained what "kosher" meant. For Sylvia, noticing what foods her father would and would not eat became a game. "A Jew doesn't eat pork," he would declare. Then Sylvia saw him eating pork—a staple in Czechoslovakia—and she said, "Hmm, what's that you're eating?"

"Do you know the main mitzvah in the Torah?" he replied.

"No," Sylvia answered, puzzled. "What is it?"

"Protect life. When these damn Communists have nothing in the shops but pork, you don't want your own father to eat? So your old father will collapse in the middle of the road and a car will hit him and he will die. So what is more important—that I eat pork or that I die in the middle of the road?"

Sylvia did not understand what her father was talking about.

Sometimes, when something bad happened, Alena would say to Sylvia, "Oh, I wish I were a Christian! Their God is so kind: He always forgives them." When things went well and Sylvia was feeling proud, Alena might warn her, "Keep silent. Our God doesn't like us to be too proud. Our God is very tough—a tough guy."

Czechoslovakia is a country rich in churches and religious artwork. As a girl, Sylvia loved to go inside churches; she loved the architecture and the smell of incense. When Sylvia asked about Jesus and the crosses and churches, her father turned harsh. "Don't go in there," her father told her. "Look at the architecture. Look at the beauty of the art. But don't go into these places. Don't allow these people to talk to you. I hate these places."

When Sylvia asked her mother about Jesus, Alena told her: "Well, he was one of our smart people. Many people made fairy tales about him, and that is not something we should learn about."

It was all confusing to Sylvia. She knew that her family were not Communists and not atheists. They celebrated Christmas but did not go to church. There was a God, but Jesus was just a fairy tale. At one point when she was small, Sylvia started believing that Jesus was a hairy animal with wings who brought presents at Christmas. When someone gave her a hamster, Sylvia thought the hamster was Jesus and was afraid to touch it. At grammar school, some children called Sylvia "Zhid Arishid"—a Czech nickname meaning "Jew the peanut." She liked the way it rhymed. One day, coming home from school when she was nine, Sylvia saw that someone had scratched a six-pointed star on her family mailbox and written the word *Zhu*—Jew—in the center. It meant nothing to her. It was just a star.

As odd as it may seem to most Americans, the Wittmanns were not atypical. Across Eastern Europe, still smarting from the anti-Semitic campaigns of the early 1950s and the relentless pressure against them, Jews buried their identity. They did not speak of it in front of their children. Many denied it outright. A handful of synagogues in Prague, Warsaw, Budapest, and East Berlin remained open, but they were quickly beginning to look like old age homes. The Communists wanted a small Jewish community that they could show to tourists and visiting officials as a sign of the new Communist "tolerance." But they did not want a Jewish community that was vibrant or one that would make demands or cause problems. They kept Jews under close surveillance. No one dared go to synagogue unless he or she was deeply religious—which most Jews, like the Wittmanns, were not. In Prague, the small synagogue near the center of town that had been open for worship since the thirteenth century remained open. But only a handful came to pray.

The other synagogues in the old ghetto were now museums. When the Germans conquered Czechoslovakia, they had seized these synagogues and over the next three years filled them with stolen Jewish ritual objects from across Czechoslovakia. As Jews from city after city, town after town, were deported to the concentration camps, the Nazis, carrying out a grand plan, carefully bundled up Torah scrolls and candelabras, Passover plates and Hanukkah menorahs, embroidered tablecloths and prayer shawls, and shipped them to Prague. There they were examined and catalogued by Jewish scholars under Nazi supervision, then placed on display inside the synagogues. The scholars were shipped to concentration camps and killed. The synagogues constituted a new museum—the Museum of an Extinct Race. Under Hitler's plan, the elite SS, Hitler's storm troopers, would visit the museum to familiarize themselves with the people they were in charge of annihilating. Other Germans would later visit the museum the way tourists go to archaeological museums to see the artifacts of stone-age man and long-forgotten civilizations. Only a few SS groups saw the museum before the war turned against the Germans. After the war, the Communists turned the collection of Jewish artifacts into the official Jewish museum—a lure for tourists. Czech Jews were discouraged from coming. The richness of the exhibits never failed to awe visitors: the shining silver goblets; the intricately woven covers for the temple ark that housed the Torah; the exquisitely tooled candlesticks that graced the tables of Jewish homes on the Sabbath. People marveled at the artistry and beauty of the Jewish objects. They were always stunned when they were told how and why the objects had been collected. The exhibit stood as testimony to the monstrousness of Nazi crimes.

As the 1960s unfolded, the Jews of Czechoslovakia and Eastern Europe had, almost miraculously, avoided extinction. But what the Nazis had tried to accomplish in five years of frenzy the Communists were now achieving through decades of slow and steady strangulation. They had closed down the Jewish school that Tamas Raj attended in Budapest. They had driven committed Communists like the Gysis out of their jobs because they were Jews, or partially Jewish. The communists had so terrorized the Wittmanns that they would barely speak the word "Jew" to their children. The Communists were gradually snuffing out Jewish life, as if to ensure that the synagogues in Prague would become, as Hitler had planned, a museum of an extinct race.

In 1960, Vaclav Wittmann moved to Prague to find better-paying work. He landed a job in construction and by 1962 had saved enough for the rest of the family to join him in a cramped apartment. Soon they were able to swap their tiny space for a four-room flat on the top floor of a five-story building in the center of the city.

It was in Prague that the Wittmanns heard the stunning news, in June 1967, of Israel's surprise attack on the Arab states. Vaclav and Alena quickly supplemented what they were hearing on the official radio station by tuning in the shortwave broadcasts of the BBC and the Voice of America. They reacted with glee at the humiliation little Israel was heaping on the bigger Arab armies,

backed by the Soviet Union. The Czechs could not attack the
Soviets directly. But they could enjoy the Soviet Union's humiliation in this proxy war a thousand miles away. Many non-Jewish
Czechs gloated as well. All over Prague, ordinary citizens began
circulating petitions denouncing the Arab countries.

In their apartment on Martynska Street, Vaclav made a decision. He walked down the stairs and headed over to the Jewish
Community Center opposite the old synagogue. A man who until
then had considered Judaism just part of his ethnic background
volunteered to fight in the Israeli army.

"Are you crazy?" the head of the Jewish community asked him.
"You would have to emigrate! Don't do it, and don't tell anyone
about it!" Discouraged, Wittmann went home.

The excitement caused by the Six Day War was minor com-
pared to the furor the next year when a group of Communist Party
reformers led by Alexander Dubček introduced the Prague Spring.
Declaring he wanted to introduce "Socialism with a human face,"
Dubček lifted censorship laws and eased political controls.
Czechoslovakia blossomed. Robert Wittmann, now twenty-three,
emerged as one of the country's leading avant-garde artists. When
the poet Allen Ginsberg came to Prague, he asked to see Robert's
work. In one installation, Robert placed a large white panel in the
middle of a busy square in Prague. He cut a large hole in
the middle of the panel and painted the edges so they looked like
film sprocket holes. Then he placed white chairs in front of the
panel, inviting passersby to watch the "film" of people going about
their business on the other side of the panel. Intoxicated by the
new freedom, Robert and his friends began mixing art with politics. They printed posters saying: "Everyone who is preparing war
should be assassinated"—a thinly veiled warning of the Soviet
invasion that everyone feared might come.

On a hot August night in 1968, Vaclav Wittmann went to the
theater to see the premiere of a friend's play. Afterward, he went
with friends to the Artists Club, where they drank late into the
night. Coming home, Vaclav heard the drone of aircraft. But he
was too drunk to pay much attention. He climbed the four flights
of stairs, unlocked his door, undressed, and fell into bed. As dawn

broke, Alena was shaking him. "We are occupied! We are occupied! Go out and get potatoes and milk."

Soon the buildings of Prague were shaking with the rumble of tanks. The Soviet Union was invading Czechoslovakia, to put an end to the Prague Spring. Vaclav, hungover, stumbled outside with two shopping bags, to stock up on provisions in case the Soviets closed the stores. The scene was chaotic. In front of the main radio station, a Soviet tank was burning. On other streets, Czechs who spoke Russian were pleading with Soviet soldiers to abandon their tanks and cease the invasion. People were pulling down street signs so the invading troops would not know where they were. They were ripping out lists of tenants in the lobbies of apartment buildings to stymie soldiers who came to make arrests. Wittmann bought his potatoes and milk and then joined in. He climbed atop a garbage can, reached up, and ripped down the sign for Martynska Street. While he was up there, he pulled down a neighboring street sign as well.

Because it was August, twelve-year-old Sylvia was at her grandmother's house in the country. She saw Czechs speaking to a young tank driver in Russian. Why was he invading a brother Socialist country? The driver seemed confused; he seemed to think he was supposed to invade Germany. A Soviet officer came up to him. "Stop talking to these people, or you will be shot," he admonished.

In Prague, Vaclav volunteered to drive an ambulance; Czechs had been injured as they battled the Soviet tanks. Loudspeakers blared requests for donations of blood. In scenes broadcast around the world, the Czechs fought valiantly against the massive invasion. But they were outmatched. The Soviets hustled Czechoslovak Politburo members onto a military plane in chains and flew them to Moscow, where they were forced to sign a declaration saying they welcomed the invasion and had invited the Soviet troops into Czechoslovakia.

In the rapidly closing political window, Michael, who was eighteen, received word of his admission to school in Paris. He decided to seize the opportunity and go. His father was proud; it took courage to take a chance on freedom. Vaclav was sure

Michael would come back after a year or two. He had been accepted into the university in Prague. The situation in Czecho-slovakia would calm down, Vaclav reasoned. Alena was not so sanguine. In her heart, she believed that Michael, who as a boy had been taken away from her so cruelly for two years, would not return. He would not want to return to the country she was sure Czechoslovakia was becoming—once again muffled by the Com-munists. On their way to the railroad station to see Michael off at Christmastime, Alena told Sylvia that she did not believe Michael would return.

"Why don't you stop him?" Sylvia asked.

"I cannot keep my child from his freedom," Alena responded. "Who knows what will happen to this country?"

In the bitter chill of a Prague winter, Alena watched the train pull out of the station, as again her youngest son was taken away from her.

The Soviet crackdown was brutal and fierce. The new hard-line regime in Czechoslovakia wreaked havoc with intellectuals and dissidents, purging the Communist Party of all supporters of the Prague Spring, stripping dissidents of their jobs, forcing workers to sign loyalty oaths to remain at work. Most Czechs turned their backs on the government and focused inward. This seemed at first a kind of surrender, the surrender of a small country, once again, to the larger power of invaders. But in fact it was a form of silent protest and rebellion, the way the Czechs kept their spirits up and their hopes alive. Instead of fleeing their country, which was not possible, Czechs fled into the privacy of their souls and passions.

Sylvia's rebellion took an odd turn. Emboldened by some friends, she decided to visit the old synagogue in the center of Prague. It was 1969, just after the invasion, and she was thirteen. Her going was a sign of teenage rebellion more than any yearning for religion or prayer. Everyone was doing what was forbidden, Sylvia reasoned. Religion was forbidden, so Sylvia and some of her friends went to the synagogue a few times to see what it was like. The visit seemed inconsequential and quickly faded from memory.

The next year, however, Sylvia was intrigued enough with her background to accept an invitation from the Jewish community to take some courses in Jewish history and culture and participate in a ritual *mikvah* or bath. Although Sylvia's mother had been born Jewish, she had been baptized a Protestant by her father during the patriotic fervor that gripped Czechoslovakia before World War II. If Sylvia wanted to be considered a member of the Prague Jewish community, she had to undergo a ritual conversion. Accompanied by a friend, she decided to take the requisite classes. They turned out to be simple; the ritual bath unpleasantly cold. But in undergoing the conversion, Sylvia felt she was establishing some connection with this mysterious thing called Judaism that had been whispered about so often in her home. Her mother did not object. Her father, Sylvia suspected, was secretly pleased.

The following year, Sylvia received the report card that signified her graduation to high school. She had applied for a special school that taught photography, one of her passions. She was rejected. On her grade report, the teacher wrote: "Individualist. Not suitable for organizations. Never member of Young Pioneers or Socialist Youth Movement. Zionist ideas and attitudes. Part of family in Israel, out of the Socialist camp."

None of Sylvia's family lived in Israel. Sylvia was not even sure what a "Zionist" was. She brought home her report card and showed it to her mother. "What is Zionism?" she asked.

"Aha!" Alena exclaimed. "It is starting again!" For the first time, Alena told her daughter about what had happened to her in the 1950s—her arrest, her interrogation, the two-year separation from Michael. Alena then visited the school and complained that her daughter was being unfairly treated and unfairly labeled. It made no difference. The entries were now part of Sylvia's permanent school record. Like her mother, fifteen-year-old Sylvia was now labeled a Zionist and an outcast.

# Chapter Ten

# "My Word Will Be Heard Under the Newly Built Walls"

The year of Stalin's death, 1953, was the year of Tamas Raj's bar mitzvah. Vilmos Raj, his grandfather, expected that Tamas would be bar mitzvahed in the family synagogue, a large temple near their apartment.

Vilmos was a warm and friendly man, a beloved figure in the Raj family, who loved to sing and seemed content to stay in the background while his wife and his elderly mother-in-law ran the house. While little Tamas and much of the family had hidden in one of the Wallenberg Houses in Budapest in the closing days of the war, escaping deportation to the death camps, Vilmos and his wife had been sent to the countryside to dig ditches against the advancing Soviet army. For months, they had been forced to live in a barn, sharing space with pigs and other animals.

Tamas and his brother, Ferenc, idolized their grandfather in the way small children naturally gravitate to the gentleness of indulgent grandparents. Religion, and the rhythms of Jewish life, still mattered very much to Vilmos. In the heady days of freedom following the end of the war—before the Communists seized power in 1948—Vilmos Raj decided to open a small shop in Budapest. He did not want to work in an office or a factory, because that could mean working a six-day week, and Vilmos would not break God's commandment to rest on the Sabbath. With the help of a relative who sold wholesale cloth, Vilmos opened a tiny fabric shop. Tamas loved to visit him there. And on Saturdays, when his grandfather closed his store for the Sabbath, Tamas would walk with him to synagogue to pray.

Soon after the Communists took control, they declared war on private shops. Vilmos's store was seized and closed down. So Vilmos moved to a stall in an open-air market, where he could still keep his own hours. Within a few months, the Communists decided to move the entire market, many of whose small shop-keepers were Jewish, to a remote site outside Budapest. Getting to work would be hard, and business was sure to drop off. But Vilmos prepared for the move. It was the only way he could work and, on Saturdays, pray.

But the Communists refused to give him a permit at the new site. Their intent was clear: to make it impossible for Budapest's Jews to both earn a living and be devout. In an effort to help Jews being squeezed out of a livelihood, several Jewish organizations overseas gave money to set up special cooperative factories that would close on Saturdays. Vilmos applied for a job at one of the factories. As they prepared to open, the Communists ordered them dismantled. There would be no special factories for the Jews.

Unable to find a workplace where he could follow his religion, Vilmos began doing piecework—weaving baskets by hand. It was hard work and paid little. But Vilmos did it well—so well that the Communists, who had taken away his store, gave him a medal. Vilmos had not been trained to weave baskets, however. He was old and getting weak. The thin strips of wicker cut his hands as he bent them into shape. He never complained, and he never grew bitter. Day after day, young Tamas watched as his beloved grand-father's hands turned coarse and bloody because he was a Jew and would not work on Saturday.

As the day of Tamas's bar mitzvah approached, he practiced his prayers and his reading from the Torah. But his father, Sandor, grew more and more uneasy. He was remembering his pact with the Soviets as a condition of his release from the prisoner-of-war camp: to join the Communist Party. His practice as a lawyer in Communist Hungary had flourished as a result of that pact.

Though Tamas's father was a Communist, the family kept a kosher home. The Communists had closed down the Jewish schools, but Tamas's mother still taught at the temple religious school and took the boys to a Jewish holiday camp on summer vacations. Tamas's approaching bar mitzvah, however, provoked a crisis.

Sandor did not want his son to have such a visible bar mitzvah. The "Doctors' Plot"—when nine Moscow doctors, six of them Jews, had been arrested on charges of conspiring with the CIA and other western intelligence groups to assassinate Soviet leaders—had just been announced in Moscow. The smell of anti-Jewish purges was in the air. Two days after the Doctors' Plot was proclaimed, Hungary's official newspaper denounced Zionism, and Matyias Rakosi, the Jewish head of the Hungarian Communist Party, began a purge of the party. Rakosi, mindful of the fate of the Jewish head of the Czechoslovak Communist Party, Rudolf Slansky, who was hanged in a Prague prison, was determined to escape the same fate. He quickly sacrificed one of his top lieutenants, the Jewish head of the secret police, along with the Jewish chief of Radio Hungary, the chief physician at the Jewish hospital, who had treated several members of the Politburo, the head of state economic planning, six generals and colonels in the secret police, thirty doctors, the director of the Jewish museum, and the official in charge of Jewish affairs within the party. The Hungarian ambassadors to the United States and France, both Jews, were recalled and arrested.

In such an atmosphere, Sandor announced he could not risk going to a synagogue, much less be seen bringing his son there to be bar mitzvahed. It could derail his career as a lawyer—or worse. The boy had to be bar mitzvahed, Vilmos insisted. Then do it out in the country, Sandor proposed, in a small town outside Budapest, away from the prying eyes of the secret police. It was finally agreed that Tamas would be bar mitzvahed in a small synagogue on a Budapest back street. It was well known that the Communists had seeded the larger synagogues with informers and even stationed members of the secret police outside them, keeping track of who entered. But they did not bother with the small, Orthodox synagogues tucked away on narrow side streets. Indeed, on those few occasions since his return from prisoner-of-war camp when Sandor felt the pull to attend synagogue—on Rosh Hashanah and Yom Kippur, the holiest days of the Jewish year—he himself had gone to such a synagogue, confident that the worshipers would not betray him. He had often spotted other Jewish Communists there, seeking refuge as well.

So on the day of his bar mitzvah, Tamas went with his grandfather to a small synagogue several blocks away from his house. A few moments later, his father walked a circuitous route to the same temple. He slipped in through the back door, sidled into a pew, and saw his son proclaimed a Jewish man.

As the Communists tightened their hold on Jewish life—closing schools, shutting down businesses like Vilmos's, infiltrating synagogues—the official Jewish community remained eerily silent. Budapest's Jews, like Jews in most of Europe, were much more centralized than in U. S. cities. Headquartered in a stone building just behind the great synagogue in downtown Budapest, the Jewish community offices served as the funnel through which flowed money and advice on community affairs. Here, behind oversize wooden doors and beneath vaulted ceilings, the installation of rabbis and the funding of social programs for Jews were supervised; the Jewish newspaper was published and, most important, Jewish interests were represented before the government.

In 1945, at war's end, the Soviets and the Americans had agreed to set up a democracy in Hungary, with free elections and guaranteed rights for all political parties. As part of this democratic spirit, most of the old leadership of the Jewish community was tossed out of office. Some had been discredited by their dealings with the Nazis during the war as they strove to save the Jewish community; others were part of the "Jewish aristocracy," who were now thought to be out of touch. The various factions in the Jewish community agreed on Louis Stoeckler—a factory owner and a member of the old leadership, who had tried to hold the Jewish community together during the Nazi occupation—to serve as president until a permanent leader could be chosen. Few knew much about him or his politics.

Shortly after Stoeckler was selected, a committee was formed to organize community elections so a permanent president could be chosen within six months. The date set for elections came and went without any action. Stoeckler blamed the delay on administrative confusion and logistical problems. Another date was set.

When anti-Jewish riots, inspired by the Communists, erupted in the countryside in 1946, Stoeckler was silent. Instead he wrote an article in the official Jewish newspaper, praising the occupying Soviet army: "Hungarian Jewry! Don't forget! You owe your very life to the Red Army! Help it, strengthen it, it is your defender, your liberator, the preserver of your life."

Delegates at a national convention expressed their anger and dissatisfaction with Stoeckler. They criticized him for failing to demand the return of Jewish property and for failing to combat anti-Semitism aggressively. Stoeckler announced another delay in Jewish community elections. His office, he said, was still having trouble assembling a complete list of Jews in Hungary. Elections would again be postponed—until 1948.

What became clear—what many had suspected—was that Stoeckler was a Communist informer, placed at the heart of the Jewish community to systematically weaken the position of the Jews in Hungary and leave them defenseless. In 1948, the Communists took over in Hungary. Stoeckler announced elections. But, in fact, only one slate of candidates was presented, and it was made up entirely of Jews loyal to the Communist Party.

Running unopposed, Stoeckler was elected president of the Jewish community. Shortly afterward, just before Hanukkah, Stoeckler signed a document closing all thirty Jewish schools, including the one attended by Tamas Raj.

When the Communists began turning against the Jews and accusing opponents of being part of a Zionist conspiracy, Stoeckler joined in, denouncing "Zionists" and "Zionist spies." The Jewish newspaper, Uj Élet, became a government mouthpiece, parroting anti-American propaganda and attacking Israel. When the Communists began deporting Jewish businessmen and middle-class intellectuals to the countryside, stripping them of their homes and household goods, Stoeckler's newspaper chortled: "No tear will be shed for the Jewish capitalists who, interested only in their profits, have been allies of the slaveholding lords and the flayers of the common people. . . . People of this ilk have excluded themselves from the community of our working coreligionists. . . . [Jews] approve of the decision that the . . . exploiters and torturers of the people, and the counterrevolutionary rumormongers, should have no place" in Hungary.

Stoeckler's loyalty to the regime, involving the betrayal of his own community, could not protect him from the fact that he was, after all, a Jew. On a winter evening soon after the Doctors' Plot was announced in Moscow, police raided Stoeckler's home and found two hundred dollars in American currency and some Swiss francs. They issued a warrant for his arrest. The charge: currency fraud—the same charge the Communists had invoked to arrest Vaclav Wittmann in Czechoslovakia. Stunned, Stoeckler fled toward the Austrian border. It was too late. The Communists captured him, and Stoeckler—the informer, the man who helped the Communists crush much of what was left of the Jewish community of Hungary—was arrested and put in prison, charged with being a spy and a Zionist.

The Communists now prepared to make Stoeckler the center of an anti-Semitic show trial. They took him to a basement room and photographed him and another Hungarian with guns in their hands. The contrived photographs were to be the centerpieces of a trial that would "explain" one of the enduring mysteries of World War II: What had happened to Raoul Wallenberg, the savior of so many Jews, who was last seen heading down the road to meet advancing Russian troops in 1945. In fact, Wallenberg had been arrested by the Soviets and would later die in a Soviet prison. Those running the trial of Stoeckler were determined to "prove" something different—that the Jew Stoeckler had murdered Raoul Wallenberg in the basement of the American embassy before the Russians ever arrived.

The trial never took place. Stalin died. After several months,

Stoeckler was released and allowed to emigrate to Australia. But the leadership of the Jewish community remained firmly in the hands of Jews loyal to the Communist Party—Jews who were about to have their authority challenged by another Jew, Tamas Raj.

As teenagers, Tamas and Ferenc plunged deeper and deeper into Jewish life. They began teaching at the Jewish summer camp they had attended as children. The memory of a rabbi uncle who had died in Auschwitz loomed ever larger in their minds. In 1958, Tamas, who planned to become a teacher, applied to Budapest University. He had to write an essay and then submit to an oral examination by several professors. He chose to write on two popular Hungarian writers: Gyula Illyes and Laszlo Nemeth. It was a good paper; Tamas handed it in, full of confidence.

On the morning of his oral exam, Tamas rose late and rushed to the university without reading *Nepszabadsag*, the party daily. There, in an editorial, the chief Communist Party historian had denounced Illyes and Nemeth, the writers Tamas praised in his essay, as "enemies of Socialism." Tamas's hopes of entering the university were doomed. At the oral exam, a sympathetic professor tried to persuade him to apply to a lesser university. Tamas thought about it but decided instead to enroll in the only seminary left in Eastern Europe that still trained rabbis. The Communists had kept it open as a public relations gesture, a symbol of their "tolerance" for Jewish life. Being a rabbi also meant being a teacher, Raj reasoned. And it meant a chance to influence and touch the lives of young people—young Jews. Tamas's father disliked the idea of his son becoming a rabbi. Though Sandor did not object to his sons' maintaining a Jewish life in the privacy of their home, to become a rabbi, like having a bar mitzvah in a large synagogue, was to invite too much attention, to court trouble. But Tamas was almost an adult now, and backed by his mother and his grandfather Vilmos, he decided to enter the seminary.

The rabbinical seminary was woefully underfunded; many of the rabbis teaching there had been vetted by the Communists and presumably reported regularly to the Communist authorities. But the seminary was a place where Tamas could study Hebrew and the Bible and begin to forge his own destiny.

Tamas became close to Jozsef Schindler, a charismatic young rabbi in the southwestern city of Szeged, who commuted to Budapest to teach at the seminary. When Schindler fell ill and died, in 1962, he asked in his will that his student Tamas Raj replace him as rabbi in Szeged. Tamas, only twenty-one, was two years away from completing his studies, but he decided to try to fill Schindler's shoes. As boys, Tamas and Ferenc, who did not have many toys, had often played imaginary games. They created an imaginary country they called Heroland. In the spirit of the Cold War, there was an East Heroland and a West Heroland. Each brother ruled one country and established the laws. Outside, in the real Hungary, Hungarian freedom fighters were shot to death just outside Tamas's window. But in Heroland, justice always prevailed. Tamas had not played Heroland with his brother in years. But he gathered up his books and headed for Szeged, to see if he could create a Heroland there.

Like Budapest, Szeged reflected the success and assimilation of Jews in Hungary. The city's first Jewish temple, located near the waterfront, literally turned inward. A forbidding, mausoleum-like structure, it had few windows and a stern, unadorned facade. Over the years, as Szeged's Jews grew wealthier and more influential, they had built a new synagogue next door, a grand and extravagant building in the Moorish style, more suitable to Istanbul than to southern Hungary. It rivaled the great Dohany Synagogue in Budapest and attracted admirers from across Eastern Europe. When, in the nineteenth century, city leaders decided to build a statue commemorating one of Hungary's national heroes, Jewish businessmen in Szeged paid for it. Fifty years later, when the Nazis ordered Szeged's Jews deported to the concentration camps, the city council urged—in vain—that they be spared. The Nazis killed most of Szeged's Jews and used the great synagogue to warehouse old clothes. About two thousand Jewish families returned to Szeged after the war. But by the time young Tamas Raj arrived, in 1962, old age and Communist harassment had reduced the city's Jewish population to just six hundred people, two hundred of whom were elderly widows.

What attracted Raj most to Szeged was not the grandeur of the synagogue or the remaining Jewish community but the city's university. Among its students were Jews who had no connection to official Jewish life. Many, like Tamas, came from homes of Jewish Communist parents. But unlike Tamas, they had not had a Grandfather Vilmos to keep the spirit of Judaism alive. It was these young Jews—not much older than himself—on whom Raj set his sights. He began calling on students who had never considered their religion important. He organized a youth group and religious classes for young people and sent university students invitations to the synagogue. On the walls of one meeting room he hung posters of young Israeli women lying on a beach. Every Saturday afternoon, he hosted a Sabbath meal and lectured on Jewish subjects or encouraged the students to research a topic and present it.

Soon the old synagogue in Szeged was hopping. Raj arranged youth celebrations for Hanukkah, Purim, and other festive holidays. He scheduled events where students learned Israeli dances and listened to lectures by diplomats from the Israeli embassy in Budapest. He started a Saturday youth group that began with lunch and a talk about Jewish life, then continued with field trips around Szeged. Dozens of students began to come regularly to Raj's Saturday lunches. They would adjourn afterward to a café or go for a walk to Jewish sites or a stroll in the woods. Though only a few years older than the students, Raj dressed formally in a dark suit, top coat, and black bowler hat. Always the "rabbi"—slightly aloof, a bit arrogant, but immensely learned—he breathed life into what had been a dying community. In a short time, he had begun to inspire great loyalty in people who felt confident that Rabbi Raj would not let them down, that he would not back down from his principles.

Raj completed his rabbinic studies and was formally ordained as Szeged's rabbi. Word of his success with the young people of Szeged soon reached Budapest and, inevitably, the Communist secret police. A few days after sending out invitations to one of his youth meetings, Raj received a long-distance call from the head of the official Jewish leadership in Budapest. Cancel the meeting, the man ordered. What is the problem? asked Raj. "If you organize a youth group like this, then the Catholics and the Protestants will organize youth groups, and they are bound to be anti-Semitic," was the response. "What you need is to ban anti-Semitism, not youth groups," Raj replied. He hung up. Later that day, an official from the local office of church affairs, the Communist department that oversaw religious activity, appeared in Raj's office. He carried with him one of the letters of invitation Raj had sent. He did not say how he had got it, but it didn't require much imagination to assume that an informer existed inside the Jewish community. Though Louis Stoeckler had fled the country, the official Jewish leadership remained under the control of the Communists—who expected supervision of misbehaving Jews like Tamas Raj.

"You will cancel this meeting, because you are planning to leave Szeged on Friday for the entire weekend," the Communist official told Raj.

"I have no plans to leave," Raj responded.

"If you do not leave Friday, the police will come Saturday and arrest you," the official explained calmly. Fearing now that any Jews who attended the meeting would be arrested or put under surveillance, Raj hurriedly phoned around Szeged to make sure no one came.

But the youth activities at the synagogue continued. Raj became more careful, spreading the word through young people whom he knew and could trust, encouraging them to bring friends.

The secret police responded by stationing a plainclothes policeman near the entrance to the synagogue to monitor Raj's comings and goings. The man always carried a briefcase. Sometimes he stood on one side of the street; sometimes on the other. He never came inside and never acknowledged any greeting. Raj nodded at him politely every morning when he went to his office in the synagogue and every evening when he left.

One day Raj arrived at the synagogue to find that someone had scaled the ornate wall surrounding it and thrown a stone through a window. He went up to the plainclothesman and asked, "You are always here—why didn't you prevent it?" The man, nonplussed, stammered that he was just passing by.

Up in Budapest, concern over Raj's activities was increasing. In 1966, the new head of the official Jewish community—Geza Seifert, a lawyer hand-picked by the Communists—sent a secret memo to the Communist authorities informing them of meetings where Israel was discussed and of groups of Jews learning modern Hebrew. He denounced three rabbis. One of them was Tamas Raj, whom Seifert accused of teaching Zionism and maintaining contacts with Yugoslavia, a rogue Communist country that had declared its independence from Moscow.

The Six Day War accelerated Communist surveillance and harassment in Szeged. At first Raj, like others, greeted the news of Israel's surprise attack and swift advance with shock and amazement. As the dimensions of Israel's victory became clear, Raj fielded enthusiastic telephone calls from many of his students. Not only was Israel winning; it was humiliating Arab armies backed by the Communists. "We have captured Sharm el Sheikh!" an excited teenager shouted to Raj over the phone one afternoon. Aware that his telephone was probably tapped, Raj cut the student off. "OK, we'll talk about it later."

As the Sabbath approached, Raj copied out a prayer urging support for Jewish nationhood that had appeared in Hungarian prayer books before the war. He sent copies to all the synagogues in the region, urging congregations to read it on Friday-night and Saturday services. Friday evening, with the war still being fought in the Middle East, Raj gave a sermon on the need for Hungarian Jews to show solidarity with Israel. At the back of the great synagogue, sitting as usual by himself, was a man whom Raj had always suspected of being a Communist informer. As Raj began to speak, this man walked up the center aisle and sat in the front row. The better to hear, thought Raj.

Any sense of personal invincibility Raj had felt in the face of secret police monitoring vanished at dawn on September 4, 1967. Three months had passed since Israel won the Six Day War. Raj was in Budapest, visiting his mother. The police walked up the three flights to her apartment and rang the doorbell at six o'clock. Margit Raj hurried to open the heavy wooden door. Gathered on the grimy landing were five plainclothes policemen, the caretaker of the house, and a neighbor. The police needed two witnesses in order to make an arrest. From his bedroom, Raj heard a commotion and then the police telling his mother that her son was under arrest.

An unmarked car drove him to a special prison run by the minister of the interior for spies and enemies of the Communist state. Once inside, Raj was blindfolded and told to take off all his clothes. He stood there until the police returned. They removed the blindfold and gave him his shoes without the laces and his pants without the belt, a common practice to deter suicide by hanging. He was marched off to another room, where again he was made to strip. Naked, he waited until a man came in, the prison warden. "You should know that you are only a number now, and your number is 4490," he said.

Raj was put into solitary confinement. The police interrogated him for three days, taunting him: "Why are you here? Who do you think is in the neighboring cells?" Raj was unprepared for the interrogations, which went on for hours. The interrogators would use things he had said to trap or humiliate him. Once, after a particularly exhausting session, Raj asked, "Why? What is the purpose of all this?" The interrogator puffed on a cigarette and answered, with surprising candor, "Since the June war the Jews have become very insolent. We have to show them who is the master."

After three days, Raj was released. Ordered to return to Szeged and report to the police station there every day, he was given a warning: Unless he stopped his activities, the Communists would transfer him to a city without university students.

As Yom Kippur neared, the police called Raj to remind him that he would be expected to report to the police station on that holiest day of the Jewish year. Raj said he could not. He would be spending the entire day leading services in the synagogue, and in any event, he told them, it was forbidden for a religious Jew to do anything on Yom Kippur but pray. The evening before Yom Kippur, a policeman appeared at Raj's house. He said that if Raj did not report the next day, the police would send two officers to the synagogue and drag him out. "Very well, you can do that, but then I'll walk through the city in my rabbi's robes." Raj waited for the police; they never came.

The harassment escalated following the Soviet invasion of Czechoslovakia in 1968, as nervous Communists across the East Bloc tightened their hold on dissidents. Walking home late one night after visiting a Jewish family in Szeged, Raj was attacked just outside his house and struck on the head with a stick. His head still bloody, Raj called the police. "It's probably just a case of robbery," the police officer said. "This is not surprising; people attack Jews because everybody knows that they have money even on their skins." Raj spoke to his neighbors and discovered that the man had been waiting outside his house for hours. The "robber," he was convinced, had been sent by the Ministry of the Interior to deliver a warning.

In Budapest, his brother, Ferenc, also a rabbi now, was coming under similar pressure. Clandestinely he had begun helping Jews flee Hungary through Yugoslavia. The State Office of Church Affairs summoned Ferenc to a meeting. An official warned him, in a message aimed at his brother as well: "What we don't like about you is that you are rabbis of the young people. We don't care—you can teach all the old people. You can have all the classes you want. But don't touch the youth."

Like Tamas, Ferenc ignored the warning. The two brothers became bolder in their defiance of the regime. Ferenc began recruiting Jewish artists and actors to travel down to Szeged and perform in the synagogue to show their support for Tamas. At the grand Dohany Synagogue, Ferenc slid into a pew next to Rabbi Shlomo Carlebach, a Hasidic folksinger from America, and asked him to sing at his brother's synagogue in Szeged. Carlebach agreed. So did the comedian Kabos—the Jerry Lewis of Hungary—who was a concentration camp survivor.

When Kabos stepped off the train in Szeged, he was recognized immediately. People swarmed around him, clamoring for autographs. "Watch what I do," Kabos said to Ferenc. He began to run. The crowd ran after him, eager for a wave, an autograph, a handshake. At Tamas's synagogue that evening, Kabos recounted the tumult surrounding his arrival. "There was a time when I was a child that I was running and everyone ran after me. But they were running after me because I was a Jew. Now the people run after me because they want to shake my hand. How things have changed! But," he added, "we cannot let the children forget."

The Communists were not pleased. Tamas Raj was more than just an irritant now. His synagogue was becoming a symbol of open defiance, attracting not just Jews in Szeged but nationally known figures like Kabos, who had never before made a political issue of their religion. Then, in 1970, Tamas Raj hatched his most audacious plan yet. Like many learned Jews, Raj had a legalistic mind that loved to burrow through the intricacies of Jewish law. He now intended to use this to turn Communist law against itself.

Back in the nineteenth century, Imre Madach, one of Hungary's best-known writers, had written a play, *Moses*. Raj planned to stage a performance of the play—on Israeli Independence Day, May 10. It was a defiant gesture in a country that had broken off diplomatic relations with Israel after the Six Day War and regularly denounced Israel's "aggressive war" and "expansionism."

Raj went about preparations carefully, obtaining all the necessary permits from the fire department, the local Jewish community, and Szeged's Office of Cultural Affairs. Then, a few days before the performance, the Communists realized what Raj had planned. A Communist cultural affairs official in Szeged summoned Raj to his office. He had learned, he said, that Raj intended to speak before the performance. The play was now canceled.

"I gave permission for the performance," said the official, "but not for you to address the audience."

The strategy was clear—to deny Raj the benefit of a heavy-handed cancellation that would create a cause célèbre and rally support. The Communists wanted the event quietly smothered to death by the bureaucracy.

Raj said he would accept the consequences of his own words

and that both his remarks and the performance would be tape-recorded. If there was anything the official did not like, Raj would pay the penalty—after the play.

The official looked at Raj nervously, his hands shaking. He told Raj that two people from the Ministry of the Interior had come down from Budapest to the Cultural Affairs Office to talk with him in person. They had told him to use any pretext—just ban the performance. Raj walked out. The performance would go on.

Next, several non-Jewish actors in the play came to Raj's office and announced that the Communist-controlled actors union had forbidden them to wear hats while they performed. Because *Moses* was to be staged in Szeged's grand synagogue, all the actors had agreed to cover their heads, in accordance with Jewish tradition. If the actors would not cover their heads, the performance could not be held in the temple. It might be moved to another place, but there was no other building that Raj could get on such short notice with as much seating capacity.

Raj called the temple's cantor into his office. He had a plan. The two men talked, then headed downstairs across the courtyard and into the temple. Placing yarmulkes on their heads, they carefully took the Torah scrolls out of the ark at the front of the temple and carried them, silver ornaments clanking, across the courtyard to the temple offices. With the Torah gone, the temple was no longer a sacred place. It was now just a big building with eighteen hundred seats. The actors did not have to cover their heads.

On the night of the performance, cars jammed the streets bordering the synagogue. Jews came down from Budapest—though not the official Jewish leadership—and from other cities. One of Hungary's Catholic bishops hurried through the temple doors for a seat. More than two thousand people squeezed into the building. It was standing room only.

Raj rose and looked out over the crowd. Among the crowd, he knew, were members of the secret police, eager to jump up and cancel the performance at the first sign of criticism of the regime. Few in the audience knew the pressure Raj was under, the constant efforts of the Communists to derail the performance, the harassment, the beating. How to communicate all this? How to show solidarity with the Jews—especially his young Jewish students—crammed into the synagogue, without bringing down the fury of the police?

Raj walked to the ornate pulpit at the front of the synagogue and mounted the steps. In his deep, gravelly voice, he welcomed the audience and described the history of the play they were about to see. Then he began to recite a well-known poem by Miklos Radnoti, a young Jewish poet from Szeged who had been put in a concentration camp by the Nazis and shot in 1944. A few months before he was killed, at the age of thirty-seven, Radnoti had written a poem, later discovered in his papers, "Neither Memory nor Magic," which Hungarian students, especially students in Szeged, read in school and were often required to memorize. After describing the horrors of the concentration camps and Nazism, the poem soared with an assertion of hope:

> *The world will be rebuilt, and even though it is forbidden*
> *   to me*
> *My word will be heard under the newly built walls.*

Standing before the audience, Raj recited the well-known lines, lines that many young people in the audience knew by heart. " 'The world will be rebuilt,' " he concluded. Then he paused. The audience waited, expecting the words "and even though it is forbidden to me." They never came. Instead Raj recited the final line of the poem: " 'My word will be heard under the newly built walls.' " That pause told Raj's listeners all they needed to know. He, too, had been forbidden to speak freely. Like Radnoti, he was imprisoned by silence. But like Radnoti, Tamas Raj had hope in the future.

The performance was given a tumultuous ovation. Even the official Jewish community in Budapest, increasingly apprehensive about Raj's activities, seemed enthusiastic. Geza Seifert, the community's head, wrote Raj a letter congratulating him on *Moses* and passing on the compliments of the bishop who had attended.

The day after he received that letter, Raj found another letter from Geza Seifert on his desk. It informed him that he was being dismissed as the rabbi of Szeged.

The Communists had spoken. Raj had gone too far. The Communists now saw him as a dangerous dissident. They had not been tricked by Raj's use of the Radnoti poem. They understood all too clearly Raj's contempt for the regime and his influence among Szeged's young Jews. They ordered the Jewish community to strip Raj of his post.

Raj drove to Budapest and confronted Seifert in his cavernous office, with its phone linked directly to the State Office of Church Affairs. Seifert informed Raj he was being transferred to the towns of Nagykanizsa and Kaposvar—towns as obscure as their names were long. They had no university. The only Jews living there— forty of them—were confined to an old age home. The synagogue was virtually abandoned. There was no place to obtain the kosher food Raj insisted on. Raj visited the towns and then returned to Budapest, demanding a meeting with Seifert. He would go, Raj declared, but first he wanted to take six months to learn the art of ritual slaughter, so he could prepare kosher meat for himself and for the Jews there. Seifert glared at Raj. He was flanked by Hungary's chief rabbi and by the head of the rabbinical seminary. "We don't need you," Seifert told him. "You are dismissed from the rabbinate."

Raj stood up. "Gentlemen," he said, "you have judged not me but yourselves." He strode out of the room and down through the gloomy staircase and out into the sunlit street. The great Dohany Synagogue stood to his left, the site of the former ghetto where so many Jews had died to his right. Tamas Raj stood between them, no longer a rabbi.

Back in Szeged, five hundred Jews signed a petition demanding Raj's reinstatement and sent it to Seifert. Seifert ignored the petition. Raj returned to Szeged, unsure what to do. He considered fighting his dismissal. Within a few days, however, Raj was summoned to the local office of church and state affairs. If he did not leave Szeged voluntarily, he was told, the police would remove him by force. And if he continued to seek signatures for a petition, the police would arrest him for "incitement." Raj was ordered to

move out of the apartment that had been allocated to him as
Szeged's rabbi.

Raj refused to give in. He might no longer be allowed to serve
as a rabbi, but he would not abandon Szeged. In addition to his
rabbinical training, Raj had acquired a degree in history. Szeged
was home to a well-respected museum, which stood near the river
in the center of town. Raj applied for a position there as a historian and researcher. The museum staff was interested in hiring
Raj, but all appointments had to be approved by the Office of
Cultural Affairs—the same office that had tried to stop the performance of *Moses*. When Raj's application arrived there, it landed
on the desk of the same man who had tried to persuade Raj to
stop the performance at the behest of the Ministry of the Interior.
The official passed the application on to the Szeged Communist
leadership. The response was a single sentence: "We do not support your further presence in Szeged."

Without a job and lacking official approval to remain in Szeged,
Raj had run out of possibilities. But he was determined to fight
on. He filed a court suit demanding that he be allowed to keep his
apartment. His brother called him from Budapest. A friend who
was a judge had told Ferenc that the suit was pointless: It had
been decided at a high party level that Raj would be dismissed
and driven out of Szeged. Ferenc himself was under increasing
pressure and was considering fleeing the country.

Tamas still balked. Then a friend of his came to Szeged, saying
he needed to meet with Tamas urgently. He was bringing with
him a trusted friend who knew people in Hungary's secret police.
"Leave Szeged as quickly as possible," the man told Raj. "Your life
is in danger."

Raj quickly packed his belongings and drove to Budapest. He
moved into his mother's large apartment in the Eighth District,
where he had lived as a boy. At twenty-four, he had been one of
the youngest rabbis in Hungary. Now he was thirty-one, and
his rabbinical career was over—for the moment. In Szeged the
plainclothesman stopped his surveillance on the sidewalk outside
the temple. It was no longer necessary. Szeged no longer had a
rabbi.

# Chapter Eleven

# "What Is a Jew? Is It a Devil?"

Leokadia was still young and pretty, with the looks of a movie star. Back in ravaged Warsaw, where housing was in short supply, and with a little daughter, Leokadia realized she did not care much for raising a child. The Nazis had leveled much of the city. Leokadia's entire family moved into a one-room apartment that had once been owned by Jews. Her mother slept in a bed in one corner, Leokadia in another corner, and little Barbara in a third corner. In the center of the room stood a crude wooden table, where the family ate. When Leokadia invited men over to the apartment, which was frequently, Barbara was told to hide in the bathroom and be quiet. Like many children in Warsaw after the war, poorly fed and sleeping in drafty apartments, Barbara had developed tuberculosis. While her mother entertained men on the other side of the door, Barbara crouched in the bathroom, trying desperately not to cough.

In 1949, when Barbara was six, Leokadia finally married—a simple man, who, until the day he died, emphasized that he had accepted and married Leokadia even though she already had a child. Leokadia dressed her daughter in white for the Catholic wedding. Barbara stood with the couple before the priest, holding a garland of flowers.

It was Leokadia's mother who truly raised Barbara. Her grandmother was a religious woman who made sure that Barbara was a good Catholic. She sent her to Catholic schools and got her up every Sunday morning for church. When Barbara was eight, she received her first communion. The smell of incense swirled toward her from the front of the church. The vaulted ceiling soared above. Dwarfed by the magnificence around her, Barbara, in her white communion dress, faced the long walk down the aisle to the raised pulpit where the priest stood. Barbara swayed a bit and tried to clear her head. Then she swayed again and fainted. The excitement, the smells—it was all too much. It was an inauspicious debut, but Barbara's family was nonetheless pleased. As the walls of Communism had closed in on Poland, religious faith reasserted itself, and the Church, with its comforting rituals, had become a prized sanctuary.

Barbara settled into a typical Polish Catholic girlhood. She was a diligent student both at school and in the religion classes at her parish. Just as the Communists had shuttered all the Jewish schools, so too had they closed all the Catholic schools. But at home, the child's mother and her grandmother both insisted that Barbara go to church and keep up with her Catholic studies. When she was twelve, Barbara read a popular girls' book about the life of a nun and thought for a time that she would like to be a nun herself. But as she entered adolescence, she began playing hooky from Sunday church services and religion classes. She would meet her school friends and go off with them. The others could laugh and joke about not going to church. But Barbara always felt uneasy, as if she were committing a sin.

Growing up in Warsaw in the early 1950s, Barbara did not know many Jews. Most of the fifty thousand Jews who remained in Poland did not consider themselves Jewish. Many had married non-Jews or, like Klaus Gysi in Germany, imagined they had discarded their Jewish identity when they joined the Communist Party. Given Poland's history of anti-Semitism, the pogroms after the war, and the waves of anti-Semitic purges that engulfed East Germany, Hungary, and Czechoslovakia in the 1950s, most Jews in Poland realized it was safest to push their Jewish identity as far into the background as possible. For a girl like Barbara, a Jew was something alien and strange, as rare as kiwi fruit in a Warsaw market. She heard her parents tell occasional jokes about Jews; in them, the Jews were always wily and crafty, not to be trusted. Once she was washing clothes, and her mother, looking over at her as she wrung out shirts, said, "Oh, you're doing them the Jewish way." Barbara thought that odd. What was "Jewish" about wringing out clothes? And what were Jews, anyway? All she really knew about Jews was that they had curly black hair and brown eyes.

In 1956, however, the anti-Semitism that had swept across the rest of Eastern Europe touched down in Poland, and Barbara discovered that in fact she knew someone who was Jewish. A power struggle between different factions in the Polish Communist Party unleashed a virulent anti-Semitic campaign that attacked Jews first in one faction, then another. Nikita Khrushchev, the Soviet Union's new leader, flew abruptly to Warsaw to veto the appointment of a top Jewish Communist as head of the party. The Polish secret police set up a special department to monitor Jews, creating files on all people of Jewish origin. Jews began to flee. And as with the Nazi invasion, many Poles seemed to be not at all unhappy that the Jews were under attack. Amid the rising anti-Jewish hysteria, a friend of Barbara's from school, Elzbieta, came to her to say that she was leaving Poland. Barbara's mother had always discouraged Barbara from playing with Elzbieta. The girl's parents had told her that the family had to leave Poland because they were Jewish. Barbara was sad, but after a few months, she began receiving letters from Elzbieta, describing her new life in Australia. With every letter, Elzbieta included a small gift, something that would fit in the envelope, like a few raisins—tokens that teenage girls exchange around the world to cement a friendship. Leokadia was unhappy with the letters; she read them before handing them to Barbara. Then, suddenly, the letters stopped. Barbara would never learn what happened. Maybe Elzbieta had decided she was no longer Barbara's friend. Or maybe Barbara's mother had decided to intercept the letters and hide them, ending the correspondence. For Leokadia's message was clear: She would have no discussion of Jews in her house. It was typical—many Poles turned away, not unhappy with what was being done to the Jews.

\*       \*       \*

Barbara Asendrych was born in the tiny town of Zelechow in 1943. Though her parents were Catholic, they let her play with Jewish children. Then the Nazis deported all the Jews and Barbara's mother decided to move back to Warsaw.

Barbara's first communion, 1953. In a country that was communist but still overwhelmingly Catholic, Barbara never felt especially religious. But her grandmother woke her early every Sunday to make sure she went to church.

Barbara's mother, Leokadia, outside the church on her wedding day in 1949. She told her friends and family that her first husband, Barbara's father, was a Polish resistance fighter who was killed battling the Nazis.

By 1973, Barbara was married and had a job as a statistician in the huge communist bureaucracy. She ignored the torrent of anti-Semitic propaganda unleashed by the communists that drove thousands of Jews out of the country.

Maria Wisniewska (left), with Barbara. Maria's phone call to Barbara on New Year's Day, 1987, shattered the terrible secret her family had lived with for so long.

Erna Gysi. Her embrace of communism in Germany in the 1920s irrevocably shaped the views of her son Klaus, who joined the Communist Party when he was sixteen.

Klaus Gysi with Irene Lessing, who would become his wife, in 1939. The communists decided Klaus did not "look Jewish" and ordered him and Irene to hide in Nazi Berlin. Irene considered the mission suicidal.

By 1957, Klaus's loyalty to the communists had begun to pay off. He was put in charge of overseeing East German writers and playwrights. Critics charged that he became an informer for the secret police as well.

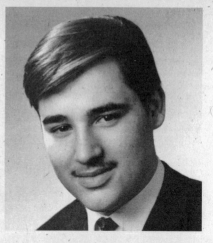

In 1965, Klaus reached the apex of power—Minister of Culture. Some saw a closet reformer eager to smooth out the rough edges of communism. Others saw a ruthless opportunist who betrayed others to fuel his rise.

Klaus's son, Gregor, 1965. As a boy, Gregor idolized his father. But in 1968, as the Soviet Union invaded Czechoslovakia, he turned on his father in rage and came under suspicion from the communist authorities.

Gregor Gysi in 1990. Eclipsing his father, Gregor was chosen to lead the communists in the first free elections after the fall of the Berlin Wall. He never considered his background important—until Germans began shouting "Jew" at him at campaign rallies. (*Edward Serotta*)

# West Berlin

A survivor of Auschwitz, Estrongo Nachama pushed wheelbarrows of coal down the ruined streets of West Berlin to heat a shattered synagogue. He soon became cantor of West Berlin's tiny Jewish community. When the Berlin Wall divided the city in 1961, he smuggled prayer books and medicine to the terrified Jews of East Germany.

Estrongo with his wife, Lilli. Born into Berlin's "Jewish royalty" of the 1920s, Lilli hid in the city during the war. She never forgot the Germans who helped her—and the ones who did not.

Lilli's father (right) and uncle. The two brothers fought for Germany in World War I. Refusing to believe the Nazis would exterminate the Jews, they delayed leaving Berlin until it was too late. Lilli's father committed suicide after Kristallnacht in 1938; her uncle grabbed Lilli and fled into hiding.

By the 1990s Estrongo was a beloved figure in West Berlin and welcomed the fall of the Berlin Wall. A year later, enraged by the explosion of anti-Semitism in both East and West Germany, he urged his son, daughter-in-law, and grandchildren to flee. (*Edward Serotta*)

Estrongo's son, Andreas (far left), leading the President of Germany through the Topography of Terror exhibit. When he was bar-mitzvahed in 1964, his rabbi predicted that the Jews of Berlin would soon die out. By the 1990s the Jewish community in Berlin was growing as never before.

Alena Wittmann with her baby son Robert in December 1945, seven months after the end of World War II. In 1953, the communists seized her sons and imprisoned Alena on trumped-up charges that she was a "Zionist spy." It was two years before she was reunited with her children.

Sylvia Wittmann, Alena's daughter, born after her mother was released from prison. Terrorized by the communists, Alena never mentioned that she was Jewish. But in the 1980s, Sylvia rediscovered what her mother had tried so hard to hide. *(Edward Serotta)*

Mutti, Tamas Raj's great-grandmother, survived the Nazis in a house protected by Raoul Wallenberg. She hid the family Torah beneath a pile of blankets.

Tamas's grandfather Vilmos. A shopkeeper and an observant Jew, he refused to work on Saturdays. When the communists seized power they gave him a choice: Work Saturdays or take a job weaving baskets. Vilmos wove baskets and Tamas watched helplessly as his grandfather's hands turned coarse and bloody.

Tamas's father, Sandor. Forced to join the communist party and fearful of being seen by the secret police, he snuck into the synagogue by the side door to see his own son bar-mitzvahed.

Tamas and his brother, Ferenc, in the uniform of the communist Young Pioneers. At home, the boys played a fantasy game, "Heroland," in which the communists were always defeated.

Determined to become a rabbi, Tamas defied the communists, encouraged young people to attend synagogue and praised Israel. After the Six Day War in 1967, he was arrested, imprisoned and stripped of his job. He did not work as a rabbi again for almost twenty years. Then, triumphant, he was elected to parliament. (*Edward Serotta*)

A few years later, Leokadia became close to someone Jewish. The reason, ironically, was Poland's tight housing supply. With quarters so cramped, it was hard to socialize or even to think of having friends over. Leokadia's sister-in-law lived nearby in a larger apartment, and Leokadia visited her often. In 1960, during such a visit, Leokadia met Maria Wisniewska.

Maria embodied many of the stereotypes that Leokadia tossed around about Jews. She had dark hair and dark eyes; she indeed had the prominent "Jewish nose" that Poles so often sniggered about. She spoke Polish with a noticeable Yiddish accent and gestured often with her hands.

Maria had been born in 1917 in Drohiczyn, a small Jewish town—a shtetl. Her father was a deeply religious man who ensured that his daughter learned Hebrew and sought to protect her from the temptations of a sin-filled world. Once, when Maria made herself a fashionable dress with short sleeves, her father became enraged and forbade her to wear it. When she went to a dance, her father sent her brother to fetch her: Dancing was not a proper activity for a pious Jewish girl.

Though it had always been a fact of daily life in Poland, in the 1930s, as economic conditions deteriorated and Polish nationalists came to power, anti-Semitism worsened, especially in small towns like Drohiczyn. The nationalist parties ordered Poles to boycott Jewish shops and businesses. The boycott was endorsed by the archbishop of Warsaw. Maria's father worked as a roofer; Maria sometimes assisted him. In 1939, just before the war began, Maria and her father went to repair some roofs just outside Drohiczyn. A group of Poles lined up and hurled stones at them. Maria and her father hurried home.

On September 1, 1939, Germany and Russia, temporarily allies, invaded Poland—Germany from the west, Russia from the east. The Russians occupied Drohiczyn. Twenty-two-year-old Maria learned Russian and began to work as a barmaid. She married another Jewish resident of the town and in February 1941 gave birth to a son. She had rebelled against many of her father's strictures while growing up, but she was still a Jew and so had a ritual circumcision for her son.

In the summer of 1941, Hitler declared war against the Soviet

Union. Advancing German troops swiftly pushed Russian soldiers out of Poland. Drohiczyn fell to the Germans, and as in Zelechow, the Germans confined the Jews in a ghetto. Maria and her family were herded inside. A little over a year later, in November 1942, the Germans began the deportations to Treblinka. Maria's husband was taken away; she would never hear from him again. As the last of the Jews were nearing deportation, the Germans began to demolish the ghetto, building by building. Maria's father tried to resist. The Germans shot him in the street. In the chaos that followed, Maria and her sister fled to the woods with Maria's twenty-one-month-old son and her sister's two children.

The Polish winter had begun, and it was raining heavily, a cold, driving rain. Maria, her sister, and the children found a hut in the woods and took refuge inside. A man appeared. He knew immediately that the women were trying to escape. "Get out, you Jews," the Pole shouted. "You are supposed to be dead. I will call the police!" Maria begged him to have pity on the children. He refused. Fleeing, Maria and her sister sought out homes outside Drohiczyn where their father had put on new roofs. Surely *these* people would help this fugitive band. From house to house they went. At each, they pleaded for shelter. Maria's little son began crying, "Mama, I want bread!" But at each house, they were turned back into the cold. The Poles knew the Germans were killing all the Jews—and would kill any Pole who tried to save them. In the cold rain, Maria and her sister and the children found a sheltered spot in the woods and spent the night, without food, with all the children sobbing. "Mama," cried the eight-year-old daughter of Maria's sister. "Why do I have to die?"

The next morning, the sun came out. An old woman came by with some hot soup. Maria, leaving her baby son with her sister, snuck into a nearby village. Using gold she had kept hidden from the Germans, she bought a German identity card from a Russian black marketeer. The card could offer protection for only one person—if the Germans did not realize it was fake. Card in hand, Maria headed off to look for help, for some way that the others could survive. Days later, when she returned to her family's hiding place, they had all disappeared.

After a few days, Maria no longer trusted her fake German identity card. She decided to try to pass herself off as a Pole. The Nazis hated the Poles only a bit less than they hated Jews. To be Polish meant to suffer, but it meant a chance to live.

Maria was rounded up by the Germans as a Pole and sent to Germany to work as a slave laborer. She lived under constant fear that her fellow captives would expose her as a Jew and thus condemn her to death. Though the Germans seemed not to suspect that Maria was Jewish, many Poles taunted her: "Here comes a Jew!" One seven-year-old Polish boy kept saying, "Oh, you're a Jew!"

But the Nazis were never the wiser. Maria survived the war. She returned to Drohiczyn, hoping to discover that her son had survived. Instead she learned that the Germans had found Maria's son, her sister, and her sister's children and shot them. Maria resolved that if she ever had another son, she would not circumcise him. Perhaps, had her son not been circumcised, a Polish family would have taken him in.

The Poles who lived in Drohiczyn did not welcome the approximately fifty Jews who returned to the town. Seven young people were killed in an anti-Semitic pogrom. Maria fled to the city of Bialystok, but pogroms there caused her to flee again. She applied to emigrate to Palestine, but the new Communist government denied her permission.

In the labor camp in Germany, Maria had met a Polish man who had helped and protected her. After the war, they married, and over the next five years Maria gave birth to three sons. True to her vow, none of them was circumcised.

Nevertheless, Maria's Jewish background haunted them. The family moved to Warsaw in 1956. When Poland's Communists unleashed an anti-Semitic campaign as part of an internal power struggle, many Poles seized upon the chance to turn, once again, on the Jews. Maria's seven-year-old son came home from school one day and asked, "Mom, what is a Jew? The children call me a Jew. Is it a devil?" Maria sat down with the boy and explained that a Jew is a human being. But that was all she could tell him, she said. She would explain more to him when he was bigger. The taunting continued, and Maria's husband asked his boss, who controlled housing assignments for workers, for an apartment in a different neighborhood.

And so by 1960, Maria, in an attempt to help her children flee the schoolyard taunts, settled into the Warsaw neighborhood where she met and became friends with two Polish Catholics—Leokadia and her sister-in-law.

The women met regularly for coffee. Neither of the Polish women knew about Maria's experiences during World War II. Maria rarely shared those. But they did know that Maria was Jewish, and they talked about the kind of work she was doing. In 1961, a Jewish organization from the United States had contacted Maria and asked her to look after one of the legacies of Poland's war years: Jewish girls who had been given to Catholic families and raised as Catholics. No one knew how many of these "hidden Jews" existed in Poland or where they were.

One girl whom Maria found had been saved by an elderly couple. When the husband later died, there was no income, no electricity, no running water. Maria took the girl, who was nineteen, into her home, even though she and her husband and her three sons shared just two rooms. After six months, the girl moved to Israel, where she discovered she had an uncle. But something went wrong. After a few months, she returned. Perhaps under pressure from the secret police or perhaps out of spite over some minor infraction, the girl denounced Maria to the Polish secret police—accusing her of enticing Jews to emigrate to Israel, a criminal offense in Communist Poland.

The Polish police came to arrest Maria on July 21, 1964. She was accused of being a spy and working for an organization that conspired against the Polish state. The court sentenced her to two years in prison. The coffees with Leokadia and her sister-in-law ended.

In March 1965, Maria was released as part of a general political amnesty. But she was marked now as a "Zionist." The casual coffees resumed. No one talked about what had happened or why Maria had been imprisoned. Maria did not hold that against the other women. They were frightened by what had happened to her, she knew. And there was not much anyone could have done.

Leokadia went even further, however. The women often talked about their children, but Leokadia was careful never to invite Maria to her house. And she never let her meet her daughter, Barbara. It was as if she feared the contamination of someone Jewish—as if her daughter might be tainted by association.

In 1967, following the Six Day War, anti-Semitism flared anew in Poland. The head of the Polish Communist Party, Wladyslaw Gomulka, ascended the podium at a party conference and declared that Jews were "Poland's fifth column," seeking to sabotage the country. On March 8, 1968, as the Prague Spring burgeoned in Czechoslovakia, several thousand Polish students gathered in the courtyard of Warsaw University to demand the reinstatement of two Jewish students who had been expelled for taking part in protests against a Communist ban on the performance of one of Poland's most popular historical dramas. Students chanted slogans and applauded an announcement that university officials had caved in—they would meet with a student delegation. Then several busloads of Communist Party activists and reserve soldiers pulled up and began attacking the students as "counterrevolutionaries." Police, swinging truncheons, came in to break up the demonstration.

Two days later, the official Communist newspaper printed a list of the student "ringleaders" of the demonstration. All but one of the accused were Jewish. Demonstrating against the brutal beatings, five thousand students took to the streets in Warsaw, and similar protests erupted across Poland.

The Communists shut down Warsaw University and began mass arrests of the students. Then the Ministry of the Interior, which controlled the secret police, began compiling lists of Jews. Jewish Communists began receiving in the mail copies of their birth certificates, which noted their religion. Jews were purged from the army and stripped of their positions at newspapers and book publishers. The Communist-controlled press rattled on against the dangers of a Jewish conspiracy undermining Poland's economy and endangering Polish stability. On national television, hard-liners interrupted a speech by Gomulka, who was trying to cling to power, with chants of "Expel the Zionists!"

One of the targets of this latest anti-Semitic campaign was Maria Wisniewska. After being released from prison for her "Zionist" activities in 1965, Maria had tried to blend into the background of Polish life. But the growing anti-Semitic campaign thrust her back into the spotlight. Newspapers and television news began reporting stories about her terrible anti-Polish crimes, her efforts to "entice" Polish Jews to emigrate to Israel. They referred to her as "Maria W."—eliminating her last name heightened the sense of mystery and threat. Maria considered fleeing Poland. But she could not face losing her second family the way she had once tragically lost her first. Then her husband, who had protected her in Germany and endured the pain of his children's suffering anti-Semitic taunts from schoolyard bullies, turned against her. He had always been a hard man. But for twenty-five years he had stood up against the political persecutors of his family. These news reports were too much, however. "Leave this country," he shouted at Maria one evening. "This is not your country. Your country is Israel!"

Maria fled. Her husband would not allow her to take anything with her. She headed for Rome. From there she planned to go on to Israel. It all happened very fast. There was no time to say good-bye to friends. Though Leokadia had at times seemed aloof, Maria promised herself she would write to her Polish friend once she was out of Poland and safe.

By the end of 1969, more than twenty thousand Jews had fled Poland. As the spasm of anti-Semitism ended, Poles resumed their normal lives. With many Jews gone, Poles found new openings at work. The apartment shortage in Warsaw eased a bit. Leokadia continued visiting her sister-in-law. No one talked much about Maria. Like a time bomb, anti-Semitism had destroyed the last vestiges of Jewish life. To all intents and purposes, Poland was now "*judenrein*"—free of Jews.

# Part III

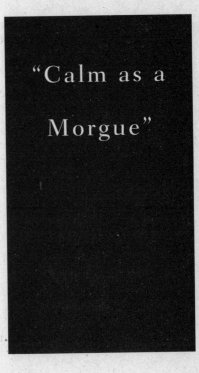

"Calm as a

Morgue"

To live in Poland, Hungary, Czechoslovakia, and East Germany after 1968 was fundamentally different than before. Any hope that the system might change, that the Soviets might allow these countries to find their own, more liberal road, was crushed. After a breath of spring, Czechoslovakia slipped back under the ice. The Soviets replaced the entire Czech leadership and began a purge that turned the country upside down. Communists who had supported the Prague Spring were dismissed from their jobs. Professors and journalists were fired and forced to find work as coal stokers, night porters, factory workers. The Protestant bishop of Prague was stripped of his office and reduced to a job delivering milk.

Once again, Jews often suffered the most. In Prague, the Soviets unleashed an anti-Semitic campaign, blaming the Prague Spring on a group of Jewish Communists who had come to power in 1968. At the Soviet-Czech summit meeting right after the invasion, Soviet Premier Kosygin eyed Frantisek Kriegel, a Jewish member of Czechoslovakia's Politburo, and snapped, "What is that Jew from Galicia doing here?" When Kriegel started to reply, Kosygin cut him off: "Shut your trap!" Kriegel, who had survived Auschwitz, was the only member of the Czech leadership to refuse to sign a statement "welcoming" the Soviet invasion.

The years after 1968 plunged the people of Eastern Europe, especially the young, into a period of intense moral and political dilemmas. Twenty years earlier, right after the war, Czechs, Poles, Hungarians, and East Germans faced a series of difficult choices. Like Alena Wittmann, pressured daily by party application forms left on her desk, they had to decide whether to join the new Communist Parties in order to advance their careers. Like Klaus Gysi, whose own son's future seemed increasingly in peril, they had to decide whether to flee when persecution began or to stay in the hope that things would change. Like Tamas Raj's father, who agreed to vote for the Communist Party in order to win release from a Soviet prison camp, they had to decide how much to challenge the system openly and how much to keep their true beliefs hidden.

Now, in the aftermath of 1968, the sons and daughters were being forced into making choices of their own. Some, like Michael Wittmann, Sylvia's brother, decided to flee. Many more stayed on, to face the day-to-day choices of life under Communism. For Sylvia Wittmann, the question was how to express her growing fascination with Judaism without triggering assault from the secret police who had tormented her mother twenty years earlier. Gregor Gysi's choice was whether to follow his father's life of compromises or risk life as a dissident. For Tamas Raj, the choice was stark. Was he to hide his religion, as his father did, or become even more open in his dissidence?

Americans tended to see the choices facing people behind the Iron Curtain in unadorned terms. There were the heroes, those who bravely defied the system and went into prison or exile for their beliefs: Aleksandr Solzhenitsyn, Andrey Sakharov, Lech Walesa, Vaclav Havel. Then there were the servants of the evil empire, who propped up the system and enthusiastically contributed to the oppression: Leonid Brezhnev, Wojciech Jaruzelski, Erich Honecker. Missing from this black-and-white view was the vast majority of ordinary people who every day faced choices in difficult circumstances—whether or not to speak out on behalf of a persecuted colleague at the office, whether or not to respond to the blandishments of the secret police, whether or not to sign a compromising document in order to get a passport to travel overseas.

The Soviet invasion of Prague slammed the door shut on Eastern Europe, even as the Prague Spring had cracked it open awhile to let in the light of hope and liberalism. "True enough, the country is calm," Václav Havel wrote in an open letter to the head of Czechoslovakia's Communist Party in 1975. "Calm as a morgue or a grave, would you not say?"

Havel's metaphor was an apt one. The people of Poland, Czechoslovakia, East Germany, and Hungary had not been killed; they'd been buried alive. As the 1980s began, there were swirls and currents: the dissident Charter 77 movement in Czechoslovakia; the early stirrings of what would become the Solidarity trade union movement in Poland; the environmental movement in East Germany; dissident groups in Hungary. For many Jews, this ferment paved the way for a renewed interest in Jewish life. Young Jews, many of whose parents were Communists, began spontaneously to return to their roots. Soon Jewish choirs and "salons," where young people met to discuss Jewish authors, were beginning to form. In Budapest, young Jews met on Friday nights to discuss Jewish history—and look for dates. In Poland, the few remaining Jewish intellectuals set up "flying universities"— professors moving from apartment to apartment every week, one step ahead of the police—to discuss psychology, philosophy, and what it meant to be Jewish.

This was part of a broader trend of disillusionment affecting young people throughout Eastern Europe. It took place underground, under the ice, out of sight of the secret police and visiting tourists. It was one of the cracks that would one day break apart the glacier.

# Chapter Twelve

# "Home Is When You Recognize Yourself in the People Passing By in the Street"

For more than thirty-five years, ever since he joined the party in 1931, Klaus Gysi had been a loyal Communist. But in the end, not even his loyalty could save him. While the Soviet invasion of Czechoslovakia had appalled the West and many East Germans, as it had his son, Gregor, what had horrified the Communist leadership in East Germany was the period of liberalization that had led up to it—the Prague Spring. The concept of writers criticizing the regime, of movies, plays, and paintings exploring forbidden questions—all this was too frightening. It could lead to instability. Culture was a sensitive area, prone to outbursts by uncontrollable artists. Always quick to sense a shift in the wind, Klaus joined in the denunciations and crackdowns that followed the Soviet invasion of Czechoslovakia.

Nevertheless, the truth was that for all his professions of loyalty, Klaus was never able to shake suspicions that he was not a true Communist ideologue. Gregor's verbal slap at his father's "foul compromises all the time" hit home. Klaus had always made compromises with his conscience to advance his career. The problem was that to the Communist leaders in East Germany, the compromises were all too obvious. Klaus Gysi was not an ideologue who could mouth party pronouncements convincingly. He was aware of how absurd they were—and it showed. A typical

Gysi speech would begin: "What mattered in the past and what matters now is the position of man and his culture in the socialist and imperialist social system and in his struggle." People looking at Gysi's face, with its lively eyes, could almost sense his stifled groan. A West German writer wrote that "to see him read out his wooden speeches, or even to listen, was a torture, probably for himself as well." Gysi was what one colleague called "a devil at the front, an angel at the back." In meetings he could deliver stern warnings and leaden Communist pronouncements to his colleagues. Then, in the hallway after the meeting, he would grab someone by the elbow, put his arm around him, and gently point out ways around a problem.

But walking the fine line between ideology and culture had damaged Gysi. His opportunism had not only eroded his standing with artists and writers but also failed to persuade his Communist overlords that he was a true believer. Despite his role as overseer of East German culture, Klaus Gysi had never been named to the Politburo, the true policy-making body in East Germany. The Communists valued him as a mediator, a middleman between artists and writers and the authorities. Gysi made the fatal mistake of believing that he was smarter than most of the Communists he had to report to. Intellectually, that was surely true. But politically, the Communists had taken the measure of their man. Surrounded by the trappings of power, Klaus Gysi thought he was using the Communists to build his own influence; in fact, the Communists were using him.

The ax fell in 1972 when Erich Honecker, who had overseen construction of the Berlin Wall in 1961, became head of East Germany. He promptly dismissed Klaus Gysi as minister of culture. It was time for hard-liners to take firmer control of the country. Klaus explained his dismissal to friends as a general political housecleaning. Honecker was new, and he naturally wanted to put his own people into the top jobs. Gysi received a generous payoff: He was appointed East Germany's first ambassador to Italy. It was the perfect place for the man who had always treasured books and women and good conversation to wait out his retirement. Free of quarrelsome artists and thickheaded bosses,

Klaus Gysi could display his knowledge of English and French on the diplomatic rounds, deploy his charm, drink his wine.

To those who saw him during these years, Klaus seemed oddly at home in Rome and the Vatican, holding forth in an almost courtly, old-world style. He met a young East German, Birgid, twenty years his junior, who was a member of a theater group touring Italy, fell in love, and married her. He lunched with priests and diplomats. He lived, as East Germans liked to say, "with a large footprint," unwilling to deny himself or his guests the finer things that were in such short supply back in East Germany. When a visiting East German friend mentioned that it was his first trip to Italy, Klaus scrunched his face in horror, gave him the embassy car for four days, turned over a clutch of spending money, and ordered him to visit Venice and Florence, to learn about the culture of the Renaissance. Being a Communist was no deterrent to enjoying the finer things in life.

Back in East Berlin, Klaus's son, Gregor, survived the political campaign mounted against him after the Prague invasion. After almost a year during which investigative committees at his law school charged him with harboring dangerous "liberal" tendencies, Gregor left one of his final exams, to find a professor standing at the doorway carrying a bouquet. Theatrically, he presented the flowers to Gregor, along with the official congratulations of the Communist Party. Over coffee, the professor explained that a top Communist official in Berlin had looked into Gregor's case personally, exonerated him, and ordered the university to call off the witch hunt. Gregor sensed the hand of his father in this: With Klaus Gysi, when it came to priorities, family was always more important than politics, blood thicker than ideology. As a sign that all was forgiven, Gregor was elected to the party committee that oversaw the law school. His excommunication was over.

But as the reality of the Soviet invasion of Prague and the freeze covering Eastern Europe began to sink in, Gregor was overcome by the realization that things would not change in Czechoslovakia—or in East Germany. While their contemporaries in the United States could say that in the 1960s they had helped bring down President Lyndon Johnson, wind down an unpopular war, usher in the sexual revolution, launch the women's movement, and triumph in the battle for civil rights, Gregor Gysi and the young people of Eastern Europe looked at 1968 and saw nothing but defeat. The Soviets made it clear that after the Prague Spring, the countries of the East Bloc would be watched more closely than ever. They would not be free to find their own path or even to experiment with liberalization. Gregor in 1968 learned a lesson Klaus had learned in the 1950s: all power rested in Moscow. For Gregor, that realization led to a kind of political lethargy—a conclusion that the time was not right for change and he had no choice but to wait.

So now Gregor, his years at law school completed, faced a choice. What to do with his life? Should he succumb to the "foul compromises" he had criticized his father for? Or, like the folksinger Wolf Biermann and the philosopher Robert Havemann, would he edge into dissidence, accepting the consequences?

Despite his run-ins with the Communist authorities at the university, Gregor still carried a reputation as an "enfant terrible," the spoiled child of a high Communist official, who was a bit too smart and facile for his own good. Like his father, he was a bright man to whom words came easily. Because of his father's power, everyone assumed that Gregor had been protected over the years. There was some truth to this. Before taking up law, Gregor had toyed with the idea of becoming a diplomat. But he was put off by the thought of intensive language training. Unlike his parents, Gregor had no gift for languages. After applying to the diplomatic corps, Gregor, accepted, changed his mind. He had his father inform the Foreign Ministry of his decision. He was too embarrassed to do it himself. Similarly, Gregor had avoided the military service required of all East German men by submitting a doctor's statement that he had a heart problem. Gregor joked that he had decided to study law because it was easy. You did not have to memorize anything, he told friends. Whatever you did not know you just looked up in a book. Gregor's natural next step—the expected step of the rehabilitated Communist son of a high party official—was to become a prosecutor and ultimately a judge, meting out Communist justice to the criminals and dissidents of East Germany.

But when he graduated from law school, Gregor Gysi surprised everyone by announcing that he wanted to become a defense lawyer.

To be a defense lawyer in East Germany was immediately to arouse Communist suspicion. In a Communist state, whomever the state put on trial was presumed guilty until proved innocent—or, more likely, simply presumed guilty. The presence of defense lawyers was a mere formality, necessary to preserve the image that the judicial system was free and fair. There were just six hundred defense lawyers in all of East Germany. It had been years since the Communists had allowed someone to open a defense practice. Gregor persevered. He agreed to serve an unusually long apprenticeship as an assistant to a judge and in 1971, at age twenty-three, was allowed to open a legal practice, becoming the youngest lawyer in East Germany.

Gregor did not fancy life as a dissident. His brief brush with the Communist tribunal in law school had not disillusioned him. He was a Communist and was prepared to accept East Germany as it was. Like his father, Gregor believed that though East Germany was an imperfect system, it was better than any other system. Gregor had been educated in East German schools. Except for a few boyhood trips to West Berlin to visit his grandmother before the Berlin Wall went up, he had never traveled to the West. He never saw Western magazines or newspapers. His images of Western Europe and the United States resembled propaganda cartoons: the Vietnam War, bloated capitalists exploiting the workers, racial conflict. After the Soviet invasion of Czechoslovakia, Gregor even found himself questioning the Prague Spring, which he had so enthusiastically endorsed. All his East German instincts and education told him that if the West was happy about the Prague Spring, there must have been something wrong with it.

At the same time, Gregor believed that even in a Communist state, a defendant was entitled to a good lawyer. When he was fourteen, his school class, brought to court, had watched the trial of a thief who had mugged and robbed an elderly man. He wrote later of his emotions: "The disgusting crime did not arouse my sympathy—rather the fact that the helplessly stammering defendant had no lawyer. Hopeless and ignorant, he sat in the dock. He had been brought in handcuffed. He was confronted with laws and mumbo-jumbo he didn't understand. I suffered with him. He got six years. I didn't know why the defendant had done what he did. But I saw through the judge and the prosecutor. For them, everything was clear. They knew beforehand how the trial would turn out. This was one reason I could not become a judge or prosecutor. I could not have passed judgments that contradicted my own sense of the law." To be a defense lawyer in East Germany was to be both inside and outside the system, a loyal Communist but a critic too. It also provided something that appealed to Gregor's ego: Gregor, like his father, was a man drawn to the limelight.

He began his legal career by handling divorces and cases of employees dismissed from their jobs. But he was increasingly drawn to criminal law. And it was here, as in that courtroom many years earlier, that he saw the naked power of the East German system at work.

In his first dozen cases as a criminal lawyer, judges always found Gysi's clients guilty and imposed the maximum sentence recommended by the prosecutor. Gysi was not allowed to speak privately with his jailed clients; members of the secret police always stood by, listening. In court, Gregor tried his best to win some leniency for his clients, whom he knew were headed for prison.

In one celebrated murder trial, Gysi and his law partner, convinced that their client was innocent, spent weeks poring over the evidence compiled by the police. In two days and nights they drew up a hundred-page brief, so damning of the prosecution's case that the accused man was set free—a nearly unheard-of outcome. The brief showed not only that the police had misinterpreted evidence but that they had deliberately ignored evidence that proved the man innocent. A few weeks later, Gysi and his colleague learned that those same police had framed two additional people for murder.

In time, Gregor's exasperation at being a defense lawyer under this system began to show. At one trial, he launched into a complex plea for leniency, based on an intricate reading of East German law. Peering down from her desk, high above the well of the courtroom, the judge looked at Gysi with disbelief. It was clear she did not understand what he was talking about. Gysi started again. The expression on the judge's face did not change. Gysi gave up and returned to the defense desk. "What the heck," he muttered loudly. "I'll put it in my appeal." The judge cited Gysi for contempt of court and filed a complaint against him with the lawyers' association.

Gysi's defense practice exposed him to the darker side of East German society—thieves, burglars, criminals—men and women who had fallen through the cracks of the supposedly perfect Socialist society. It also illuminated the arbitrariness of the East German justice system, where sentences and verdicts were determined before people were actually arrested. But he still had not ventured into the most perilous hinterland of the law, defending dissidents and "counterrevolutionaries."

Then, in 1978, almost by chance, Gysi crossed the line into political cases.

In August 1977, the Communists had imprisoned a writer, Rudolf Bahro, whose book *The Alternative* had been banned in East Germany, smuggled out, and published in West Germany. It was a dense, philosophical book that criticized hard-line Communism and favored a more liberal approach, like the Prague Spring. It was hardly the stuff of revolutions. Nevertheless, East Germany's Communists accused Bahro of "passing information to the enemy" and "betrayal of secrets." All across the country, the Communists were launching another crackdown on dissidents. They even began to target lawyers who were defending dissidents, threatening to expel them from the party. Bahro's ex-wife was a friend of Gregor's sister, Gabriele. With her former husband languishing in jail, she approached Gabriele to see if Gregor would take on the case.

Gregor read *The Alternative* and was overwhelmed. It was clear now why the East Germans were treating Bahro so harshly. The book, written by a committed Communist, was the best analysis Gregor had read of East Germany's weaknesses and problems. And it advocated the same path of liberalization and reform that Czechoslovakia had tried ten years earlier. Gregor was especially struck by a passage in which Bahro wondered about the impact on the East Bloc of reform in the Soviet Union. "Where would the tanks come from" to stop reform, Bahro asked, "if changes start in Moscow?" Gregor agreed to take on Bahro's case.

Even by Communist standards, the trial of Bahro was a travesty. Barriers were put up in the courthouse, restricting access to the courtroom where the trial took place. Admission was by invitation only. Every effort Gysi made to get evidence was rebuffed. The outcome was clear before the trial began: The Communists intended to make an example of Bahro.

Gysi did not ask for leniency for Bahro. To the shock of the court and the spectators, he asked for an acquittal. He argued as a committed Communist. If a Socialist society can't tolerate different opinions, he told the court, it isn't Socialist yet.

The court dismissed Gysi's argument. Bahro was sentenced to eight years in prison.

The Bahro trial was Gysi's first taste of dissident cases. Gysi liked Bahro. He admired the warmth and humanity the writer exuded even as he was facing a lengthy prison term. Gysi's defense of Bahro won him some attention among dissidents, but he was still a young, untested lawyer, unfamiliar with the dissident movement. That changed the next year when he was asked to defend East Germany's leading dissident, the scientist, philosopher, and writer Robert Havemann—the same man his father had declared "defeated and isolated" in 1968, after the Soviet invasion of Czechoslovakia.

Havemann was still the most widely known dissident in East Germany. A longtime Communist, who had joined the party just a year after Klaus Gysi and had shared a Nazi jail with East German leader Erich Honecker, Havemann had helped the Soviet Union develop the atomic bomb and still considered himself a loyal Marxist. But as he defined Communism, it was inseparable from freedom of speech, pluralism, and democracy. A fringe figure would have been easy to imprison or expel. But because of Havemann's principled stand and long history of loyal service to East Germany, he posed a dilemma for the East German regime. In 1976, East Germany had expelled Wolf Biermann—the other dissident denounced by Klaus Gysi in 1968. Havemann protested the expulsion and was promptly placed under house arrest, subjected to twenty-four hour surveillance. East German secret police cut off his access to any unauthorized visitors. His phone lines were cut. Soon after Bahro was sentenced, Havemann was charged with "illegal currency speculation." The Communists feared that attacking Havemann for his political views would turn him into a political martyr. Instead they planned to "expose" him to the public as a common criminal, a "speculator." The charge was minor; Havemann was only required to pay a small fine. But he would not go along with the Communists' game. Gysi was approached to represent Havemann. But when he drove out to Havemann's small house in East Berlin, through the secret police checkpoints, Havemann told him that he wanted a more famous lawyer, perhaps one from outside East Germany, who would bring the most publicity to his trial. After the Communists blocked his efforts to hire such a lawyer, Havemann agreed to let Gysi represent him. Gregor's defense was futile, and Havemann remained under house arrest. Gregor became a regular visitor.

Just as Gregor was becoming more involved defending political dissidents, his father returned to East Germany. He was sixty-seven and accepted that his career was now over. In return for his loyalty over the years, the party gave Klaus Gysi a spacious apartment in a new apartment tower built for Communist Party officials near the Berlin Wall, as well as a largely honorary post as head of a committee on international relations. Then, in 1979, Erich Honecker, who seven years earlier had dismissed Gysi as minister of culture for being too liberal, summoned him to his office in the Central Committee building, in the heart of East Berlin. He had a new assignment for Gysi: secretary of state for church affairs, overseeing the often troublesome churches in East Germany, as well as the tiny Jewish community. It was a sensitive post. For almost thirty years, the East German churches, Protestant as well as Catholic, had been at loggerheads with the Communist regime, resisting efforts to discredit them and providing a haven for dissidents and others disillusioned with Communism. Gregor's law partner, for example, was a devout Protestant, whose religious faith bolstered his willingness to work with Gregor on occasional dissident cases.

The Communists had succeeded in reducing the East German Jewish community to a tattered fragment of perhaps a few hundred old Jews. They had nearly halved the number of practicing Protestants in East Germany from fifteen million in 1950 to fewer than eight million by 1977. Now, hoping to polish his international image, Honecker wanted to begin a rapprochement that would ease the pressure on Protestants, Catholics, and even Jews—all the time keeping them under tight control. Once again, Klaus was to be the mediator between the regime and those on the margins. His skills would be useful; Honecker no doubt hoped Klaus could tame and charm the faithful as well as he had charmed writers and artists during his tenure as head of the Aufbau publishing house and as minister of culture.

"Remember," Honecker told Gysi as their meeting ended. "You will report only to me."

Klaus began his job well, impressing people with his wit and sophistication. "So bright, so eloquent," concluded Bishop Albrecht Schoenherr, the head of the Protestant Church, after meeting with Klaus Gysi. Here was "a different kind of Communist."

At an early meeting of top Communists overseeing East Germany's churches, Klaus launched into a speech in which he declared that "church politics" should not pit Marxist against churchman. Rather, the church and Communists should work together, since, after all, both Karl Marx and Jesus Christ were Jewish. His deputies listened in stunned silence. Gysi's chief of staff, Horst Dohle, a historian who was delighted with Gysi's pronouncement, began spreading the word at Communist meetings across the country. In speeches before hundreds of party members, Dohle spoke of Gysi's vision of cooperation between the churches and the Communists, of the common Jewish origin of

Jesus and Marx. Audiences were shocked and baffled. They had never heard such things. Some objected that this was not the official line of the Communist Party. With a smile, Dohle always said: "This comes directly from Klaus Gysi."

Gysi continued his efforts to woo the churches. "God will exist as long as there are people who believe in God," he declared. "Christians are perfectly normal citizens of East Germany. They are satisfied or they grumble, just like any other person in East Germany."

East Germany, Gysi now said, was not an "atheist" state. Religion and church were part of everyday life there. "We have more in common than things dividing us," he said. Christian ideals were much closer to socialism than to capitalism, Gysi declared. He even acknowledged that Protestants could protest some Communist political decisions. "That's why they are called what they are," Gysi joked.

Perhaps it was the new, more tolerant mood he sensed from Honecker about religion; perhaps he was becoming intoxicated by his own words; perhaps he was just getting older and did not care anymore. But for the first time, Klaus began to let his own Jewish identity slip out. In public, Gysi still did not acknowledge or even speak about his Jewish background, though it was common gossip among Communist higher-ups. In private meetings with Jews, however, he began to show an avuncular side that he seemed to cultivate for certain occasions. Soon after being named secretary of church affairs, Gysi received a formal delegation from the tiny Jewish community. He listened silently to their wooden, carefully worded requests, then looked at them. "At least you could have said 'Shalom,'" he remarked. He attended the annual Jewish music concert that Estrongo Nachama gave in the Rykestrasse synagogue in East Berlin. There, Gysi sat stiffly, the official representative of the Communist government. But at the reception afterward, he embraced Estrongo's wife, Lilian, and stepped into a comic routine, like an old vaudeville actor.

"Where is my gefilte fish?" Gysi asked indignantly.

"Oh, I forgot to bring it," Lilian responded in mock horror.

Gysi never made jokes about gefilte fish with the Politburo.

Indeed, occasionally his mask would slip and visitors from West Germany could glimpse the fine line he walked as a Jew in East Germany. Once, when a leading Jewish official in East Germany died, Estrongo Nachama traveled to Dresden to sing at the funeral. He brought his son, Andreas, who was then in his thirties, with him. As they walked to the grave, they passed the gravestone of the brother of Hermann Axen, one of the most hard-line members of the East German Politburo. Axen was Jewish, and his brother had been buried in the Jewish cemetery. After the ceremony, back at the hotel, Klaus Gysi pulled the Nachamas aside. Axen, he told them, was trying to get his brother's body disinterred from the Jewish cemetery. But, Gysi confided, "It doesn't matter what he does. They'll always know he's a Jew."

Klaus and Gregor Gysi, father and son, similar in so many ways, still sparred with each other, even as Gregor approached forty. Gregor was established now as one of the leading defenders of dissidents in East Germany; he was a steadfast member of the Communist Party but defended those who criticized the party, even those who protested publicly by hanging banners near the Berlin Wall. Klaus continued, as he always had, to hover near the levers of power, to be an "angel at the back," charming opponents with his learning and frank comments but in public maintaining the party line.

Gregor, his friends felt, was driven to prove himself not just to his father but to those who believed that he owed his position and success to his father's position. At Klaus's annual birthday parties, talk would turn to politics. Klaus Gysi would offer an opinion. Gregor would wave a dismissive cigarette. "That's a typical father's compromise," he would announce. Then Klaus would suggest a compromise to resolve one of Gregor's conflicts with the East German authorities—a dissident who was in prison, another forbidden to travel. Testily, Gregor would respond, "I'm not wise enough yet for such compromises."

One evening, coming home from work, Klaus found Gregor slumped against the wall in the hallway of his apartment building, holding his stepmother's violin. He looked up at Klaus and imitated a beggar.

"Of all the jobs in the world, yours only leads you to mock people," Klaus said.

Gregor replied, "See how similar we are."

But Klaus and Gregor were also different. Klaus, as even his friends acknowledged, rarely passed up a pleasure. His reputation as a ladies' man was common gossip; his leaving home had wounded young Gregor deeply. Gregor had divorced his wife in the 1980s, but by contrast, he raised his son himself, leaving the office daily at five o'clock to pick up his son at day care. Politically, Gregor was more sympathetic to the frustrations of younger East Germans, people like himself.

"Fathers and sons—it's a complicated story," Klaus Gysi once declared with a sigh. But if Klaus could not fully see the political perils to Communism represented by young people like his son, the political evolution of his daughter, Gabriele, provided further evidence that East Germany, by the 1980s, was in trouble.

As a girl, Gabriele idolized her father. But as she became more politically aware, she found herself increasingly at odds with the government's—and her father's—positions. She first crossed swords with the party in 1976, when the Communists expelled Wolf Biermann, whom Klaus Gysi and others had attacked for more than decade. Gabriele thought expelling the dissident folksinger went too far and denounced the move at a Communist Party meeting. Gabriele did not agree with all Biermann's criticisms, but she felt problems could not be solved by kicking out people critical of the regime.

She believed the Berlin Wall was absurd but, like most in her generation, had come to accept it. Yet she had a nagging sense that even in the stalwart Communist Gysi family, later generations could not be restrained within its boundaries. She once had a conversation with Gregor's son, who was six.

"Gabriele, I hate the wall," the boy said.

"But why?" Gabriele asked. He was surely too young to dream about moving to the West or visiting New York.

"Because I'm in love with Nena!"—a Western pop star whose saccharine music could be picked up on East Berlin radios. It was then that Gabriele realized the wall was doomed. "People's potential to dream is too big to limit it with the Berlin Wall," Gabriele told her father. But Klaus looked at her, unmoved. "And what do you think we should have done?" he asked her. For Klaus, the wall remained a part of the Cold War that both East and West had shaped.

When the Solidarity trade union movement rose to power in Poland in the early 1980s, Gabriele followed it with keen interest. Like her brother, she remained intrigued by the notion of reforming Communism, changing it from the inside. But the East German government feared Solidarity, and when the Polish Communists banned the movement and placed Poland under martial law, East Germany hurried to endorse the decision. Gabriele again objected, and this time she was formally expelled from the party.

She decided to move to West Germany. Her father tried to talk her out of it. They fought angrily. He arranged for her to meet with Kurt Hager, a top member of the Politburo. Hager asked her questions: Why did so many East Germans went to leave the country? What was their motive? Gabriele became emotional, raising her voice. "You can suffocate from a life not lived," Gabriele declared. "You can't restrict people's lives like this." The old Communist leader looked up. "This is good," Hager said blandly. "I'll make a note of it."

Gabriele's mind was made up. Klaus tried again to persuade his daughter to stay. It was bad enough that his son was a lawyer defending dissidents. But for Klaus, again, family came before politics. With Gabriele firm in her resolve, Klaus paid for her move to the West.

Klaus was becoming more and more pessimistic about the future of East Germany. He had always defended his loyalty to the Communist regime, his opportunism, his double dealing, by saying that every time he was ready to give up in despair, new hope for reform had glimmered, reigniting his beliefs. In 1953, in the wake of Gysi's first dismissal during the anti-Jewish purges, Stalin had died; in 1966, a liberal wave had swept Gysi into the post of minister of culture. Then in 1985, the chimera of reform appeared again—this time in the guise of Mikhail Gorbachev. The ascension of Gorbachev in the Soviet Union and his inauguration of *glasnost* and *perestroika*—openness and reform—galvanized Gysi and Communists like him, who believed that East Germany's problems lay not in the system itself but in its inefficiencies. Gysi believed Gorbachev could reform the system and make it more efficient. He saw in the Russian leader an antidote to the paralysis that had gripped East Germany, a tonic to the gray old men, inflexible and intransigent, who led the party.

But the gray old men were not feeble, and they were not about to relinquish control gracefully. They viewed Gorbachev as a dangerous reformer who should take care not to meddle in their iron-fisted control of their countries. When Gorbachev gave pioneering speeches on the importance of reform, the Communist-controlled East German press printed only summaries of the speeches, editing out the most incendiary parts.

And Klaus Gysi—with his chauffeured car and driver, his gracious apartment overlooking the Berlin Wall, his collection of fine paintings and books—was not a man who had risen so high by challenging the authorities. Even as his pessimism grew, he continued to read the reports of the secret police on the activities of churches he was supposed to supervise, passing on key information to the Politburo. The rapprochement between the churches and the Communists that Gysi had hoped for had evaporated. The churches were becoming bolder in their demands, protesting the rigid repression by the Communists and spreading an ever-widening umbrella to protect dissidents. Churches became havens for environmental and peace activists. The churches objected to the Communists' teaching military courses in schools. They pushed for creation of a peace movement that was independent of Communist control. In meetings with church leaders, Gysi tried to smooth over disagreements, but it became clear to many ministers that he was losing power and influence. He would promise meetings with top Politburo members to discuss education, ecology, and the internal state of the country. The meetings never materialized. Increasingly, many in the churches began to feel he was just leading them on, trying to pacify them.

By 1986, Klaus privately concluded that East Germany was doomed. Reform from within was really not possible. Living standards were declining. Factory production had stagnated. Economically, life was getting worse and worse for most inhabitants. East Germany, Gysi believed, might well collapse in bankruptcy by the end of 1990. Publicly, of course, he said nothing.

It was with such forebodings that Gysi approached his seventy-fifth birthday that year. Three hundred people gathered to honor the secretary for church affairs—the former minister of culture, the former head of the renowned Aufbau publishing house, the lifelong Communist who had hidden so bravely from the Nazis in Berlin. Amid toasts to long life, Gysi's staff presented their boss with a large bound book of memories: pictures of Klaus as a young boy, copies of his report cards, records of his early work at Aufbau—a fawning tribute to a powerful man. Klaus puffed a cigarette. He looked around the room.

"This is nice," he said, taking in the throng of admirers. "Let's see how many people come to my eightieth birthday."

Klaus's fall from power came two years later. It was no surprise. Feeling increasingly frustrated, Gysi had been sending his deputies to important Communist Party meetings. In July 1988, the Politburo summoned Gysi and summarily fired him. The official explanation was the ubiquitous Communist one: "health reasons." The real reason was that Gysi had outserved his usefulness. The party was about to begin a major crackdown on the churches. A notice of Gysi's "retirement" appeared in the newspaper the next day. Klaus and Birgid, who had been invited to a reception at the French embassy, pondered what to do. Gysi decided to attend; people, seeing him, would understand that poor politics, not poor health, had forced him to resign. Beneath the chandeliers, the Italian ambassador, a friend of the Gysis', glided up to Klaus. "Ah," he said. "Now I understand those 'health reasons'— you resigned to stay healthy."

One project, however, had grabbed Gysi's interest, and in a highly unusual move Klaus pleaded with the Politburo to let him stay on, even as a figurehead, so that he could see it through. This was the official commemoration of the fiftieth anniversary of Kristallnacht, the Nazis' first pogrom against the Jews—the event young Klaus Gysi had learned about the following morning when left-wing workers bicycled past his bedroom window, whistling in disapproval at the destruction the Nazis had wreaked.

Commemoration planning had started back in 1985, when East Germany began trying to improve its image among Jews in the United States, which Erich Honecker was hoping to visit. Believing that Jews influenced, if not controlled, the U.S. government, he put Gysi in charge of several of the projects designed to curry favor with American Jews. Berlin's Rykestrasse synagogue, which the Nazis had used as a stable, was renovated. Gysi announced plans to rebuild the grand synagogue in Oranienburger Strasse and turn it into a museum. Honecker dispatched Gysi to the United States, where he attended a White House prayer breakfast. Gysi invited an American rabbi to come to East Berlin to serve the small Jewish community—the first rabbi in East Berlin in twenty years.

By far the most ambitious task was the commemoration of Kristallnacht, designed to attract worldwide attention and show that East Germany was at last paying respect to Germany's Jewish history and the tragedy of the Holocaust.

Gysi relished the assignment. It spoke to many of his interests—history, culture, the cosmopolitan German-Jewish tradition he had been exposed to as a child. It was also an opportunity to address the gaps in East German history. The Communist exhibit at the Buchenwald concentration camp, which was a required pilgrimage of every East German schoolchild, barely mentioned the Jews. East German schoolbooks, while condemning Hitler and the Nazis, described them as creations of capitalism. Communists, by definition, were not capable of such acts. Like the Jews, the Communists had been victims in World War II. No one talked of German responsibility for the Holocaust.

Gysi convened a meeting of community church officials from across East Germany. He began by telling them about his memories of Kristallnacht. Then he bombarded them with questions.

Where were the Jewish cemeteries in their towns? Where were the sites of the old Jewish synagogues? Why had all this been forgotten? Suddenly Klaus Gysi was no longer the dry official coldly overseeing a party meeting but an impassioned old man talking about his history.

"Look, the Jews in Germany were not an exotic, folkloric group from the Middle East," Gysi declared. "The first thing you have to learn is that when you hear the Nazis killed six million Jews, they did not kill six million members of a foreign nation. Many of those Jews were Germans—you understand?" Gysi told the gathered officials about the Nobel Prize winners Germany had lost, the physicists, the chemists. He spoke about science, literature, and culture in Germany before 1933, totally unthinkable without Jews. The impromptu lecture lasted half an hour.

Over the next months, in conversations with aides, Gysi lamented the fate of Jewish life and memory in East Germany. When an aide reported that an East German teacher had said proudly that there was no anti-Semitism in East Germany because students at her school didn't know anymore what a Jew was, Gysi shook his head sadly. "Here you see the worst thing for anybody: universal half-education." He joked bitterly: "The Germans will never forgive us for Auschwitz."

Nor would the Politburo forgive Gysi his trespasses. They rejected his plea to stay on to preside over the Kristallnacht celebration. He cleared out his office and was replaced with a hardliner, instructed to crush dissent in the churches. Honecker never did receive an invitation to the United States.

For the third time in his career, Klaus Gysi was unemployed. He returned to his apartment high above East Berlin and added a new memento to the shelves crammed with a lifetime's worth of books and treasured objects: a menorah given to him by an actor whom he had helped get a visa to visit Israel.

While his father's career dwindled, Gregor Gysi's renown grew. His involvement in dissident cases expanded. He was named head of the national association of East German lawyers. And in a way that eerily echoed his father, Gregor began groping toward a greater understanding of what it meant to be a Jew in East Germany.

By 1986, the official Jewish population in East Germany—Jews who went regularly to synagogue and participated in Jewish events—had shrunk to just 450 in a country of seventeen million. There were an estimated four thousand other people of "Jewish origin"—people like Klaus and Gregor Gysi, who had no ties to the Jewish community. Yet even here there were signs of the Jewish revival that was stirring, underground, across Eastern Europe. In an effort to bring together some of these other Jews, a sociologist named Irene Runge organized a meeting in East Berlin of a group she dubbed We Ourselves.

Runge was born in New York City in 1942, the daughter of two Jewish Communists who had fled the Nazis. Her parents, like many German leftists, returned in 1949 to East Germany to help build up the new, Communist society. In a short story she wrote some years later, Runge described growing up as a Jewish girl in East Germany—the awkward silences, the strange looks that greeted a little girl who did not have any aunts or uncles or grandparents, because they had all been killed by the Nazis or fled Germany:

> Susannah gives chocolate, chewing gum and candy to the others so that she is not alone. That helps to find friends. These friends ask her how they celebrate Christmas at home and whether they really killed Jesus. Susannah doesn't understand the questions and her parents stop her from seeing these friends. . . . Susannah has no grandparents in the new country, no aunts, no uncles. She has no brothers and sisters.
>
> In other people's living rooms, she sees photos from their family history. There they are, framed and respected: fathers, uncles, brothers, killed in action, missing, captured somewhere. They invite her to festivities reuniting aunts, uncles, grandparents, cousins, some visiting from the west. The others can easily fill entire apartments with relatives. When it becomes crowded and cozy at the end of such days, aunts and mothers pass around old pictures, complaining about

those who bombed their house, their city, who did not distribute food fairly enough. Before songs are being sung, Susannah leaves. She has no pictures of her dead, whose murderers she doesn't know.

"Home," wrote Runge, "is when you recognize yourself in the people passing by in the street."

Determined to re-create some sense of "home" and belonging, Irene Runge organized a meeting of Jews like herself—from Communist families, little interested in Judaism as a religion but eager to explore their Jewish roots. She persuaded the official, Communist-controlled Jewish community to organize a meeting in a drab social hall in the Jewish community building next to the once great Oranienburger Strasse synagogue, which was now a gutted shell with a tree growing in the center. In a small room set up with small tables, like a café, she soon was scheduling regular meetings to discuss Jewish holidays and explore Jewish culture.

Gregor Gysi came the first evening and attended many subsequent lectures. His feelings about his background had remained unsettled since those nighttime talks when he and his sister tried to puzzle out just what it meant to be Jewish. Sometimes, the intensity of his feelings surprised him. In 1974, six years after he was married, Gregor went with Jutta, his non-Jewish wife, to Auschwitz. It was his first visit, and he felt both moved, as a Jew, and guilty, as a German. In the death records there, he found the names of many of his relatives, including the aunt who had sent her nephew Klaus a postcard saying all was well. Gregor still had the postcard.

Gregor disliked the way East Germany trotted out its "alibi Jews" at official occasions—as if to say, "We had nothing to do with this Holocaust." He did not want to be singled out as a Jew, given any special treatment. He wanted to be an equal among equals. But his Jewish background nagged at him, and he pursued it in a typically intellectual way, attending Irene Runge's meetings, reading books, trying to puzzle out just what it all meant.

\*       \*       \*

By the summer of 1989, the internal despair affecting East Germany broke the surface. Thousands of East Germans began fleeing to West Germany through Hungary and Prague. By the end of the summer, nearly fifty thousand people had left, many of them young East German families, who told television audiences around the world that they were only seeking a better life for their children. The Politburo was paralyzed, unable to decide what to do.

In September, crowds began to gather in Leipzig every Monday to protest. Each week the crowd increased, marching in silent protest, carrying signs declaring "We Are the People," demanding the freedom to travel to the West. Plunged into crisis, the Communists worked feverishly on a travel law that would satisfy popular demands. By opening the borders a bit, the Communists hoped to dissipate the anger that had built up over the decades.

When the party issued a draft travel law, Gregor, as one of East Germany's leading lawyers, was asked to join a television panel to discuss it. Gregor himself had visited the West for the first time as an adult only a year earlier, when his mother arranged for the East German Culture Center in Paris to invite her son to speak about human rights in East Germany. It had taken Gregor a year to get a visa, and he had been called by the secret police before he left and when he returned. Gregor understood the frustration of East Germans trapped behind the Berlin Wall. As a panelist, he criticized the proposed law as too bureaucratic and conservative. Over the next few days, Gregor received six thousand letters from East Germans supporting his call for a more liberal travel law. Gregor and members of the lawyers' association began working on a travel law of their own. They planned to submit it to the Politburo on November 11, 1989.

But events were moving too fast. Gregor was asked to attend a public meeting of actors and directors at the Deutsches Theater—where, forty-four years earlier, Gregor's parents had seen a performance of *Nathan the Wise* in bombed-out Berlin. The theater people were agitating for a demonstration in Berlin to match Leipzig's demonstrations. They feared that the police—who had cracked down on smaller antigovernment demonstrations in East Berlin in recent days—would attack and beat the demonstrators. When Gregor arrived, the theater was packed. He mounted the stage and was asked to comment on the possibility of police retaliation if East Berliners took to the streets in mass protests. Gregor suggested a novel approach. Why not apply for a permit to hold a "legal" demonstration? Like every Communist country, East Germany insisted on a veil of "legality" over a brutal and oppressive system. The East Berlin police chief had the power to issue such a permit.

Realizing that they could no longer contain the momentum, the government approved the rally. The date was set for November 4, 1989, and the rally would be held in Alexanderplatz, the heart of East Berlin. Gregor was chosen as one of the speakers.

The night before the rally, Gregor met his father for a drink at the bar in the Hotel Stadt Berlin, overlooking Alexanderplatz. Gregor was nervous. In twelve hours, he would be taking the most daring political risk of his life, speaking to a mass rally calling for reform of the Communist regime. Two decades earlier, Klaus had lectured Gregor on the art of compromise. He had lambasted him for being politically naive and stubborn. But Klaus did not lecture Gregor tonight. The two men agreed: only dramatic reform could save East Germany.

The crowd the next day swelled to one million people, the largest demonstration in the history of East Germany. One after another, speakers rose to call for more democracy, free speech, and the right to travel. The speakers list was a roll call of East Germany's most prominent dissidents and such literary figures as Stefan Heym and Christa Wolf. Others, like Markus Wolf, the former head of the secret police, spoke as loyal Communists who nevertheless demanded reform. Many in the crowd were party members as well. Standing near the front, unnoticed, was Klaus Gysi, come to hear his son speak.

Gregor stepped to the podium, and the crowd stilled. East Germany needed democratic control of the Stasi, Gregor declared, and of the regular police as well. "Every abuse of power has to be ruled out or at least severely punished. We need new rules for elections and a constitutional court. And we need more lawyers." The crowd cheered. In East Germany, lawyers represented a challenge to the system, a chance to fight for their rights in a system that had always been arbitrary. Gysi spoke of the day-to-day harassment that was experienced by millions of East Germans, the constant surveillance and fear of the secret police. "If I try to summarize demands for a state of law in one sentence, I'd say, 'Every household should have a telephone, and the words "I shouldn't tell you this on the telephone" should forever belong to history.' "

Gregor built to his conclusion. "We have adopted many English words and phrases, which I don't mind. But from the Russian language we have adopted only the word *dacha*. It's about time we adopted two more words: *perestroika* and *glasnost*." The crowd roared.

But talk of *glasnost* and *perestroika*, while daring for a lifelong Communist like Gregor, was old news. What Gregor Gysi was envisioning was a "third way," an East German version of the Prague Spring, in which Communism would be reformed but in which the Communist Party would still run the country. However, events were moving too fast for that. In Leipzig, the placards now read: "We Are ONE People," signifying unification with West Germany, Communism thrown off and the democratic, capitalist West embraced. This was not a revolution that could be led or managed from the top. It had begun in the grass roots, in the trenches, and now it was about to march down the streets leading to the Berlin Wall.

In the days immediately following the East Berlin rally, the East German leadership held emergency meetings.

The Communist Party, in a new spirit of openness, began to brief East German as well as Western reporters on its meetings. Every evening, reporters from both sides of the wall crammed into an auditorium in East Berlin, cameras rolling, to record comments by Gunther Schabowski, the Politburo member chosen to give the daily briefing to the press. On November 9, as the 6:00 P.M.

deadline for the news conference neared, Schabowski asked Communist Party head Egon Krenz what he should report.

Krenz handed him a sheet of paper containing the new travel law. Most of it concerned regulations that would allow East Germans to emigrate directly to West Germany from the East instead of passing through Hungary or Czechoslovakia.

It also contained two key sentences: "Private trips can be applied for. Permission will be granted in a short period of time." Schabowski waited until the end of the news conference to read the travel law. He did not think it was the most important decision to have come out of that day's meeting. The reporters seemed puzzled, especially about "private trips."

A reporter jumped up. "Mr. Schabowski, what about the Berlin Wall?"

Schabowski paused. Berlin was still an occupied city. At the very least, the Allied powers, including the United States and the Soviet Union, should have been informed of any changes in travel between East and West Berlin. But Schabowski did not know: Had they been told?

Deciding to avoid the question, Schabowski called the press conference to an end. But as it broke up, around seven o'clock, the question—What about the Berlin Wall?—hung in the air.

What the East German government expected was that at eight o'clock the next morning, East Germans would begin obediently lining up at local police stations to get their identification cards stamped for authorized visits to West Germany. Border guards were to be notified of the new regulations and new procedures at 4:00 A.M.

It had never occurred to the Communists that in East Berlin, in the shadow of the Berlin Wall, people listening to their radios and televisions, swept up by the excitement of the imminent changes, might simply walk to the wall that evening and find out what was happening.

Which was what they did. The crowds began massing at checkpoints at 9:00 P.M., waving their identity papers and shouting questions to the police. "Can we go over?" they shouted. "Can I cross this border with this personal ID card tonight?"

The police were confused. They told the East Germans filling up the streets to come back the next morning at eight to get a proper visa stamp at the police station. But the people thronging the street would not be turned away. The crowds kept getting larger. At some checkpoints, lines of cars a half-mile long were forming.

Then, at the Bornholmer Strasse crossing point, a border guard appeared. The crowd pushed forward. "Can an East German citizen with a personal ID card cross over to West Berlin tonight?" a man shouted.

The guard looked at him. "Yes, whoever wants to," he replied. "Go ahead."

The crowd surged forward. The Berlin Wall had come tumbling down.

In the apartment on Leipziger Strasse, the Gysis had finished their Chinese food and toasted their anniversary. They heard a roar in the distance and stepped out on the balcony to look. They could see nothing. Klaus flipped on the television, and there, on West German television, were the pictures of tinny East German cars, Trabants, puttering through the wall, their roofs being pounded by jubilant West Germans, who were spraying East Germans with champagne and offering a yellow delicacy rare in East Germany: bananas. It was good, Klaus thought. It was long overdue. East Germany would continue, but in a more normal, more open way. Klaus and Birgid said good night to their friends and went to bed.

Earlier in the evening, Gregor had attended a conference on the future of the Protestant Church in East Germany. The events of the past weeks had left him exhausted, and he went home to sleep. Around midnight, the phone rang. It was his lover. "The wall is open," she said. Crowds were pouring into West Berlin. She wanted to go. Gregor demurred. There would be too many people. The situation was still too unclear. Gregor settled in front of the television set. He was mesmerized by the images flickering across the screen: the tears running down the faces of East

Germans as they stepped into West Berlin, the joyous poundings on cars, the people dancing on the wall, popping open champagne, and swigging it from upturned bottles.

Gregor called his lover. He was far less sanguine than his father. "This is the end of East Germany," he said.

He was right.

# Chapter Thirteen

# The Worst Address in Berlin

In 1972, Andreas Nachama left his parents' home to begin university, where he majored in history and Jewish studies. Unlike Estrongo, whose life revolved around the synagogue, Andreas had interests ranging from German and Jewish history to contemporary events. In many ways, he was heir to the teeming numbers of cosmopolitan Jewish intellectuals and editors who lived in Berlin in the years before the 1930s. He wrote his doctoral thesis on Prussia. His first job was as a teacher of Western European agricultural history at a German university. Soon he began making radio and film features on the history of skyscrapers, the history of Sunday, the history of foreigners in Europe, the history of migration.

Andreas was a more sophisticated man than his father. He spoke English fluently and traveled often to the United States, France, and Israel. His wife was the daughter of an Indian-born Israeli diplomat. Unlike his father, who had been uprooted and tossed into Berlin by the winds of the Holocaust, Andreas had roots in Germany. He had been born and raised in Berlin, and when he was a boy his father took him across the Berlin Wall and out to the Weissensee cemetery, so he could see where his mother's family, the Schlochauers, had been buried, how proud a family they had been, how deeply entrenched in Germany.

Estrongo had always lived as an outsider in Berlin, holding on to his Greek passport, speaking simple German. His entire presence as a Jew in Germany was a historical accident. But his son considered himself German, and he was a Jew. The question facing Andreas was profound: Was it possible, after the Holocaust, after the Nazis, to live as a Jew in Germany?

In December 1979, Andreas landed a job as a curator for an upcoming exhibition in Berlin on the history of Prussia, the German state that had given birth to Bismarck as well as to many of the least admirable traditions associated with Germany: militarism, bureaucracy, and a rage for order. These traits had all shaped Prussia into the most powerful German-speaking state ever, until Bismarck united Germany in 1871. The exhibit was to take place in the Martin Gropius Building, an ornate red-brick edifice, backed up against the Berlin Wall, that had been damaged by the relentless Allied bombings and was being reconstructed.

Andreas visited his parents to tell them about his new job. His mother stared at him. "That's one of the worst addresses in Berlin," she said.

The Martin Gropius Building, on what had once been called Prinz Albrecht Strasse, was now surrounded by a parking lot and piles of rubble. It had always been a school of industrial arts, but across the street, the Nazis had taken over several buildings and turned them into Gestapo headquarters. It was a factory of terror. Cars passing through the entry gates into a courtyard were shielded from the stares of outsiders by a high wall. Inside the building, the leader of the SS—Heinrich Himmler—planned and oversaw the policing of the Nazi state, the imprisonment and torture of political opponents, and the destruction of the European Jews. Adolf Eichmann had an office there before he moved to larger quarters a few blocks away. In the cellar of the Gestapo building, in a warren of jail cells, some of Nazi Germany's best-known prisoners were tortured. Erich Honecker, who now ruled East Germany from the other side of the Berlin Wall, had been interrogated there. Hiding in different parts of Berlin, with very different backgrounds and politics, both young Klaus Gysi and young Lilian Nachama had lived in fear of being discovered by the men who worked at Prinz Albrecht Strasse.

By 1980, when Andreas showed up for work across the street, nothing remained of the old Gestapo buildings. They had been damaged during the war and torn down in the years afterward. The rubbled site now contained garbage—an old conveyor belt, a huge mesh filter for gravel. Old cars were left behind from a time when the area had been turned into an "autodrome," where West Germans without driver's licenses could drive cars around a small circular track. The activities of the 1950s, 1960s, and 1970s had literally buried evidence of the crimes of the past. The Gropius Building rose up amid a ruined landscape.

When Andreas arrived at his office for his first day of work on a chill January day, he announced the "good news" that the exhibit on Prussia would be held at the "worst address" in Berlin. A colleague said he had heard the same rumors. The staff began to research the history of the street. When the exhibit opened, the last room was devoted to the Nazi legacy of Prussia. A window opened onto the rubbish-strewn lot below. There was a map alongside the window, showing where the various Gestapo buildings once stood. "Here were the torture cells of the Gestapo and SS," the map declared in German, English, French, and Russian. The exhibit left to the visitor's imagination what lay underneath.

The sight of postwar rubble burying the site of one of the most gruesome episodes of German history was, Andreas believed, a fitting metaphor for postwar Germany's continuing unease with uncovering its Nazi past. In the decades since the end of the war, West Germany had taken initially tentative and then bold steps to confront and acknowledge its Nazi legacy. The West Germans had built synagogues and opened a Jewish theological seminary. They had given reparations to Israel. They had built monuments and memorials to Jews. German writers, like Günter Grass, returned again and again to the question "What made Auschwitz possible?" In 1979, the year before Andreas started work at the Gropius Building, German television broadcast the American miniseries *Holocaust* and attracted a record viewership—40 percent of the nightly audience. The broadcasts provoked a flood of emotional and shamed responses from many younger Germans, who said they had never fully understood the Holocaust before.

At the same time, many West Germans—two-thirds of the population, according to polls—believed that it was time to shed the burden of the Nazi past, to draw a line beneath the Holocaust and move on into the future. Many resented the unending burden of guilt others expected them to carry. In 1972, West German Chancellor Willy Brandt visited Poland and fell on his knees before the memorial to the Warsaw ghetto, at the spot where tens of thousands of Jews had been loaded onto trains and shipped to their deaths. The picture of the leader of West Germany on his knees before a memorial to Jews slaughtered by Germans made the front pages of newspapers around the world. It enhanced Brandt's stature as a moral leader. But in West Germany, a poll found that 48 percent of West Germans thought Brandt's gesture was "overdone." Only 41 percent found it "appropriate."

In the 1980s, a number of historians began to argue that the cruelties of the Nazi regime were not unique. In fact, they asserted that Hitler had been inspired by the excesses of Stalin during his purges in the 1930s. Some even went further, claiming that the Jews bore some responsibility for the Holocaust because Chaim Weizmann and other Jewish leaders had declared that they should join Britain's war against Nazi Germany, thus making Jews Germany's mortal enemy. This would explode in the mid-1980s in what became known as the Historians' Debate, a controversy so bitter that eventually the president of West Germany intervened to stop it. In a way, the specifics of the debate were less important than the impulses behind it: on one side, an effort by historians to confront West Germany's guilt; on the other, an effort to alleviate it and place Germany among "normal" countries. The intention, Andreas believed, was to relativize the Holocaust, to show that Auschwitz—the methodical killing of an entire race of people simply because of their race—was no different than the wartime bombings of Dresden or Hiroshima or the atrocities of Pol Pot. By extension, Jewish victims of the Holocaust were no different from the German or Japanese victims of Allied bombings.

In June 1984, West Germany and its new chancellor, Helmut Kohl, were barred from ceremonies commemorating the fortieth anniversary of D-day on the beaches of Normandy. Kohl, a historian by training, was angry and hurt. He was the first West German chancellor who had been a child during World War II. He was just fifteen when the war ended and thus had been too young to face the moral choices it raised. Kohl was driven to make Germany a normal country, a country that could acknowledge its catastrophic past—and move on. Stung by the refusal of the Allies to welcome him to Normandy, Kohl urged Ronald Reagan to visit a German military cemetery in an act of reconciliation. It soon emerged that in the cemetery, in Bitburg, forty-nine members of the brutal Waffen SS had been buried along with German soldiers.

Despite a firestorm of protest, including a personal appeal from Nobel Peace Prize winner Elie Wiesel, Reagan decided to go to Bitburg and to the concentration camp at Bergen-Belsen.

Andreas and his father, who felt that honoring members of the Waffen SS with a visit was an insult to the Holocaust, wrote angry letters to the West German government and signed petitions protesting the American President's visit. Reagan's decision to visit Bitburg was a political coup for Kohl. The West German parliament voted 398 to 24 in favor of the visit to Bitburg; only the left-wing, environmental Green Party opposed it.

A few weeks before Reagan arrived, the head of Germany's Jewish community, a friend who had also survived the Holocaust, telephoned Estrongo at home. Would he, as Germany's best-known cantor, as a survivor of Auschwitz, chant the Jewish mourner's prayer at Bergen-Belsen when the American President visited? Estrongo did not even have to think it over. "No," he declared. He would not be part of this effort to trample on the victims of the Holocaust. On May 5, 1985, Reagan and Kohl visited the graves of the German soldiers at Bitburg, then helicoptered to a memorial ceremony at Bergen-Belsen. Like millions of other West Germans, Estrongo watched the proceedings on television. It was the moment, he would say later, when everything seemed to start going wrong in Germany.

\*     \*     \*

As the 1980s wore on, the mounds of rubble covering the site of the former Gestapo headquarters in West Berlin lay undisturbed. Berlin approached its 750th anniversary, and the Gropius Building, with its beautiful exhibition spaces, was to be a centerpiece of the city's celebration. Andreas believed it was time for Berlin to dig out the rubble and unearth the remnants of the Gestapo headquarters that lay beneath. It was time to uncover this wound. Other groups in Berlin demanded that the headquarters be turned into some kind of memorial.

The museum initiated the digging, a gruesome archaeology. Excavators first uncovered the foundations of the entrance through which prisoners had been whisked into a courtyard, there to be dragged inside for interrogation and torture. They found toilets and showers that had been used by guards. Downstairs, they discovered the cold stone floors of basement cells where prisoners were locked up and beaten. They found the cellar of an annex that housed the cafeteria for the guards and officers. Most of the dreaded work of the Gestapo—the beatings, the torture, the planning for the "Special Actions"—had taken place in the upper floors of the demolished buildings. The remains of the basement cells were like a ghostly footprint.

Scholars and historians gathered over the rubble and began to assemble an exhibit. The result was "Topography of Terror," which opened on July 4, 1987, the anniversary of the day American troops had marched into Berlin right after the end of the war. Andreas invited his parents to the opening, so they could see—and relive—the terror of the Third Reich. Visitors entered the exhibit at ground level and walked down a flight of stairs into the old Gestapo basement. They passed from room to claustrophobic room, confronting pictures of prisoners. Alongside each photograph were excerpts from their letters and final words, graphic descriptions of beatings and torture, and evidence of their courage in facing death. For decades, many West Germans had retreated from questions about why they did not resist the Nazis. There was nothing they could have done, they said. The Nazis were too powerful. Resistance was futile. But here the mute walls that had echoed with so many screams testified to the fact, as the exhibit itself declared, "that there were people who refused to bend, who did not take the easy route of accommodation or of closing their eyes but who opted for resistance and did not hesitate to risk their lives in order to prevent, lessen or shorten injustice."

The exhibit reproduced the dry documents of genocide: lists of Jews who received "special treatment"—execution; descriptions of anti-Nazis who received "intensified interrogation"—torture. Some of the memos bore the familiar signatures of Nazi leaders; others bore the scribbled names of German clerks and bureaucrats, who responded with laconic approval to requests for deportations, for more efficient gas chambers, for expansion of the death camps. The requests for more efficient killing machines for the camps were phrased like requests for an increase in the production of timber and coal.

The exhibit space was cramped. The ceilings were low. Every wall contained a horror. There was no escape in these basement rooms without sunlight, with concrete pillars pressing in. The walls screamed with pain. When visitors finally emerged from the warren of terror, they ascended a staircase and stood on a platform overlooking a pile of rubble from the old Gestapo headquarters. Less than a hundred yards away loomed the Berlin Wall and, beyond it, the grimy, black-sooted buildings of East Berlin—all the tragedies and horrors of fifty years of German history within the space of a few city blocks.

In its first year, more than 300,000 people visited "Topography of Terror." What was originally to be a temporary exhibit quickly became one of the few places in West Berlin where Germans could confront their history.

Estrongo was proud of Andreas's work on the exhibit. It confirmed for him that West Germany was a different place than the Germany that had annihilated his family and driven Lilli's underground. Estrongo had been upset by the controversy over Bitburg, but he blamed that on Kohl and the politicians. He had no quarrel with the West German people. He glided through West Berlin as a respected Jewish leader, beloved by Jews and respected by Germans. When he crossed over into East Berlin, he was greeted like a Jewish pope, with embraces and delighted smiles as he led the dwindling Jewish population in Purim and Hanukkah celebrations. He visited elderly Jews in nursing homes and delivered toys for the Hanukkah party held every year in the grand Café Moskau on Stalin Avenue, in the heart of East Berlin. Amid the red velvet seats that usually held well-heeled Communist officials, Estrongo would light the menorah and lead his small band in Hanukkah songs.

Once, on a trip to Magdeburg, in East Germany, to minister to the handful of Jews there, Estrongo met the conductor of the local church choir. Impulsively he asked, "Shall we have a concert together?" Within a few months, the state secretary of religious affairs—Klaus Gysi—had granted the necessary approvals, and Estrongo led the choir in a concert of traditional Jewish religious music in the Magdeburg cathedral—to an East German audience that was 80 percent non-Jewish. The concert was so popular that the group was soon flooded with requests to perform. Thousands of East Germans wanted to hear in person the man they had heard on the radio Friday nights for so many years, singing for twenty minutes those haunting religious tunes. It was as if they wanted to catch one last bit of Germany's Jewish past before it faded away completely. Soon invitations arrived from West Germany as well. Eager to polish its image among worldwide Jewish groups, the East German government approved visas for the choir to travel with Estrongo over the Berlin Wall and into West Germany. Estrongo exulted, then fretted. He pleaded with the members of the choir: Whatever you do, please do not defect. All the choir members returned home to the East.

Estrongo studiously avoided politics. He tended to his Jewish flock, doing what he could to lighten lives with a present or a favored song. He despised the Communists, but East Germany and the Berlin Wall were facts of life. In 1988, to honor his years of work on behalf of East German Jews, the East German government awarded Estrongo a medal. Erich Honecker himself bestowed it on Estrongo, as flashbulbs popped. The picture was published in the next day's newspaper. Neither man in the picture—the Communist leader nor the Jewish cantor—was capable of imagining that the Berlin Wall would collapse in less than a year.

Nor was Estrongo's son. Andreas accompanied his father occasionally to official functions in East Berlin. The grayness and drabness of the East never failed to depress him. He always returned to his home with a sense of relief, and sadness, the inevitable shaking of the head with which so many West Germans confronted the implacability of Communism.

In the summer of 1987, shortly after "Topography of Terror" opened, Nachama received a phone call at his office. Two people had shown up at the exhibit entrance, saying they were journalists from East Germany. They wanted a guided tour. Nachama rushed to the exhibit entrance and showed the East Germans around. They were especially impressed with the cell devoted to Erich Honecker. At the end of the tour, the visitors asked whether the exhibit could be displayed in East Germany. Surprised, Nachama said that would be no problem.

Andreas did not hear from his East German visitors for a year. Then they reappeared, this time disclosing their true identities—one represented the East German Cultural Ministry, the other the Foreign Ministry. In January 1989, after elaborate negotiations, "Topography of Terror" opened in East Berlin.

The response astounded Andreas. The East Germans had expected to sell two thousand catalogs during the month-long exhibition. The catalogs were gone in three days. Long lines formed at the entrance. From Berlin the exhibit traveled to the concentration camps at Sachsenhausen and Buchenwald, both in East Germany.

On the day the wall fell, Andreas was as stunned as the rest of the world. He went, on that anniversary of Kristallnacht, to the headquarters of the West Berlin Jewish community, to hear his father chant the Kaddish before a gathering of German and Jewish dignitaries. At home with his family that night, he switched on the television for the eight o'clock news and settled in for a night of television viewing. Suddenly, there on the screen were reporters at the border checkpoints. Crowds of East

Germans were surging through, bathed in champagne by their West German brethren. It all seemed unreal. Had the wall really fallen?

The next morning, Andreas made his way to work. He had planned to meet a friend at the "Topography of Terror" exhibit, just fifty yards from the wall. The streets were thronged with dazed East Germans gawking at shop windows, inhaling their first breath of freedom. At the exhibit, Andreas heard an unusual noise and stepped outside. It was the clink-clink-clink of hammers striking the Berlin Wall. From both sides, East and West, Germans were striking at the concrete with hammers and chisels, chipping it away.

# Chapter Fourteen

# "Will It Ever End?"

The last customers had left hours before. Alena Wittmann pushed the broom a final time across the narrow shop floor, pulled the door behind her, locked up, and began the walk to the trolley that would take her home. It was 11:00 P.M. Ahead lay the long ride to her apartment and the long climb up four flights of stairs to bed. Ever since her work in the sulfurous metal factory in the 1950s, Alena's health had not been good. She was convinced she had been poisoned by fumes. Now she was exhausted all the time.

In the years right after the 1968 Soviet invasion Alena had managed to avoid the purges that swept Czechoslovakia. She had left the oppressive factory jobs behind her and, using the German she had learned as a child, found work overseeing the gift shop that sold Czech crystalware to departing tourists at the airport. She supervised the staff and was able to speak with foreign tourists, even the occasional American. Meeting Americans was always a thrill to Alena, who treasured the memories of the American soldiers who had liberated her town from the Nazis and introduced her to big-band music and Jimmy Stewart movies. But as the Communists widened their purge in the 1970s, Alena came under suspicion. Because she had been arrested as a Zionist spy in 1953 and interrogated for three months, her loyalty remained in question. One day an official approached her and offered her a chance to reform and become a member of the Communist Party. All she had to do was fill out an application. Alena smiled and refused. "I had some experiences in the 1950s," she told him evenly. Soon her salary was cut in half. Then she was dismissed from her job. After months of searching, she was given a job by the Communists, running a tiny, one-room crystal shop in an industrial part of Prague. No foreigners ever went there. Alena had to do everything: place the orders, unpack the glassware, deal with customers, keep the books, then clean up every night.

As they had two decades earlier when they placed Michael in an orphanage and made Robert live with his grandmother, Communists had split Alena's family. Her son Michael never returned from Paris after the Soviet tanks invaded.

Robert, the Wittmanns' older son, was in trouble. Many of his artist friends were in jail or lying low to avoid arrest. Robert had associated himself with people who would become the core of Czechoslovakia's dissident movement. He signed petitions against the government. His life in Prague was becoming untenable. The police called him in for questioning. Thugs loitered outside his apartment building. When they beat Robert, the police said there was nothing they could do. Alena was sure the thugs were being paid by the secret police. Robert decided to leave the country. Alena agreed that there was no other choice. In the mercurial way in which the Communists operated—approving some applications, while denying others—they approved Robert's visa. In 1978, he left for Australia.

That left Sylvia, Alena's youngest child and only daughter. Sylvia, born in 1956, had inherited both her mother's stubbornness and her disdain for Communist authority. But her rebellion took a different road. Disdaining dissident politics and refusing to abandon her mother by emigrating, Sylvia was returning to Judaism and embracing Jewish life—rediscovering what her parents had tried so hard to forget.

As she approached twenty, Sylvia realized that whenever she found a friend whom she could call a soul mate, almost always the friend turned out to be from a Jewish or mixed Jewish family. Like

Jews in other Eastern European countries, most Jews in Czechoslovakia had abandoned their identities or tried to obscure them.
This coming together of Jews, Sylvia felt, was a kind of homing
instinct. There were sociological explanations, of course. Like
Jews in the United States or Europe, those in Czechoslovakia
were usually well educated and had flocked to professions like
academics and publishing. Even through political upheavals, they
had remained interested in culture and politics. Because so many
Jews in Czechoslovakia had been scarred by the Stalinist purges
of the 1950s, several of Sylvia's friends came from homes that
took a jaundiced view of Communism.

But all these factors only partially explained why so many of
Sylvia's friends were Jewish. In East Germany, Gregor Gysi, too,
occasionally mused that so many of his friends were Jewish in
background. In Hungary, the young people showing up at Tamas
Raj's synagogue in Szeged marveled at the other faces in the room.
They had long known these people as friends. Only now, in the
synagogue, did they discover that their friends were Jews. Across
Eastern Europe, the Catholic Church, energized by the election
of the first Polish Pope in 1978, was beginning to attract
Catholics seeking safety and a challenge to Communist systems
that they had found empty and brutal. Now, after decades of
Communism, it was as if the Jewish instinct for survival had
reasserted itself and was preparing to confront the forces that had
earlier tried to destroy it.

In 1981, Sylvia, who had just turned twenty-five, set up what
she grandly called a "Jewish salon" in her parents' apartment. The
Wittmanns had a large front room with a piano and family pictures, which was heated separately from the rest of the apartment.
Whenever Alena became impatient and wanted Sylvia's boisterous friends to call it a night, she would invite them into this
"salon." The room was little used in the winter, and there, with
people bundled in sweaters, taking turns shoveling coal into the
stove, Sylvia began her "Jewish salon." Tentatively, at first, friends
began coming to the weekly salons with a copy of a book by Kafka
or a musty volume of Jewish literature taken from a remote corner
of their parents' bookshelves. After more than a dozen years of

repression following the crushing of the Prague Spring, anything that smacked of the forbidden had become a magnet for Prague's disenchanted young people. A friend of Sylvia's visited from Slovakia. His father had taught him Jewish songs. Soon the cold air of the salon was filled with the voices of young Czechs singing Hebrew songs, reading Jewish poetry, and discussing Jewish authors. Occasionally, Sylvia and some of her friends walked to services at the old synagogue a few blocks away. Some of them began going every week. They could not follow everything that was going on; few spoke Hebrew. But they liked being with the handful of elderly Jews who had faithfully attended services every Friday night and Saturday through all the years of Communism. Simply being in these people's company seemed more important than praying. They asked the elders about the significance of the old buildings in the former Jewish ghetto. They requested stories about their lives before the war. The older Jews were a link to the past and to this still mysterious religion that seemed to be reasserting its hold on the young.

In 1983, after several attempts, Sylvia received permission to visit her brother Michael, now living in Brussels. It was her first trip out of the country. For months, she had helped a friend clean the old synagogue and the Jewish community building, in the hope that tourists would ask her questions and she could guide them through the synagogue. The tourists tipped her in West German marks, American dollars, or British pounds. The treasured Western currency—hard currency—which was impossible to get in Czechoslovakia, would be needed when she visited her brother.

She stepped off the train in Brussels with $260. The city overwhelmed her; it seemed so clean and new. Sylvia marveled at the plants that flourished in the store windows and restaurants, until she realized they were artificial. She had never seen plastic plants before. Michael, now an investment banker living in a swank part of the city, escorted his little sister around town. At restaurants, Sylvia ordered little, conscious of her limited funds. She always ordered mineral water, despite her brother's urgings to try forbidden pleasures such as Coca-Cola. In Prague, Coca-Cola could be bought only with scarce hard currency. Then, one day, Sylvia sneaked a look at the menu and found that Coca-Cola cost the same as mineral water. What a country! thought Sylvia. From then on, she ordered only Coca-Cola.

Sylvia had illicit plans. She wanted to visit Israel, despite the Czech Communist prohibition. Israel was still a pariah state, regularly attacked in the press. But for Sylvia it represented an opportunity to reconnect with her Jewish roots, to find out more about this mysterious thing called Judaism.

Her brother offered to lend Sylvia money for the trip, and she and Michael worked out a plan. The Israeli embassy in Brussels agreed to put Sylvia's visa on a separate sheet of paper so it would not appear in her passport. Sylvia was due to return to Prague in a few days. Her brother called the Czech embassy, claiming that his sister had a terrible case of flu; she could barely speak. Michael was ordered to check in every few days, to apprise them of Sylvia's status. Before every phone call, Michael arranged to have a friend in the background, to cough and wheeze and talk to Michael in a hoarse voice, posing as Sylvia, who had left for Tel Aviv.

Sylvia landed in a time warp. Jewish life in Prague had been suspended in time; little had changed since the 1930s. Those Jews who were left still talked of the old traditions. The few services that Sylvia had attended at the old synagogue in the center of Prague were conducted as they had been for centuries, with old men in prayer shawls standing and praying in Hebrew, swaying back and forth, while the women peered from a hidden gallery. But in Israel, Czech Jews who had settled in Tel Aviv took Sylvia to a Reform synagogue, where women read from the Torah and there was a woman cantor. Sylvia sat through the service but didn't like it. It reminded her too much of the Czech Protestant Church. On a day trip to the Sea of Galilee, Sylvia looked through the windows of a yeshiva—an Orthodox religious school—and saw the boys with their yarmulkes and side curls. In the synagogue at this school, the men bobbed and swayed and prayed, just as they did in Prague. This Sylvia liked; it was the Judaism she wanted to become more familiar with.

It was a confusing week. Sylvia met up with some Czech acquaintances who had emigrated to Israel. They invited her to speak at their university about Jewish life under Communism. They put up a poster announcing that a "Czech Jewish woman who has come to Israel secretly will speak."

Hastily, Sylvia tore it down. "There could be secret police everywhere," she shouted. "If you want to do it, do it in your home, inviting only your friends."

Just before her return to Brussels, Sylvia learned of a demonstration to take place in front of the Knesset, the Israeli parliament, protesting Israel's occupation of the West Bank. Curious but fearful, Sylvia approached the Knesset gingerly: Surely the police would intervene. The protesters were not even Israelis. They were Americans, and they were brazenly chanting, "Give the West Bank back to the Arabs." Even more amazing to Sylvia, the police were protecting the demonstrators. They were not beating them or bombarding them with torrents from water cannons. She approached one of the Israeli police. Why were these Americans allowed to protest so freely in Israel? "Well," said the policeman, "they're Jewish."

Sylvia returned to Brussels and headed home, happy as the train rumbled back to Prague. It was spring. Outside the train window bright-yellow flowers in mustard fields blanketed the countryside. Israel had been wonderful but strange. Prague, her home, was familiar and comforting. But Sylvia's euphoria lasted only a few days. The drab buildings, the petty, self-important bureaucrats, the scramble for food or a nice dress when something new materialized in the stores . . . Sylvia sighed. She had seen how her brother lived. She found herself returning again and again to one thought: "I have to emigrate." It would mean leaving her mother alone; Alena and Vaclav had divorced, amicably.

Her mother's difficult years—her months in prison, her two years waiting for Michael to be returned to her, her work at the factory, her demotion from the airport crystal shop to the forlorn storefront—had taken their toll. Alena's kind, intelligent face had become drawn and tired. But Alena had never said or done anything to stand in the way of her children's wishes. She had not protested when Michael left after the Soviet invasion or when Robert left a few years later. Whether to abandon Czechoslovakia was a personal decision everyone had to make alone—it was a decision Alena herself might have made if she had had such an option in the 1950s. Now she felt she was too old, too set in her ways, to begin a new life in another country. But her daughter? Her whole life still lay before her.

Sylvia met with a handful of friends and decided to leave. They plotted their escape—by train through Yugoslavia and then out to the West. They wrapped up what little foreign currency they had in tinfoil and jammed it inside their backpacks; someone heard the tinfoil would mask their money from the X-rays that examined luggage at the border. On the day of her daughter's departure, Alena accompanied Sylvia and her friends to the train station. And there, on the platform, Sylvia changed her mind. She looked into her mother's eyes and decided she could not leave.

Sylvia said good-bye to her friends and returned home with her mother. She resumed her job as a receptionist at the ornate Ambassador, one of the Prague hotels designated for use by foreigners. Every day, she saw the work of the secret police firsthand. The hotel was full of hidden cameras and microphones. The room holding the recording equipment was always locked; only the hotel manager, a member of the Communist Party, had the key. A secret policeman was regularly assigned to the hotel. Sylvia and the other front desk workers joked about the policeman—so awkward and clumsy as he lounged in the hotel lobby with his newspaper.

Sylvia joined the "home university"—clandestine meetings of students with dissident professors banned from teaching at the university. When the secret police discovered one of the locations, the students moved to another house. It was like a game of cat and mouse.

Frustrated with her hotel job, Sylvia in the late 1980s found a job with one of the government-sanctioned agencies that shepherded groups of Russians, Bulgarians, and other East Bloc visitors, plus the occasional tour group from Western Europe. Sylvia, who had excelled in languages since grammar school, spoke both

Russian and English. She was often assigned to take groups of English-speaking tourists from Denmark and other Western European countries around Prague. These groups always insisted on visiting the concentration camp at Terezin, or Theresienstadt, a forty-five-minute drive from Prague.

As with Buchenwald in East Germany, the true history of Theresienstadt and the suffering of the Jews there had been replaced with a history that exalted the role of the Communists in fighting the Nazis. Officially approved tour groups and school-children were taken to the "small fortress," a red-brick fortification in the heart of the town, which the Nazis had turned into a prison for political offenders. It had housed 32,000 inmates, most of them Czechs accused of resisting or criticizing the Nazi regime. Many had been tortured to death.

But visitors were rarely told of the town that surrounded the prison, which the Nazis had entered in 1941 and then filled with Jews deported from towns and cities across Europe. The Nazis had turned Theresienstadt into a "model" concentration camp and paraded representatives of the Red Cross through it in June 1944. Only carefully selected inmates were shown to Red Cross inspectors. Healthy-looking children were given haircuts and fed before the visitors came. Fifty amateur singers performed Verdi's *Requiem*, as German propaganda cameras whirred. Satisfied with the conditions, the Red Cross left. The singers were sent to their deaths in Auschwitz.

More than 140,000 Jews passed through Theresienstadt. Almost 34,000 died in the camp; another 87,000 were shipped to Auschwitz and other death camps, including many of Klaus Gysi's relatives. Of almost 10,000 Jewish children who entered the gates of Theresienstadt, only 150 survived. The official Communist exhibit barely spoke of these Jews.

After the war, the town of Theresienstadt returned to normalcy. The boys' barracks was turned into the police barracks. The buildings still bore the faded numbers painted on by the Nazis, but the citizens who moved in after the war went quietly about their daily lives. Visitors driving from Dresden to Prague passed through the town and saw the fortress. Many thought that the fortress, with its walls, was the ghetto, not realizing that the streets where they walked, bought a soda, asked for directions to Prague, were the same streets where 140,000 Jews had suffered and almost 10,000 Jewish children had lived their final days.

Tourists to Czechoslovakia were not allowed to travel independently. Their itineraries were always prearranged by the official Communist travel agency or by one of the semiofficial agencies, like Sportourist. The itinerary always included Theresienstadt but stopped off only at the small fortress.

Sylvia had pieced together the real history of Theresienstadt from her friends and family. In 1987, she was assigned her first tour group from Western Europe—handicapped students from Denmark. At Theresienstadt—the students wanted to see it, having read about it in school—Sylvia lowered her voice, as other guides passed, and pointed out the lies and omissions of the Communists. Because of her fluency in English, Sylvia was assigned more groups from Western Europe. And when they expressed interest, she always told them the true history of Theresienstadt.

Though Czechoslovakia was still under Communist control, Jewish groups began visiting in the late 1980s, stimulated in part by a traveling exhibit, "The Precious Legacy," that had highlighted the holdings of the synagogues in the old Jewish ghetto. One day Sylvia's boss called her at home. "Are you Jewish?" he asked. Memories of the problems that had plagued her mother flashed through Sylvia's mind. Had the tourist agency come to know what she had been saying at Theresienstadt? She braced herself for what would come next.

For the first time in the Wittmann family, being Jewish turned out to be an advantage. "We have no other Jewish guides," the head of the agency said. Sylvia was asked to guide Jewish tourists and instruct the other guides not only in answering questions about Theresienstadt but also in these tourists' dietary and cultural requirements.

Spurred by her secret trip to Israel, Sylvia continued her exploration of her Jewish background. She continued to meet with Jewish friends. But when she heard that the secret police had stepped up surveillance of the old synagogue in the center of

Prague, Sylvia stopped going. It had become too dangerous. Sylvia questioned her decision to stay in Prague. Rarely did a day go by when she did not ask herself: Will it ever end?

When it did end, Sylvia was in Paris; Michael had taken her on a sightseeing tour of Europe. She saw the fall of the Berlin Wall on television, and by the time she could get a train back to Prague, the revolution that would topple Communism in Czechoslovakia was well under way. Every night, people streamed into Wenceslas Square to call for the resignation of the Communists. When students went on strike to call for democracy, one of Alena's neighbors cooked for them every night and brought them food. For the first time in decades, Alena said, people are treating each other like people, not wolves.

Standing amid the crowds in Wenceslas Square, the giddiness of freedom enveloping her, Sylvia savored the momentous changes taking place. Unlike her brothers, who had fled Czechoslovakia for freedom, she had stayed. And now, without even leaving Prague, she was stepping into a new world.

# Chapter Fifteen

# Kaddish

Stripped of his pulpit, hounded out of the university town where he had defied the Communists and reenergized Jewish life, forced to live now with his mother in Budapest, Tamas Raj pondered his next move. He filed suit against the official, Communist-controlled Jewish community, saying they had wrongfully seized his apartment in Szeged. Raj's father, a lawyer who knew the head of the Jewish community, spoke to the official Jewish authorities on Raj's behalf to see if his son could get his job back. He was told no. Raj's sister-in-law contacted a cousin who was a Communist judge. "It doesn't matter whether your brother-in-law is right or wrong," the judge told her. "The Communist Party has already decided."

Amid the growing pressure on Raj, his brother Ferenc decided to flee the country. The two rabbis, Ferenc in Budapest, Tamas in Szeged, had together endeavored to keep Jewish life alive, bringing in singers from Israel and even smuggling Jews out to the West through Yugoslavia. Ferenc himself had been denied appointment to the prestigious Dohany Synagogue because of his charismatic appeal. Ever since the Six Day War, the secret police had increased their harassment of Tamas and Ferenc. Unlike his brother, who was not married, Ferenc had a wife and two young children. He felt he could not endanger them any further. In

1977, Ferenc and his family snuck out of Hungary through Yugoslavia and into Italy, following the same path on which he and his brother had sent hundreds of other Jews.

Tamas Raj never considered leaving. He decided to continue teaching Hebrew and Jewish history. Raj had, in a sense, crossed over to a far more dangerous place. No longer a brave young rabbi struggling to keep Judaism alive in Eastern Europe, he was now a dissident.

For a year and a half, Raj looked fruitlessly for work. He was a marked man—unemployable. Finally, he landed a job as an editor with the publishing house run by the Hungarian Academy of Sciences, which was compiling an encyclopedia of literature and a general encyclopedia. His first job was to write entries on famous Jewish writers of the past. Dead Jews were the only Jews the Communists would allow Raj to deal with.

Several times a week, Raj left his apartment and headed for Budapest's main library, a cathedral-like building alongside the Danube. Up the broad staircase, he headed into the main reading room, one of the most extraordinary places in Eastern Europe. As in Czechoslovakia, the Communists in Hungary had purged the universities, publishing houses, and newspapers of anyone suspected of "bourgeois" ideas. Dismissed from their jobs as the Communists cracked down, some of Hungary's most eminent writers now whiled away the time at the library amid the tattered books and manuscripts. Some seemed almost to live there. Raj began to speak with the writers in furtive whispers, continuing in small coffee shops and bars. Several were already well-known dissidents. Others, like Raj, had suddenly found themselves cast adrift. None of them were allowed to publish anymore. Raj began to farm out work to them, assigning them historical entries in the Academy of Sciences encyclopedia—topics so dry and academic that no censor could object. The work helped the men to earn a living and feel useful. Even more important, there, just down the street from Communist Party headquarters, the seeds of Hungary's dissident movement were being sown.

Raj began quietly to teach Hebrew classes in his apartment on

Friday afternoons and Sunday mornings. Anyone giving private language lessons to more than five people had to report the classes to the tax authorities. Raj was sure that if the police got wind of his Hebrew classes, they would use this law to close him down. He spaced his students out so those leaving his apartment would never encounter the group entering. Larger groups were told to dress as if they were coming to a party. Occasionally, they would commandeer a table at a restaurant to burnish the impression that these were just friends eager to unwind after a long day at work.

In 1981, Raj met and married a university student. Raj's reputation as a teacher had spread. Friends of his new wife were eager to sign up for Raj's Hebrew lessons. Raj decided to offer more classes. On the afternoon of his first lesson, he bet his wife that someone would ring the doorbell to ask if he had a room or an apartment to let. It would be the secret police, Raj said, checking on him.

The students arrived and settled in for their lesson. As predicted, the doorbell rang. Indeed, two men were at the door, asking if they could look around; they had heard the apartment was for rent. Raj's wife politely told them they were mistaken. There were no rooms here. The mysterious men went away.

The Hebrew classes expanded Raj's contacts among Hungary's dissidents. He taught the wife of Gyorgy Konrad, Hungary's best-known writer, as well as a well-known Protestant minister who had been dismissed from his church by the Communists. Raj still did not consider himself a dissident. He was a rabbi and a teacher, deprived of his pulpit, continuing to teach as best he could.

Despite Raj's experience, Hungary had become a more liberal country—by Communist standards—than any of the other East Bloc satellites. After nationalizing all small shops in the 1950s—Tamas's grandfather's store among them—the Communists eased up and allowed some privately owned shops to open. What was forbidden in East Berlin and clandestine in Prague was often winked at in Budapest.

The thaw of the 1980s extended to Jewish life as well, and it finally reached Raj. After teaching his private classes for over a decade, Raj was invited to teach modern Hebrew at Budapest's university—the same university to which he had been denied entry thirty years earlier when he had the temerity to praise two Hungarian writers who had fallen into Communist disfavor. Raj began a newspaper column on Jewish life and Jewish subjects, especially the history of the largely Jewish Eighth District, where his parents had grown up and had hidden in a Wallenberg House at the end of World War II. Raj enjoyed cooking, and in 1983 he approached a popular magazine, proposing a series on Middle Eastern food, its focus on the connection between food and culture. In keeping with the prevailing pro-Arab political policy, the editors insisted that the first article be about Arabic cooking. Raj submitted an article on Arab cooking and another on Jewish cooking. That winter the magazine published the first article in the series; on the cover was a picture of gefilte fish.

Raj began to ponder applying for reinstatement as a rabbi. Sandor Scheiber, the elderly head of the rabbinic seminary, had long been a mentor to Raj. The two shared a common desire to sustain and nurture Jewish life among Hungary's young. For years, much as Raj had done in Szeged, Scheiber had hosted Friday-evening gatherings in his Budapest apartment, where young Jews could mingle and talk about Jewish topics. People joked that Scheiber ran the best matchmaking service in town. But now Scheiber was ill, and Raj knew that if he died, Hungary would lose not only a great scholar but a powerful force that held the Jewish community together.

In February 1985, Raj sat down and wrote a letter to Hungary's chief rabbi—a man closely connected to the Communists—applying for "reactivation" as a rabbi. He did not ask for "rehabilitation." He had done nothing wrong. He simply wanted to resume his rabbinic duties. Soon after Raj wrote his letter, Scheiber died. Raj knew that he had lost a powerful ally. The chief rabbi began to speak of closing the seminary. Raj wrote to him again, protesting this and reiterating his request for reinstatement. Then the chief rabbi died as well. Old age was accomplishing what the Communists had been seeking to do for decades—wipe out the Jewish leadership.

That summer Raj was summoned to a meeting of the board of rabbis at the Office of Church Affairs, the Communist bureau he had tussled with so often in Szeged. The rabbis offered Raj his job back if he would admit his past mistakes. He refused. They dangled more attractive offers in front of him—all on the condition that he renounce his activities in Szeged. Raj refused again.

A few weeks later, just days before Rosh Hashanah, the Jewish New Year, the Office of Church Affairs informed Raj that he was being reinstated as a rabbi, assigned to a small synagogue with a leaky roof a few blocks from his house. Two days after Raj was told of his reinstatement, he was visited by two secret policemen. If you don't behave yourself, they told him, you will never advance to a better synagogue. You will remain at this small, leaky synagogue for the rest of your life. Raj said he did not care. All he wanted was to be a rabbi again.

Raj's new congregation was a mirror image of the one he had inherited in Szeged a quarter of a century earlier. Though there were between two and three thousand Jews living in the neighborhood, only a handful of elderly people went to the synagogue. Once again, Raj began by establishing study classes for children. On the first day, five children showed up—Raj's two children and the children of a couple he knew. Within a year, the classes had swelled to a hundred children. As he lectured about the Bible, explaining the stories of Abraham and Isaac and Jacob, God giving the commandments, the Jewish exile in Egypt, the students listened attentively. Behind them sat their parents, taking notes. The generation of Hungarian Jews born right after the war had become cynical like other Hungarians about a system they saw as void of ideas and offering no prospect of a better life. As their children grew and began to ask questions, these Jewish parents found themselves searching for their roots. In the classroom, huddled around small desks, listening to Raj talk in simple terms of the meaning of the seder plate and the lights of Hanukkah, they were rediscovering their Jewish identity.

Visitors from abroad came to Budapest and saw only the nearly empty synagogues and the Communist-controlled Jewish high school, named after Anne Frank, which had but nine students.

But quietly, Jews were meeting, learning, and laughing. At the same time Raj was attracting more and more parents to his classes, teenage Jews were forming discussion groups that met after soccer tournaments. Plans were afoot for an underground magazine devoted to Jewish life. In apartments across the city, young Jews were meeting on Friday nights to discuss Jewish history—an echo of the salon Sylvia Wittmann was running in her Prague living room and of the meeting hall in East Berlin where Gregor Gysi sat around café tables, talking to fellow Jews about Jewish writers and thinkers. On the surface, Jewish life in Hungary looked moribund. But just out of sight, ferment was growing. Younger Jews, those born after World War II, were thirsting for knowledge.

In June 1989, five months before the fall of the Berlin Wall, Hungary took its most dramatic step yet toward liberalization: It agreed to hold a memorial service for the leaders of the 1956 anti-Soviet Hungarian uprising. Young Tamas Raj had watched the street fighting from his parents' apartment overlooking Joseph Boulevard. He had seen the Soviet tanks rumble down the street to crush the Hungarian patriots who had wanted to pull Hungary out of the U.S.S.R.'s orbit and expand freedom. After the invasion, the leaders had been put on trial, summarily convicted and executed, and buried in an unmarked grave outside Budapest. Now, thirty-three years later, under pressure from dissidents, the Communists had agreed to allow a proper burial and memorial service. Rabbi Tamas Raj was invited by the dissidents to say a prayer for one of the leaders of the 1956 uprising, a Jewish Communist who had fallen in the fight against Soviet power.

The ceremony filled a vast, open public square in front of the National Gallery of Art. Six coffins rested on the steps. The building's pillars were wrapped in black. Huge red-green-and-white Hungarian flags draped the museum's neoclassical facade. In each flag, the hammer and sickle, the symbol of Communism, had been cut out of the center, leaving a gaping hole. Somber funeral music flowed from loudspeakers. Two hundred thousand people crammed the square, laying flowers at the base of the coffins, listening to old speeches from the 1956 uprising, paying their last respects. Before the crowd, Raj mounted the rostrum. The crowd quieted as he bowed his head. In the stillness of downtown Budapest, Raj began to speak in Hebrew, reciting the Kaddish.

After twenty years underground, the tables were turned. The Communists had tried to silence him. Now Rabbi Raj stood before a crowd of two hundred thousand, saying Kaddish for Communism itself.

# Chapter Sixteen

# "We Have One Thing to Discuss . . ."

Leokadia had been lying, paralyzed by a stroke, in a Warsaw hospital bed for five and a half weeks. It was early October 1986. Barbara had visited her every day and strained to understand her mother's slurred words.

"We have one thing to discuss . . . ," Leokadia whispered as Barbara hovered by her bedside. "We have one thing to discuss. . . ." Barbara leaned closer. But no matter how hard Leokadia tried, she could not complete her thought. She died on October 19.

Barbara called a priest to administer the last rites, and she buried her mother from the neighborhood church Barbara had attended as a little girl, where her own son, Leokadia's grandson, had been baptized.

Leokadia's death was a blow. But Barbara was honest enough with herself to know that she and her mother had had a difficult relationship. In recent years, the two very different women had drifted further and further apart. Leokadia had always done what she wanted, Barbara felt. She was an impractical daydreamer, who could not control her spending and was always short of money, always. Leokadia frequently came home, out of money, saying it had been stolen; everyone in the family knew she had gambled it away in the state lottery.

Barbara was far more careful and thrifty, planning out moves with deliberation. Life in Poland required patience, and so, methodically and successfully, Barbara had moved from her mother's one-room flat to a room in an aunt's apartment that she shared with her husband and baby son to a small place on the top floor of an apartment block a half hour's drive from the center of Warsaw. For the first time in their married lives, Barbara and her husband had a room of their own—an alcove, really, off the small living room. Their son slept in a small room behind the kitchen. After years of living in one room and sharing a bathroom with neighbors, it was a palace.

Barbara returned from the cemetery to gather her mother's belongings. There wasn't much she wanted to keep—some old photographs, a few pieces of china, a box of papers. On the wood-veneer dining table that took up most of her living room, Barbara began to sort through her mother's papers. There seemed to be little that was remarkable. Then, tucked amid the old bills and documents, Barbara found some ragged pieces of paper—return addresses torn from envelopes. One was from Australia, another from Sweden, a third from Israel. No letters were attached, no hints of the envelopes' contents. Barbara had never heard her mother talk about friends overseas. Still, she decided that since Leokadia had corresponded with these people, they ought to be notified that she had died. She copied the addresses onto fresh envelopes and informed each recipient that Leokadia had died.

Barbara thought no more of it. She returned to her job at the statistical office, where she endlessly processed agricultural production figures. Coming home in the evening, she began to find letters with strange postmarks in her mailbox. The people she had written to were writing back. The letters were strange, cryptic. "We know you but you don't know us," one letter began. "We know everything about you." Another, from Israel, referred to the "blessed late doctor, your father." Barbara assumed they were referring to her stepfather, who had died a few years earlier. But her stepfather had worked as a security guard and night watchman. Her father, of course, had been a Polish resistance fighter killed during the war, when Barbara was a baby.

She puzzled over the letters but pushed them from her mind. Just another of her mother's mysteries, she assumed. Best to leave it alone. Besides, Christmas was approaching, and Barbara looked forward to the time together with her family. On New Year's Day, bright and cold, Barbara's son and daughter-in-law came over for holiday dinner. Barbara had just poured the coffee when the phone rang in the kitchen. It was an overseas call, from Sweden; Maria Wisniewska—Leokadia's Jewish friend, who had fled Poland in 1968 when the Communists denounced her for helping Jews emigrate to Israel—was on the line. Barbara recognized the name from one of the torn envelopes in Leokadia's box.

Barbara had never received an overseas call before. The connection was clear. It sounded as if she were calling from another part of Warsaw.

"All the best for the new year," Maria began. "Thank you for your letter. I knew your mother."

Barbara interrupted her. Would Maria explain the strange references to her father the doctor and tell her who these people were who said they knew all about her?

There was a long pause. "Then I will tell you," Maria blurted out. "Leokadia was not your real mother. Your father was a doctor, and your name is Zajdler. You are a Jew."

Barbara stood in the doorway to her kitchen, clutching the phone. She began to cry. Her daughter-in-law rushed across the small hallway from the living room and tried to grab the phone. Barbara would not let it go. Her whole body was shaking. Maria, on the other end, was trying to comfort Barbara. But Barbara was not listening. She heard the words, but they meant nothing.

As she hung up the phone, dazed, her cries turned to sobs. Huddling around her, her family asked, "What's happened? Who was on the phone?"

Barbara looked around. "I am a Jew," she announced. She turned to her son. "And Granny Lodja, your granny, was not my mother."

Silence descended on the small living room. If Leokadia was not her mother, who was? And if she was not Catholic, but Jewish, what did that mean?

Barbara asked her daughter-in-law to go the very next morning to find some books on Judaism. The Communist-controlled bookstores had nothing, but in a secondhand-book shop, Barbara's daughter-in-law found a copy of *Born in Warsaw*, the reminiscences of a Jewish man who lived in Warsaw before World War II, and a volume of poetry about the Warsaw ghetto.

Barbara began to trace her family. She started with a search for her baptismal certificate, which should have listed her real parents and birthplace. Learning that the church where she had received her first communion and later been married had retained the certificate since her wedding, Barbara, together with her son, her daughter-in-law, and her three-year-old granddaughter, hurried to the church. It was raining heavily, and they arrived dripping wet. A nun told them she would have to get the vicar's permission to show Barbara her baptismal certificate. After a few minutes, the nun returned with a piece of paper. "Well, I can show it to you, because there is nothing in there, nothing special," she said. The certificate recorded Barbara's birth date as December 26, 1943, her place of birth as Warsaw. Barbara's "parents" were Leokadia and her stepfather. It had been signed not by the priest at the church in 1943 but by the priest who had married Barbara nineteen years later. It was all a lie. Barbara remembered now that her mother had not allowed her to have anything to do with planning the wedding, especially discussions with the priests. Leokadia, she realized, must have persuaded the priest to sign a false baptismal certificate.

The nun expressed surprise that Barbara and her family had come rushing to the church in such a downpour. "I'm Jewish," Barbara said. "I'm looking for my past."

"Don't do anything else," the nun cautioned Barbara. "Just say your prayers for this baptism that was never celebrated."

Another envelope soon arrived from Israel. Inside was a letter dated March 4, 1972. It had been written in Polish by Leokadia, in careful script over four pages of paper. There was no indication of who it had been addressed to. But in it were the first glimpses of Barbara's true life story.

Barbara sat down at her table and began to read.

Warsaw, March 4, 1972

Dear Madame,

The letter I received yesterday seemed strange to me. How did you find me? Where do you know Mrs. Zajdler from? This is an old story from 28 years ago, from 1943. This story is known only to me, to a doctor who is already dead, and to Mrs. Zajdler herself, whom I saw only once when she came and kissed the baby and asked me to bring it up as if it were my own baby, since she didn't know what would happen to her and she wanted the baby to survive. And this is the story.

[I married a man named Bruno.] I was in the hospital in Garvolin [a town near Zelechow]. On December 26, 1943, I had a baby daughter, who died immediately afterward. I was mad with despair because the doctor told me I would have no more children. My despair was limitless. On the third day a doctor brought me a baby to nurse because he said her mother had no milk. It brought great happiness to me. At that point I did not think that it was not my own baby but imagined it was mine because she looked very much like my own daughter. At that time my husband was away. He was with a partisan group, so I didn't tell him anything and he was killed three months later and no one knew about this.

On the fourth day the doctor, who was already very old, asked me to come to his room and asked if I wanted to keep the baby as my own baby because he would like this very much because this was the baby of his close friend who was in hiding and his wife wants the baby to survive because she doesn't know what will happen to her and whether she will survive. He told me that they are a Jewish family but very decent and wealthy. I naturally agreed right away. I asked the doctor not to tell anyone about this. When I was leaving the hospital, my mother-in-law came to pick me up with the baby. Just before that, Mrs. Zajdler came to kiss the baby and asked me to raise it as my own. If she survived the disaster either she or somebody from the family would get in touch with me. She knew my maiden name and my married name. She wanted the baby to be called Basia [the Polish diminutive of Barbara]. She gave me a little note on which it said, "E. A. Zajdler, born Szapiro." She was a petite, dark-haired, nice-looking and, one could see, intelligent woman. She begged me to keep the only memento she had with her—a lady's watch with a gold casing. I didn't want to take it. I asked her to keep it because she might still need it. But she didn't want to.

The works of the watch still exist. I think my grandson plays with it. I had the case made into a ring that I gave to Basia and she still has it. I looked for Mrs. Zajdler after the war but in vain. The daughter was christened, with me as the mother, because I had a certificate from the hospital saying that she was my baby with the dates of my baby daughter's birth—December 26, 1943. This difference could have been a few days or none at all.

Basia is with me. She is my dear daughter, and so are my son-in-law and my grandson. They love me dearly too. I have been very sick recently. I have had a very serious operation and I was already near death. I had a letter prepared with the secret, but since I recovered I destroyed the letter, so nobody knows about it and I would not like to cause her distress because I know how much she suffered when I was sick.

If you are Mrs. Zajdler, please contact me but discreetly and we will discuss how to solve this problem. For I understand the heart of the mother who gave birth. But you must also understand me as a mother who has lavished all these feelings on this daughter. If you are Mrs. Zajdler, I suppose you will not want to hurt my daughter's heart or mine. I always hoped that Mrs. Zajdler was dead. And I would tell the secret on my deathbed. But if you are truly Mrs. Zajdler, I would like us both to be able to share their happiness, because she really has a very good husband and a dear son. This is all I can say. Please contact me, but cautiously because of my present husband, who does not know anything about it and also loves the three of them very much. We are very attached to them. I do not work now. I am on pension even though I am 49. But I help them as much as I can, for the young need more than the old.

I close now. Please answer me soon. I am very concerned with all this because I fear I am losing my child although I feel Basia would still love me as she has loved me so far.

Sincerely yours,
Leokadia Pieniazek

At first Barbara was incredulous. Then she remembered the watch. When she was twelve or thirteen, her mother had given her a beautiful gold watch, far nicer than anything else the family had. Leokadia, even when she had little money, always insisted on being nicely dressed, and Barbara had thought it odd, even as a child, that her mother did not wish to wear the elegant timepiece herself.. Inside the box with the watch had been a note that read: "E. A. Zajdler, born Szapiro."

The watch had not worked very well. Barbara had to keep taking it in for repairs. And even though Leokadia had little money, she never complained. At a certain point, the gold rim around the crystal had become loose. The jeweler recommended replacing it with a nickel rim. He offered to turn the gold rim into a ring. Barbara remembered wearing the ring when she turned sixteen. She still had the watch and the ring somewhere in the house. The watch still worked.

Yet there were passages of the letter that Barbara knew were not true. Bruno, already married, had been her mother's lover, although she had sometimes used his name as her own. And Bruno had not died fighting the Nazis. He had returned to Warsaw at the end of the war. Then there was the most maddening mystery of all. To whom had Leokadia sent the letter? Was the anonymous "Madame" Barbara's real mother, the E. A. Zajdler who had turned her three-day-old daughter over to the Catholic Leokadia as she anticipated deportation to the death camps? Had the woman ever written back to Leokadia after receiving this letter? The questions multiplied, but there were no answers—only the story laid out in the four thin pages that Barbara read again and again until she had committed all the details to memory.

In June 1987, six months after her phone call to Barbara's apartment, Maria Wisniewska returned to Poland for the first time since she had fled the country. Barbara met her at the train and brought her home, eager to discover more details about her hidden life. Although Maria had been traveling for twenty-four hours, the two women talked until dawn, Maria spilling out the details of her own experience during World War II—her escape from the ghetto, the Poles' refusal to help her, her son's death.

She spoke of the anti-Semitic campaigns against her and of how she had come to meet Leokadia.

Barbara's mother, she said, had never mentioned anything about her daughter's true identity until Maria had written to Leokadia that she was now living outside Poland. Leokadia had replied to her letter, confessing to Barbara's history. Please, Leokadia had asked, now that Maria was outside Poland, could she write to people in Israel to find out if perhaps the Zajdler family still existed? Had Barbara's mother survived the war? Were there any Zajdler relatives? Over the years, Maria, who had gone first to Australia and then to Sweden, had written to Holocaust archives in Israel and had contacted groups that kept records of concentration camp survivors to find some trace of Barbara's family. She had no luck. In her letters to Leokadia—letters that Leokadia had apparently destroyed except for a few return addresses—she had urged her again and again to tell Barbara the truth. Others in Israel who had heard of the search had apparently written to Leokadia too. But Leokadia had always said it was too great a risk. Her daughter, who had suffered from tuberculosis as a child, was always in such frail health. The shock might be too much.

As the night wore on, Barbara pummeled Maria with questions. Was there anything else she could remember, any clue that could help her trace her real family? So persistent was Barbara that Maria was taken aback. "Are you ashamed of being Jewish?" she asked suddenly.

No, Barbara replied. She just needed to know more.

# Part IV

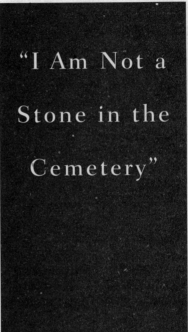

"I Am Not a
Stone in the
Cemetery"

O ver the next few weeks, democratic revolution hurtled through Eastern Europe. The Berlin Wall fell on November 9, 1989. A week later, students marched through the streets of Prague, singing "We Shall Overcome" and demanding the overthrow of the Communists. Ten days later, the Communists had resigned. In Poland, a democratic government endorsed by Lech Walesa assumed power. The speed of events prompted a joyous Vaclav Havel to declare: "In Poland it took ten years, in East Germany ten weeks, in Czechoslovakia ten days!"

By Christmas, the hated tyrant Nicolae Ceauşescu lay dead in Romania. Hungary was planning free elections. In city after city in Eastern Europe, citizens, including Jews, walked the streets with the hesitant steps of people who have been living in a cave and now blinked wide-eyed at the new world around them. Winter had settled in with its bleak days and chill winds, but it felt like spring.

Despite the burgeoning freedom, signs of the disasters that had befallen Jews over the decades in these countries were everywhere. On Oranienburger Strasse in East Berlin, the crumbling shell of the once great synagogue stood surrounded by plywood walls, its windows still shattered from the Kristallnacht pogrom. In more than fifty years, no one had bothered to sweep up the glass inside.

Poland was a land of silences and empty spaces. There was no relic of the old Warsaw ghetto; everything had been leveled by the war and new construction. In villages, questions about Jews were met with mute stares. The remnants of graveyards were all that were left.

After forty-five years, the Iron Curtain had been lifted, allowing Westerners a first uncensored glimpse of the fate of Jews on the other side. American reporters fanned out across Eastern Europe. We all, it seemed, were filing stories with titles like: "The Last Jews of Eastern Europe," "The Last Jews of Warsaw," "The Last Jews of Prague."

What had happened to the Jewish underground that had flourished in the 1980s? Where were the young Jews who had flocked to Sylvia Wittmann's literary salons and Tamas Raj's illicit Hebrew classes? Where was the underground Jewish choir in Prague and the Jewish group Gregor Gysi had visited in East Berlin? Were these all casualties of the fall of the Berlin Wall, like hothouse flowers that could not survive the open air of freedom?

In March 1990, six months after the fall of the Berlin Wall, I went back to Budapest. My translator, who was Jewish, urged me to take a detour to visit a new Jewish nursery school. We stepped through the shabby door. The inside was a riot of color. Children were scurrying across brightly swept floors, drawing pictures for Purim on green and red construction paper. Their bright eyes looked up and greeted us. The teachers hustled their charges down the hallway with gentle prodding. Blue-and-white Jewish stars decorated many doors; posters of Israel filled the stairwell walls. The school was oversubscribed—not just with Jewish children but with the children of Christian Hungarians who had heard that Jews knew something about education. The teachers taught a regular curriculum but also Jewish tradition and Hebrew. Most of the parents were not religious. Many were sons and daughters of Communists. But they wanted to give their children the education they had never had. When the teachers spoke about the holidays, they had to add dozens of chairs, because huddled behind the children, listening to storybooks and following every word, were their parents, many of whom had taken time off from work to come to the school.

In Prague, the Jewish Town Hall and the neighboring Jewish community building had been transformed. The official Jewish leadership, long in thrall to the Communist Party, had been voted out of office. The buildings bustled with activity. Six months earlier, before the "Velvet Revolution," I had visited Prague's only kosher restaurant, housed in a former synagogue. I had shared an empty, cavernous room with a tourist couple from Germany. Now the dining room was packed. Lively dinner chatter competed with the clanking of china and silverware as waiters hustled between tables crowded with Prague Jews and tourists, the waiters' trays laden with chicken soup, brisket, and potatoes. Upstairs, cartons of Hebrew-language texts were being opened. The Jewish choir, underground for seven years, had been invited to sing at Prague City Hall. In an appropriately dramatic gesture for a man who had gained fame as a playwright, President Vaclav Havel appointed as the new Czech ambassador to the Soviet Union the son of Rudolf Slansky, who had been executed on Stalin's order as a "Zionist agent."

In Warsaw, the editor of the newest and most influential newspaper, *Gazetta Wyborca,* was Adam Michnik, the revered Jewish intellectual and dissident whose protest at Warsaw University in 1968 had sparked the Communist government's anti-Semitic purge that had caused thousands of Jews to flee Poland. Michnik had become one of Lech Walesa's top advisers in the new Polish parliament; the head of the Foreign Affairs Committee was Bromeslaw Geremek, another Jewish adviser to Walesa.

Jews were reappearing in top positions in other countries as well. In Romania, Peter Roman, the grandson of a rabbi, was chosen as prime minister. And Gregor Gysi was beginning to step even further into the political spotlight.

Like many of my fellow reporters, I set out to write an obituary about Jews in Germany and Eastern Europe. Now, I suddenly realized, I was writing a birth announcement.

# Chapter Seventeen

# "How Can I Be Attacked for Something I Can't Help?"

In the new world created by the fall of the Berlin Wall, the pace of events had stepped up dramatically. East Germany was near collapse, and the drive to reunify the country was becoming irresistible.

And the new head of the East German Communist Party was a Jew—Gregor Gysi.

Gregor's speech five days before the Berlin Wall fell had catapulted him to center stage. A few weeks after his speech, Gregor stepped forward again and, in a rally in front of the Communist Central Committee headquarters in East Berlin, called for the resignation of the Communist leadership.

The next day, Gregor was handed a note summoning him to a meeting at Central Committee headquarters. He expected a rebuke. "What the country needs now is peace and stability and no experiments at the top," he imagined them reprimanding him.

Instead the Communists asked Gregor to be their savior. The Politburo, discredited, had resigned. Allegations were surfacing about lush villas in the East German forests for party leaders, private hunting preserves, foreign bank accounts stuffed with cash. The Communist Party was in a state of near panic. It was hemorrhaging members, thousands of whom, disillusioned, were sending in their party cards, resigning from the party that had ruled East

Germany for almost forty-five years. Gysi entered the cavernous lobby of Communist headquarters and was escorted to a room filled with smoke and people he did not know. There, he was asked if he was available to take over as the new head of the Communist Party. He was stunned. Several party leaders urged him to accept. As a lawyer well known for defending dissidents, he would have credibility, they argued. As a critic of the regime in the past few weeks, he would distance the party from the collapse of the Politburo. He was still a loyal, card-carrying Communist, they pointed out. Without him, who knew what chaos would unfold.

Gregor faced the same choice his father had confronted at the end of the war. He was a smart, shrewd man with a reputation as a defender of dissidents. He could easily mail in his party card and return to his law practice. Or he could join one of the new political parties, untainted by Communists, formed by the dissidents he had defended. Or he could sign on with the left-of-center West German Social Democrats, who were scouring East Germany for young, charismatic recruits they hoped could help them in what was sure to be a united Germany.

But Gregor, though he had rebelled against the leaden hand of East Germany's leaders, was still a leftist and a Communist. He was still repelled by the excesses of West Germany and believed in the dream of a Socialist, egalitarian society.

For him, the entire Communist movement had been interlocked with the history of his family since the 1920s, when his grandmother Erna joined the party because of its early support of abortion and women's rights. His mother and father had worked underground for the Communists during the war and served it loyally since then. Gregor had been groomed to succeed in the best Communist institutions: the Young Communist League, Humboldt University and its law school. The thickheaded, dictatorial leaders of East Germany had discredited Socialism, Gregor believed. They had tarnished his father's and his grandmother's dream of utopia. Now Gregor had the chance to restore the shine to Socialism, to show that the political ideology that had entranced his family for more than sixty years was still solid at its core.

Perhaps most important, Gregor, like his father, was drawn to power and to the spotlight—to the center stage of publicity. Klaus had always doubted Gregor's mettle. Even now, as Gregor pondered his decision, his father scoffed, "How can this disorganized guy be party chairman?" By accepting the Communist Party's offer of leadership at age forty-one—an age when his father had just begun *his* climb up the cultural hierarchy in East Germany— Gregor could lay to rest once and for all questions about his seriousness of purpose. He would be stepping onto the world stage at the moment of Communism's greatest crisis.

And so Gregor agreed. He put on a blue worker's cap that contrasted incongruously with his lawyerly blue suits. At the party congress in late 1989, he was elected by 90 percent of the vote and presented with a broom representing a "clean sweep." Journalists and photographers pressed in on him like cattle to a feeding trough. "Do you feel you are a Communist?" a reporter shouted at him. Gregor hesitated, then, showing the fast thinking that had served him well in the courtroom, he replied, "The Communist utopia hasn't been achieved yet. But the term tends to be misunderstood. So in order not to be misunderstood myself, I prefer to call myself a Democratic Socialist." Within months, the Communist Party had renamed itself the Party of Democratic Socialism.

The torch had been passed within the Gysi family. An artist visiting Klaus presented him with a cartoon he had drawn. It pictured Klaus and his older friends, heads in hands around the dining room table, trying to puzzle out how everything in East Germany had all gone so terribly wrong. Off to the side, the artist drew a caricature of "little Gregor," wearing a worker's cap, carrying high the "red banner" of the Communist Party. The older generation had failed, was the unspoken message of the cartoon. With East Germany's first free elections scheduled in a few months, the future now rested with Gregor and his contemporaries.

Gregor's Jewish background was noted immediately in every article or television report about him, especially in the United States. His backers saw several political advantages to letting Gregor's Jewishness be known. The parties running against the

Communists in East Germany's first free elections might restrain their campaigns, for fear of being accused of anti-Semitism. It might also increase Jewish support, internally as well as abroad, for halting, or at least slowing down, the reunification of Germany.

Gregor played the "Jewish card" deftly. In meetings with German Jewish groups, he emphasized his opposition to unification, summoning up memories of Germany's past. He encouraged several American Jewish groups to help stop the rapid drive for unification. In his first speech as head of the Communist Party, he announced that the party's policy toward Israel would change. He called for restoring East German diplomatic relations with the Jewish state, which had been broken in 1967 after the Six Day War, and announced that he himself would visit Israel.

Some of Gregor's initiatives were heartfelt. He had long been bothered by the way older East Germans tried to find small justifications for having done nothing to stop Nazi crimes, or even for participating in them. An elderly typist had once told Gregor that it was wrong the Nazis gassed the Jews, but it was also wrong that the Jews always pushed to the front of the line in the shops. Gregor's Jewish background was beginning to receive a lot of attention. He joked that suddenly everyone knew about his Jewish ancestors but no one seemed to know about his mother's mother, a noblewoman of great prominence in turn-of-the-century Saint Petersburg. "I'd like to read about myself also being blue-blooded, for a change," he observed wryly.

Gregor was turning out to be a skilled and cunning politician. Like his father, he was not above using his religion, deploying it as a weapon. It never occurred to Gregor, in those early, heady days after the fall of the Berlin Wall, that his Jewish background could become a weapon that would be turned against him.

The first catcalls came at a rally in Dresden. Gregor had just begun campaigning for the elections that would be held in a few months, in March 1990. "Jews out!"—the words hit him like stones. Across Germany, the fall of the Berlin Wall was unleashing a surge in anti-Semitism and attacks on foreigners. The head of East Germany's tiny Jewish community received anti-Semitic letters. Several Jewish cemeteries in East Germany were defaced with swastikas. Someone sent a severed goat's head to the synagogue in Leipzig. Soon the floodgates opened. In Dresden, more than five hundred neo-Nazis with shaved heads and jackboots marched through the streets, their arms lifted in the Nazi salute; beating drums, they chanted, "Foreign pigs, we'll get you all!" In Stuttgart, West Germany, vandals ripped out seven tombstones at a Jewish cemetery and spray-painted them with black swastikas.

The outbreak of anti-Semitism seemed insane. East Germany was a country with virtually no Jews; in reunited Germany, Jews made up less than 0.1 percent of the country's population. But still the attacks continued. Soon they expanded to include foreigners, immigrants, anyone who was "different." In Dresden, a man from Mozambique was thrown to his death from a trolley car. In Leipzig, a Vietnamese was stabbed to death. In September 1991, right-wing extremists laid siege to an apartment building in Hoyerswerda, near the Polish border. The building was full of refugee families, mostly from Mozambique and Vietnam. The extremists tossed bottles and Molotov cocktails through the windows, while several hundred German townspeople looked on, doing nothing. The refugees fled. By the end of 1991, there had been more than two thousand right-wing attacks. Seventeen people had been killed.

Intellectually, Gregor understood what was behind the rise of anti-Semitism and nationalism. East Germans were scared. Their country had collapsed. Millions were being told they would be put out of work, that their factories were too inefficient to compete with West German factories. People were angry and confused. Unification was happening too quickly. People felt politically, psychologically, and morally marginalized. They were being told by West Germans that their system was all wrong, that they had never learned to work properly, that they had all collaborated with the secret police. For some, especially young people searching for an identity, right-wing extremism offered a chance to lift their self-esteem at the expense of others. Jews and foreigners provided convenient scapegoats.

But that these anti-Semitic attacks were being focused on him, the new head of the reformed Communist Party, shocked Gregor. He had been caught unawares. He did not really consider himself Jewish. It would have been understandable if the skinheads on the fringe of the Dresden crowd had shouted "Socialists out!" or "Communists out!" But this was incomprehensible. Gregor, puzzled and hurt, complained to his top adviser, André Brie, whose father was also Jewish. "I can understand people attacking me for my views. But how can I be attacked for something I can't help?"

It was an eerie echo of Klaus Gysi's dilemma fifty years earlier when he had been forced to go into hiding in Berlin. Klaus had always insisted to his children that he faced the greatest danger because he was a Communist, not because he was a Jew. Gregor always believed this distinction was important to his father because being a Communist was something Klaus could control, while being Jewish was something he could not. Now Gregor faced the same predicament. He wanted to be admired, criticized, or attacked for what he believed, not for what he was.

The catcalls in Dresden were just the start. Gregor began receiving anti-Semitic mail and threats. He now traveled the country with bodyguards. One evening Gregor attended a reception given by the Israeli ambassador in Bonn. The ambassador came up to Gregor. "Strangely enough, since you are in Bonn, I've been getting less anti-Semitic mail," the ambassador said.

At rallies and meetings, Gregor found more and more evidence of the rage against foreigners that was tearing through Germany, especially among young people. Confronting one young thug in East Germany, Gregor berated him, saying that if he really wanted to change things, he should turn against the big German banks and overthrow the monopoly structure of capitalism. "Well, *you* change the monopoly structure," the skinhead replied. "And while you are busy doing that, I'll kick out the Vietnamese and take their jobs and apartments."

Despite his concern about the anti-Semitic attacks, Gregor turned out to be a masterful campaigner. In a country not known for its sense of humor, he entertained campaign crowds and television audiences with an acerbic and self-deprecating wit. Asked what it would be like to be on the same stage as Helmut Kohl, the bear-like, three-hundred-pound chancellor of Germany, the rapid-talking Gregor replied, "There would be only one problem. You wouldn't see much of me and wouldn't hear much of him." Asked by a magazine how he would describe himself to a blind woman, the short, balding Gregor replied, "Tall, with a wonderful head of blond curls."

He loved to tell jokes about the presumed hopelessness of the Communist cause. "A Communist Party executive discusses the election situation and decides that a miracle has to happen," he began. "After a lot of thought, someone says that Gregor Gysi must walk on water. Gregor groans, but he gives in. And he goes to a lake one summer Sunday. As crowds gather, Gregor steps onto the water and walks across. 'Typical Communists,' grumbles one voter loudly. 'They can't even swim.'"

As with his father, Gregor's appeal flowed from what he was not. Most Germans, conditioned by decades of seeing dour-faced apparatchiks, expected another boring Communist. What they got instead was a witty and sophisticated man, never at a loss for a clever answer or a joke. His campaign poster, harking back to his days as a dissident lawyer in East Germany, declared him a lawyer for democracy. More accurately, Gregor was a lawyer pleading for leniency for his clients. Punish the Communists by not returning them to power, he argued. But give them enough votes to make sure that they will still speak up against the excesses of the ruling class. "Governments are replaceable; opposition is not," Gregor declared to roaring crowds. "Every decent German has to vote for the Party of Democratic Socialism at least once in his life. Vote for us in this election. Then you have it over with, and it helps us."

Gregor recognized the foreboding many East Germans felt toward the new world that awaited them. What was happening was not unification but an "Anschluss," Gregor declared—a loaded word that recalled memories of Hitler's annexation of Austria. "Unity requires unification," he argued. "Unification requires thinking about the other side and doing away with differences as best as possible. Anschluss just forces one side to submit to the system of the other side. That leads to more differences and little in common."

Gregor's goal was modest. There was no hope that the Communists would win a majority in the series of elections that followed the fall of the Berlin Wall. His hope was to stop the Communists from disappearing completely. That meant winning enough votes—more than 5 percent—to gain a few seats in the unified German parliament. Germany's other political parties were nearly united in their appeals to deprive the Communists of any representation. But as the results poured in, Gregor saw he had achieved his small miracle. He had won election representing a gritty section of eastern Berlin, crammed with impersonal, towering apartment blocks. It was far removed from the six-room house with a garden that he had known as a child, but it fitted his new image as a crusader for the poor and struggling East Germans. The reform Communists would indeed be part of the opposition in a new, united Germany. And their party leader, taking his seat as the only Jewish member of parliament, would be Gregor Gysi.

A few days after the election, Klaus Gysi telephoned his son. Klaus was quite emotional. Gregor was surprised—and a little embarrassed—by the conversation. It was not like his father at all. "Thank you," the seventy-nine-year-old Klaus told his son. "You have given my life new meaning."

# Chapter Eighteen

# Not Jewish Death but Jewish Life

Estrongo Nachama had always drifted above politics. It was true that in 1985, disgusted with Ronald Reagan's visit to the Bitburg cemetery, where several members of the Waffen SS had been buried, he had refused to sing for the President of the United States at a memorial service at Bergen-Belsen concentration camp. That had been pretty much the extent of his political involvement. But now this! Neo-Nazi criminals were marching through Dresden, brandishing swastikas. They were desecrating Jewish cemeteries and synagogues, scrawling words like "Jews out!" and "Jews bite the dust!" At Nachama's office at the headquarters of the West Berlin Jewish community, letters were arriving that read: "Jews are good people, but not here." Police with metal detectors at the Pestalozzi Strasse synagogue were confiscating knives and other weapons from German "visitors" who said they just wanted to see the service.

Estrongo and Lilian had been happy the night they flipped on the television and heard the Berlin Wall had fallen. They were happy for the Jews in the East who could now travel and speak freely. The night after the wall fell, Estrongo drove to Pestalozzi Strasse as usual to prepare the choir for Friday-night services. The choir was made up almost exclusively of Germans, of non-Jews. They had formed a strong personal bond with Estrongo over the years. As services began downstairs, Estrongo stayed upstairs with the choir for their final preparation. Down below, West Berlin's Jewish leaders were addressing the congregation. They warned of the dangers of a reunified Germany, the horrible crimes that a united Germany had committed in the past. The members of the choir shifted uncomfortably in their chairs. Nachama waved his hands dismissively. "Don't pay any attention to that," he said.

Estrongo even understood the anger in East Germany. In the months after the wall fell, he continued to travel there, singing at funerals in Erfurt, Dresden, Halle. On the train, at every cere- mony, East Germans would complain to him, Jews and non-Jews alike, about how they had lost their jobs, their job protection, their meager social security, as inefficient factories closed. Prices were rising. No one, certainly not Estrongo, had any illusions about the oppressive, dictatorial nature of East Germany. But at least under Communism people were guaranteed jobs. Now the young people had no hope for the future. A man without work, Estrongo believed, is a dead man, a man without hope, and one easily swayed into looking for scapegoats.

But the scope of the attacks, the explosion of violence in East and West Germany, unnerved Estrongo. It rekindled his fear of Germans. "This is what they are like," he began telling Lilian. "One starts the violence, and they all follow." Germany was losing its bearings. In Rostock, a port city on the Baltic coast in East Germany, a crowd of five hundred Germans, chanting "Sieg Heil," threw Molotov cocktails and rocks at an apartment building that housed Romanian refugees. More than a thousand townspeople cheered the extremists on. Romanians and Vietnamese fled the town in terror. Estrongo recalled something his father used to say: "Once the straw burns, the grass will too." The foreigners were the straw in Germany now; the Jews were the grass. They were the next target.

Estrongo believed it was time for his son, Andreas, and his young family to leave the country. The United States or Canada or Israel, he did not care where they went. Lilian wanted to leave Berlin too, but Estrongo thought they were both too old. The young, though, should pack up and move away. Yes, there were thugs in other countries too, but they were marginal, they didn't matter. Not like Germany, where violence, once somebody starts it, sweeps the country.

Andreas was not ready to leave. He was forty years old and well respected among both Jews and historians in Berlin. To be sure, Andreas had made sure that his sons, young teenagers, had learned English. They went frequently to the United States; the boys would feel comfortable there. Andreas's wife, as the daughter of an Israeli diplomat, had lived around the world; uprooting herself would be nothing new. But neither Andreas nor Sara was ready to abandon the new Germany.

Andreas was more cosmopolitan than his father, and his experience of Judaism had been more cosmopolitan. His mother had come from the cultured Berlin Jewish aristocracy. He had other relatives who had grown up in the shtetls of Eastern Europe and survived the Holocaust. His wife's family had gone to Israel from India. Andreas himself spent many Friday nights, after Shabbat services, with Jewish soldiers at the American army base in West Berlin, hearing stories of Jewish life in America. West German discussion of Jewish life, Andreas felt, had always focused on the Jews of Eastern Europe and Germany and ended with images of the massacre at Babi Yar, or the endless deportation lists, or the trains leaving for Auschwitz. Andreas wanted to show the new generation of Germans more of Jewish life, to focus less on the destruction than on what had been destroyed. And to show that even in the 1980s there were Jews like himself who lived a Jewish life, not just a life defined by the experience of the Holocaust.

Just a few months after the fall of the Berlin Wall, with right-wing violence and anti-Semitism erupting across Germany, Andreas mounted a massive exhibit at the Gropius Building—where "Topography of Terror" had planted its seed. This new exhibit was not about Jewish death but about Jewish life and culture. From across the world, Andreas gathered objects that showed the many faces of Judaism, from the Middle East to Germany to the United States. A tapestry of Jewish life, from its origins to the present day, described Jewish communities in far-flung places such as Yemen and India, as well as better-known enclaves in Europe and the United States. The Holocaust was treated as part of the Jewish story, not its end. Some criticized Andreas for not dealing more fully with the Holocaust. But there was no shortage of discussion of Jewish death in Germany, he believed. He wanted to celebrate Jewish life.

Yet even as Andreas presided over his exhibit, he discovered that the ghosts of the Holocaust and the battle over memory in Germany would not die. He was asked to join a national panel to decide what to do with the concentration camps located in East Germany. The East Germans had treated them scandalously, turning them into propaganda machines that minimized Jewish suffering and exalted the role of the Communists in combating Hitler. The worst was Buchenwald, located just on the outskirts of Weimar, up the road from a still standing hotel where Goethe and Bach once stayed. Buchenwald was not founded as a death camp, although tens of thousands died there. It was a camp for German Communists, social democrats, criminals, and clergymen. Thousands of Soviet prisoners of war had been brought to the camp and brutally executed—shot in the back of the head in the infirmary as they were told to lean against a wall for an "examination." Behind the wall were soldiers, who shot the POWs through holes drilled for that purpose. Few Jews were sent to Buchenwald, because Jews were being shipped directly to the Nazi killing centers in Poland. But as the Nazis began losing the war in 1944 and retreating, tens of thousands of half-dead Jews were marched into Buchenwald, exhausted from transports. Elie Wiesel had been one of these.

Yet Jews were barely mentioned at Buchenwald—a fact made worse because for fifty years the camp was the centerpiece of education in East Germany. The Communists required every East German schoolchild to visit there. A small marker commemorating Jewish victims stood in the left-hand portion of the camp. But upon entering, students were immediately taken to the right, to a reconstructed bunker that showed graphically how the Soviet soldiers had died. A monument was also built to show where Ernst Thälmann, a prominent German Communist leader, was killed. At no point during the tour were Jews mentioned. At the camp warehouse, they told the story of a young boy who had been hidden beneath piles of clothes. They never said that he was Jewish, or that he had later fled to Israel. The centrality of anti-Semitism to Hitler's ideology, the systematic annihilation of the Jews, the complicity of Germans, including those now living in East Germany, was erased. Hitler had been brought to power by "capitalists" and big business, not by Germans. "From the very beginning," declared the Communist guidebook to Buchenwald, "the proclaimed aims of the German Fascists were the elimination of Marxism, revenge for the last war, and a brutal terror campaign against everyone who stood in their way. Their aims were congruent with those of big business, which supported the Nazi movement generally. With its support, the Fascists came to power in 1933 and immediately began to crush the working-class movement which was the main obstacle to their plans." For East Germans, World War II was not Hitler's war against the Jews; it was his war against the Communists.

Clearly, Andreas concluded, the exhibits at Buchenwald had to be scrapped and completely redone. The true history of the Holocaust had to be told. But before Andreas and the panel of historians could begin discussing how to redo the camps, workers digging around Buchenwald and other concentration camps in East Germany discovered mass graves—of German prisoners. After the end of World War II, invading Soviet forces had turned the concentration camps in East Germany into prison camps for opponents of Communism. In Buchenwald, they ordered the American liberators to withdraw, as had been agreed by Roosevelt and Stalin and Churchill, and proceeded to fill the camp with German prisoners. Some of the prisoners were Nazis being held while they awaited trial in East Germany or the Soviet Union for war crimes. But the camps soon expanded to include victims of Stalinist terror.

Discovery of the graves created a sensation. Families of the East German victims quickly formed committees demanding that the new histories of Buchenwald and other camps recognize and commemorate the postwar history of Soviet terror. Suddenly the dominant issue facing Andreas and his fellow commission members was not how to deal with the history of Hitler's crimes but what to do about the Germans who had been imprisoned and killed after the war.

Andreas then traveled to Sachsenhausen, where another mass grave had been discovered. It was here, just outside Berlin, that his father had spent his final days as a Nazi concentration camp victim, twenty-seven years old, shriveled down to a mere sixty-five pounds, forced to gorge on a dog's food to survive. Families of Germans imprisoned by the Soviets were demanding a separate memorial to their relatives. Some non-Jewish members of the history panel wanted to create two exhibits—one dealing with the camp during the war and one to deal with its postwar history. Andreas was furious. "The proposed exhibits will invite Germans to compare how they suffered with how the Jews suffered," he declared. Andreas questioned whether many of them were victims at all. Some had been Nazi collaborators, who had deserved imprisonment after the war.

The more Andreas and other Jews raised objections, the louder and angrier their opponents became. With anti-foreign sentiment rising and anti-Semitic demonstrations spreading, many began to attack Andreas personally, saying that this historian, who had developed "Topography of Terror," whose father had survived Sachsenhausen, was "not suitable" to decide how to tell Sachsenhausen's history to future generations in Germany.

One Saturday, Andreas and Sara, with their two boys, climbed the stairs to their parents' apartment for coffee and pastries. Estrongo asked his son what was happening at Sachsenhausen. Andreas told him about the demands for a separate memorial. Furious, Estrongo began to curse the Germans. At meetings of the historians' panel, Andreas had to make sure he handled himself professionally. But here at his father's house, he faced the pain and rage of Jewish victims through his own father's violent reactions.

Andreas began receiving letters at work, denouncing him and his position.

"I object to the appointment of Andreas Nachama," one letter began, "who had the impertinence to say that after 1945 there was no one who wasn't guilty. This is an insult to all victims [of the Communists], alive or dead. As an ex-prisoner of the Gulag No. 7 Special Camp [in the Soviet Union], I vigorously protest against this brazen accusation made against all reason. I judge Andreas Nachama unsuitable . . ."

As a historian, Andreas knew that anyone who had been deported to the Soviet Union after the war had most likely been a high-ranking collaborator of the Nazis. What shocked him most was that these letters were not anonymous. They came complete with full names and addresses.

The walls that Estrongo and Lilian had built around their son were crumbling. Slowly Andreas realized that, at forty, living in Germany, he had never met a real Nazi. Andreas was not naive. He knew about the subterranean anti-Semitism that some Germans maintained. But he had grown up in a cloistered environment, surrounded by other Jews and by people who had helped his mother hide in Berlin during the war. West Germany, too, had largely kept anti-Semitism out of public discourse for forty-five years. But now, in a united Germany, German nationalism was reasserting itself more and more openly.

Increasingly, Andreas pondered his future in the new Germany. Perhaps his father was right. Sixty years earlier, on the eve of Hitler's ascent to power, Andreas's maternal grandparents had thought of themselves as German Jews. They were both German and Jewish, neither in any way inimical to the other. That identity, that sense of themselves, had been their undoing. He remembered how Siegfried, his grandfather, had refused to flee Germany. And two years later, in 1938, Siegfried committed suicide as he saw how the country he had loved and risked his life for had turned on him.

The Holocaust, Andreas felt, had forever eliminated the category "German Jew." He and his fellow Jews were now Jews in Germany—always apart from society, always examining their homeland with a watchful, wary eye. He looked at the rise of Gregor Gysi and thought of the fifty thousand other Gregor Gysis who should have been in Germany, shaping the country's cultural, intellectual, and political life.

While he turned these thoughts over in his mind, Andreas was asked by a German television station if he would move to New York as their American correspondent. It would be a chance not only to increase his visibility but to take his wife and family away from the ugly wave of anti-Semitism and right-wing violence that was engulfing Germany. Just then, the organizers of the "Topography of Terror" exhibit offered him a promotion. They asked him to become the museum's director and supervise construction of a new, larger museum they planned on the old Gestapo site.

Like Germany, the area around "Topography of Terror" had changed dramatically with the fall of the Berlin Wall. At its inception, the exhibit was housed on one of the most desolate landscapes in Berlin. The Berlin Wall ran along one side, its presence preventing any commercial construction. The surrounding area was a ruined landscape, dotted with parking lots and abandoned buildings. Potsdamer Platz, a few blocks away, once the busiest square in Germany, was deserted. Now, with the wall gone, plans were afoot to redevelop the entire area as Berlin's new business district. Sony, Daimler-Benz, and other major companies had hired architects. The entire German government would soon be moving its government buildings nearby.

It was a stark choice. Andreas could flee Germany and take up life in New York, making the choice that his mother's family should have made sixty years before. Or he could stay and cast his lot with the new Germany, dedicating his life to preserving the memory of the Holocaust and teaching that history to the reunited country's new citizens.

Andreas walked along the streets leading to "Topography of Terror" and envisioned how the new exhibit would mesh with the commercial environment that would soon surround it—the bustling office towers, the business executives hurrying to the subway. The area would be abuzz with activity and the gleam of steel and marble. And then, abruptly, Germans would come across this still barren site, a vacant swath of dirt. Below it were the old cells of the Gestapo, every concrete wall and pillar pulsing with the stark story of the Nazis and the terror of the Holocaust. How appropriate, Andreas thought. It would be like an open wound in the heart of the new Germany. He decided to stay.

Around the time of Andreas's decision, the anti-Semitic attacks unleashed by the fall of the Berlin Wall began to recede, and with them Andreas's and Estrongo's anxiety. The bitter debates over the fate of the concentration camps continued to simmer. For Buchenwald, Andreas agreed to a compromise that would set up a path around the perimeter of the concentration camp, leading through a grove of trees to a clearing beyond. There, a plaque would state that this was the site where Germans were killed and buried—separate and distinct from the concentration camp itself. A similar plan would eventually quell the debate at Sachsenhausen, Andreas believed.

Andreas recalled a conversation he had with West Berlin's rabbi when he was thirteen and preparing for his bar mitzvah. The wall had gone up just two years before. The Jewish community was elderly and dying. Andreas's was one of the few bar mitzvahs celebrated that year. The rabbi had pronounced his obituary for the Jewish community: "Today we have five thousand, six thousand Jewish community members. But in the year 2000—when you are fifty—God help us there will be only eight hundred Jews in Berlin. All the rest will be dead."

But now, as the year 2000 approached, there were more than ten thousand Jews in Berlin, fifty thousand in Germany. Jews from Russia were pouring into the city since the fall of the wall. Berlin's renewed position as one of Europe's most prominent cities was also attracting increasing numbers of Jews. On Oranienburger Strasse in East Berlin, the grand synagogue was being reconstructed. In the former Jewish quarter around the synagogue, trendy cafés were opening, with names like Solomon and Tacheles—Yiddish for "Let's talk turkey." After being closed by the Nazis in 1938, the Jewish high school in Berlin reopened its doors. Andreas decided to stay because he could see a Jewish future in Germany. The Nazis had been defeated, the Communists toppled from power. But the Jewish people lived on.

# Chapter Nineteen

# House of Blessing

Sylvia Wittmann had gone into business. She drove through the streets of Prague, pulling flyers from the pile on the back seat of her old car and taping them on walls in the old Jewish quarter and in the big hotels that catered to tourists. "Wittmann Tours," the leaflets announced. "Tours to the Old Jewish Quarter, the Jewish Cemetery, Kafka's Grave, and the Terezin Concentration Camp."

The "Velvet Revolution" of 1989 opened to the outside world the jewel box that was Prague and offered Sylvia an opportunity to go into business for herself. Quitting the Communist-controlled tourist agency, she began to handle Jewish tour groups directly. She set up a small office in the basement of her apartment building and bought herself a Western-made fax machine. After all the years of clandestine meetings in her living room, of learning her mother's history in whispers, Sylvia found there had never been a better time to be Jewish and in Prague.

Sylvia herself was intoxicated with the new freedom. She pondered becoming a rabbi. Then, one morning, she stepped through the door to her basement office and was greeted by her assistant, a friend who was helping her arrange Jewish tours.

"Hail, comrade," Sylvia's friend said. It was the greeting that Communists used to give each other. Sylvia and her acquaintances often made fun of it.

"Hail, comrade," Sylvia answered back.

"Have you seen the paper?" Her friend handed Sylvia a copy of a scandal sheet, one of Prague's multiplying new newspapers. Inside was a list of secret police informers supposedly copied from newly opened files.

Sylvia's name was on the list. Her friend looked at her, not saying a word. Sylvia was dumbstruck, then angry.

Slowly, then heatedly, she began to tell her story.

After the Berlin Wall fell, it was estimated that in East Germany, sixteen million people—one out of four—had worked as an informer for the secret police. In Prague, the secret police had wooed informers everywhere, tempting them and threatening them into providing information. The police would summon citizens just to "talk" with them. Every word was put to use. The secret police in Czechoslovakia were like vacuum cleaners, sucking up enormous amounts of information in an effort to keep people under control.

The police had first approached Sylvia in 1978, when she was twenty-two years old. Her brothers had already fled the country—Michael after the Soviet invasion in 1968; Robert in 1978, after signing the dissident manifesto Charter 77. Her mother's imprisonment in the 1950s was well known to the Communist authorities.

The summons came in a plain envelope delivered to the Wittmanns' apartment. Sylvia was ordered to appear at a police station several miles away. Stepping through the door, she was confronted by a large picture of Felix Dzerzhinsky, the feared founder of what would become the Soviet KGB. A team of two interrogators took her into a room and began questioning her about Robert. Who were his friends? With whom did he associate? As they had with her mother twenty-five years earlier, the interrogators played the Communist version of good cop–bad cop. One was arrogant, aggressive, impatient; the other smiled and tried to endear himself to Sylvia. He is pretending, Sylvia thought, that he would like to date me.

The interrogation went on for hours. Sylvia was given nothing to eat or drink. The "bad cop" warned Sylvia that her pet dog was dangerous and the police might have to kill it. He told her she would never be allowed out of Czechoslovakia to visit her brothers. "I'm much more interested in Mongolia and China and the Soviet Union, because I like Oriental culture," Sylvia said, swatting away their threats. But in fact Sylvia was terrified.

The interrogators let her go but warned that they were not finished with her. Sylvia rushed home and told her mother what had happened. Alena picked up the summons that had arrived in the mail and copied down the name of the official who had signed it: Vondracek—the aggressive interrogator, who had threatened and intimidated Sylvia. Alena had a plan.

Vondracek began calling Sylvia's home, demanding to speak with her. Alena kept saying her daughter was not home. Vondracek grew more and more impatient. Finally, Alena announced to her daughter, "Enough is enough. We can't say for a year that you are not at home." Sylvia took the phone the next time Vondracek called. He wanted to meet her in one of Prague's old wine restaurants near the Old Town Square, at ten in the morning a few days later.

When told about the appointment, Alena said, "Fine. You'll stay at home and I'll go there."

The day of the appointment, Alena dressed up in her finest clothes. She walked down the steps to the basement wine cellar. At 10:00 A.M., there was just one customer, sitting alone at a table.

"Mr. Vondracek?" Alena said. The man looked up and nodded. Alena continued, loud enough for the waiters to hear. "I see you have a wedding ring on your hand. I'm just warning you. You will not disturb my daughter anymore. A man your age, going after a young girl! A married man!"

Vondracek blanched and rushed from the restaurant. The secret police treasured secrecy. Alena had embarrassed him in public. Vondracek did not call again.

Five years later, though, the secret police approached Sylvia again. An American photographer had visited Prague and taken pictures of the Prague synagogue and Jewish community buildings. In one of the pictures, Sylvia was making a disapproving face at a Communist poster that denounced the Israeli invasion of

Lebanon, with bombs in the shape of the six-pointed Star of David. The police summoned her for an interrogation. Who was the photographer? What did Sylvia know about her? Sylvia knew the photographer well; the woman had stayed in her apartment. But she pretended she did not know what the police were talking about.

Beneath her brave facade, Sylvia again was scared. She thought: If I stop going to the Jewish community, if I don't participate, the secret police cannot ask me any questions. So Sylvia stopped visiting the old buildings near the Prague town square. When friends asked her why she did not come to the kosher dining hall for lunch or meet them there for coffee, she merely said she no longer liked the food.

A few years later, in the 1980s, a friend of Sylvia's introduced her to a lawyer who worked in the Czech Ministry of Culture. He was a committed Communist, and he and Sylvia argued endlessly about politics. When Sylvia had to have her appendix removed, he visited the hospital ·and announced that he was in love with her. Sylvia was flattered but not interested. After the Communist regime fell, he lost his job at the Ministry of Culture. Sylvia paid him to do some electrical work for her, then put him in touch with a friend who needed her apartment painted. He arrived at the friend's flat with three or four men and worked there for two weeks.

All of them turned out to be members of the secret police. When Sylvia called the man and confronted him, he said that he had wanted to spend time with her but could not be seen associating with the sister of Robert Wittmann. So he had registered Sylvia as a potential informant and listed their meetings, even his visit to the hospital, as contacts.

That was why her name was on the list, Sylvia explained to her assistant, to her friends. She was not an informer. As people saw the newspaper and began to call her, she repeated over and over again, "It's all bullshit. Bullshit!"

But in the atmosphere that had settled on Prague after the collapse of Communism, Sylvia's story struck many as unconvincing. After all, Sylvia had been permitted to travel overseas—twice—at a time when few Czechs were allowed to travel. She had worked at a hotel where foreigners stayed and in a tourist agency with foreign tourists—both sensitive positions that attracted the attention of the secret police. Even Sylvia's outspokenness was suspicious. She mocked the Communists with such freedom that some suspected she had an immunity from arrest or harassment, that she had a secret protector. The Jewish community, it turned out, was riddled with informers. Everyone had long suspected that the community's leader, installed by the Communists, had spied on Jews for the secret police. But now the newspapers revealed that Prague's rabbi had been an informer for the secret police too. A scholar at the state Jewish museum, a gentle man who had worked to protect the archives during the Communist regime, had informed for the secret police as well. People eyed one another with suspicion.

After several months, Sylvia's anger passed. Some people avoided her. Others whispered about her behind her back. Her friends, Sylvia figured, would know the truth. And those who did not like her would believe what they wanted to anyway.

She was right. Her tourism business flourished. Young people continued to come to her Friday-night basement meetings.

In an empty basement room next to her travel agency office, Sylvia assembled chairs, a table, and a piano. She filled bookshelves with histories of the Jewish people in English and German. Climbing on an old wooden bench, she pasted paper menorahs and Stars of David on the narrow windows set high in the walls. She called her room Bet Simcha—House of Blessing—and began inviting friends to join her on Friday nights to light Shabbat candles and converse and sing.

The young people who came exchanged scraps of Jewish history and experience, some of it right, some of it wrong, all fed by the heady spirit of freedom of the times. They sang Czech songs, Jewish songs, Israeli songs. They lit candles and stumbled through the chanting of Hebrew blessings—humming the parts that no one knew, breaking into embarrassed laughter as they searched for the words. A woman rabbi visited from the United States and returned a few months later with prayer books and books for teaching Hebrew. While the lights from the basement illuminated the paper menorahs and Stars of David in the window, a bearded Hasidic rabbi, visiting from London, regaled them with Jewish legends. Occasionally, a tall, elegant woman, slipping a scarf around her head, walked through the chill night air and down into the basement where her daughter had established a new Jewish meeting place. Alena Wittmann, who had only known prison and pain because her parents had been Jewish, would pull up a chair with the young people, joining in with bits of the songs when she knew them, basking in the glow of conversation and laughter.

It frustrated Sylvia that American Jews coming to Prague thought that Jewish life had died. They wanted to visit the Jewish museums with their collections of objects assembled by the Nazis, marvel over the ancient graveyard with its jumbled gravestones near the old synagogue, pay their respects at the tomb of Kafka. They were searching for the Jewish life of their ancestors, the Jewish life they had seen represented in *Fiddler on the Roof* and read about in the stories of Yiddish writers. But they didn't quite see, Sylvia felt, the Jewish life swirling all around them. Americans coming to Prague liked to think of the city as a museum. "But this is not a museum," Sylvia declared. "It is very alive here. I am not a stone in the cemetery."

As the fifth anniversary of the fall of the Berlin Wall approached, Jews in Prague prepared for Rosh Hashanah and Yom Kippur. On a late-summer evening, Sylvia gathered with a group of friends outside one of the museums opposite the old synagogue in the Jewish ghetto of Prague. The museum was closed, but Sylvia and her friends had permission to enter. They carried brooms and chairs. Methodically, they began to sweep the floors of the museum and carry out bags of dust and accumulated debris. A mouse skittered across the floor. Sylvia oriented herself and determined which side was the eastern wall, the wall facing Jerusalem. The carved niche for the Torah was still there.

More than fifty years before, this building had housed one of Prague's loveliest synagogues. The Nazis had turned the High Synagogue into a museum, part of their exhibit on an "extinct people." The Communists had maintained it as a museum for four decades, waiting for the Jews of Czechoslovakia to wither away and die. Sylvia and her friends lined up the chairs and borrowed a Torah from the old synagogue across the way. They brought in a rabbi from London to lead a service. On the first night of Rosh Hashanah, Sylvia opened the door. More than 150 Jews filed in. A half century ago the Nazis had turned most of Prague's synagogues into museums. Now Sylvia had turned this museum back into a synagogue.

# Chapter Twenty

# "Me, Too!"

For twenty years, ever since his dismissal as Szeged's rabbi, Tamas Raj had been a man with too much time on his hands and too little to do. Now suddenly he was in demand everywhere. Three Jewish schools had opened in Budapest. A former student had started a Jewish magazine. Another student was working at the Israeli embassy, closed since the 1967 war and now reopened. Budapest, with 100,000 Jews, was the largest Jewish community remaining in Eastern Europe. After forty-five years of slumber, it had exploded overnight in a burst of frenzied activity.

Raj was stretched thin. He had become increasingly active in dissident circles as the 1980s came to a close. At the outdoor commemoration of the victims of the 1956 Hungarian uprising, he said a public Kaddish. Soon afterward, he addressed a rally near his old home, on the site where Hungarians had battled Soviet tanks as they rolled in to crush the uprising. Raj spoke of the Hungarian David falling before the Soviet Goliath in 1956. "The greatest loss Hungary has suffered over the past three decades is that a generation grew up that was always lied to," Raj thundered. "The time has come to learn the truth."

The time had also come, Raj could have added, for David to triumph, and for Tamas Raj to make a decision. As Communism collapsed in Hungary, the dissident group Raj had met in the

reading room at the main library coalesced into the Free Democrats, a liberal party that was scrambling to find candidates for the
upcoming elections. For Budapest's Eighth District, once the
heart of the city's Jewish community, the dissidents approached
Tamas Raj.

Raj resisted. As a rabbi, he felt his place was in the synagogue.
He was not convinced that parliament was a proper place for a
religious leader. He feared alienating the members of his new
congregation. How would they respond to having a politician as a
rabbi—especially if they disagreed with his political views?

But Hungary was facing a crisis. As in East Germany, the collapse of Communism had unleashed a wave of xenophobia and
anti-Semitism. In Hungary, the rise of nationalism was symbolized by the rise of politicians who preached the importance of
"Hungarian" heritage. They demanded that Hungary reclaim territory that had been given to Romania after the First World War.
They blamed Hungary's economic problems after the collapse of
Communism on the Jews. They called for the dismissal of the
Jewish heads of radio and television stations. Anti-Semitic publications began appearing on newsstands.

Concerned Jews began calling Raj's office and home. Some
talked of leaving the country. Raj worried about the future of Hungary's Jews. He believed that eventually the right-wingers would be
defeated. But he did not know how long Jews in Hungary, and
Jewish life there, could withstand the rise of anti-Semitism. With
Communism's collapse, Raj had hoped for an increased number of
practicing Jews, a return to the synagogues and to religious Jewish
life. Though three Jewish schools had opened, only about 10 percent of Hungarian Jews participated in the religious education
classes he and other rabbis taught. Almost all the big Jewish institutions had opened offices in Budapest. There were at least five
Jewish youth organizations. But it was always the same people who
showed up at meetings.

The Communists had not succeeded in wiping out Jewish life
in Hungary. But, Raj feared, they had come close. They had
turned synagogues into old age homes. Only to a few, like Raj's,
did young people come. And now they were watching nervously as

the right wing expanded. High school students called him to say they were seriously thinking of leaving Hungary. They were, Raj believed, mentally packing their bags. If young people, whom Raj had always treasured and worked for, and for whom he had sacrificed his career, should leave, what would that mean for him and to the future of Hungary's Jewish community?

Beyond the fate of Hungary's Jews, what was at stake, Raj felt, was the very soul of Hungary. Would it become a progressive, democratic country or an embittered conservative backwater, overwhelmed by nationalism and hatred? Two tendencies now tugged at Hungary. On one side were modern, westward-looking politicians who wanted to end the country's forty-five-year isolation from Western Europe and embrace a free market and a free marketplace of ideas. They saw the battle against anti-Semitism as a test of becoming an open, democratic society.

The other side, the nationalists and right-wingers, looked inward and backward—to an almost mythical past when a "pure" Hungary, free of "alien influences," pursued its "national destiny." For these nationalist conservatives, Jews represented everything that was dangerous about the modern world—competition, change, democracy. Anyone who stood for broadening democracy and opening Hungary to the West was a "Jew." The new wave of anti-Semitism, Raj believed, had almost nothing to do with the reality of Jews at all. It stemmed from fear of change and the search for scapegoats.

There was another issue as well. For decades, the Communists had made sure that the chief rabbi of Hungary, appointed and controlled by them, held a seat in parliament. It provided a fig leaf of decency to the regime, evidence of how well the Jews were treated. Raj thought it important that a rabbi sit in the new, democratic parliament. The memories of Jewish Communists like Rakosi were still fresh in the minds of many Hungarians and could easily be turned into a new wave of anti-Semitism. Raj did not want to give people the chance to say: Back in the old Communist days, there were Jews in parliament. And where are the Jews now?

Raj agreed to run for parliament.

It was a heated, intense campaign. The Free Democrats ran a race that combined modern technology with hackneyed slogans and techniques that could have been lifted from 1950s America— appropriate since the last free election had been in 1948. One of Hungary's best-known actors wrote the campaign theme song, and the Free Democrats sent convoys of cars around town, loud- speakers mounted to their roofs, blaring the song to passersby. There were flags printed up for children, with pictures of the car- toon characters Tom and Jerry. The flags carried the words: "There is one thing we agree on. We want Tamas Raj for Parlia- ment." The flags were such a hit that the campaign soon printed up "Tom and Jerry" buttons too.

As election day neared, the campaign turned bitter. The Free Democrats were denounced as the "Jewish party," because several of their candidates, including Raj, were Jewish. Vandals began defacing Free Democrat posters with swastikas and Stars of David and painting the letters ZS—for *Zsid,* or Jew—in black and red.

A few days before the election, Raj was walking near his house and passed one of the campaign posters that featured his picture. On it, someone had scribbled ZS. The next day, Raj found under- neath that graffiti the inscription: "I would be proud if I were a Jew." The day after that, someone had written: "So would I." That afternoon: "Me, too." So it went, day after day, until a dozen dif- ferent hands had scribbled: "Me, too." Many of the people writing, Raj discovered later, were not Jewish at all. They just wanted to show their support.

Raj won the election. Two weeks later, yarmulke on head, he stood with the new parliament and was sworn in as a member of the first democratically elected Hungarian parliament in more than forty-two years.

# Chapter Twenty-One

# "I Have No Answer to Your Request"

Barbara pressed on. She took a part-time job at the cavernous Jewish Historical Association—a once grand but now decaying building that maintained the archives of the Holocaust of Poland's Jews. Countless file cabinets held names of Jews murdered by the Nazis, lists of Jews taken away by train to Auschwitz and other concentration camps, and records of survivors. Day after day, Barbara sifted through the rows of registers and card files in the hope of finding traces of her real parents, Jews who had turned her over to Leokadia, a Catholic woman they did not even know, before the Nazis came for them. Slowly, Barbara came to know other "hidden children." Like Barbara, many of them had found out their true identities only recently, as their adoptive parents died.

The "hidden children" began to meet. Barbara liked meeting the older Jews especially, those who had been hidden by Catholic families as young children or teenagers and remembered the traditions and the tales of Jewish life from before the war. Many were ill, and on more than one occasion, these elderly survivors were overcome by shock or neared a nervous breakdown as they made their discoveries.

In 1991, Barbara and several other Poles traveled to New York, to attend a conference sponsored by an American foundation that had heard of the plight of the hidden children. It was Barbara's first trip outside Poland. The group stayed at the Marriott Hotel in Times Square. In a lobby near the conference room was a bulletin board used by those in search of their families. It was soon covered with scraps of paper, all beginning: "I am looking for a family . . ." Barbara was reminded of bulletin boards she had seen in Warsaw after the war, when Jews and Poles kept searching for family members in the chaos and destruction left behind by the Nazis. But how possible was it that now, forty-five years later, someone who knew her real parents might still be alive—let alone her parents, if they had by some miracle survived the war. Still, Barbara pinned a note to the board and waited.

The American Red Cross offered to search for families, so Barbara, with the help of translators, carefully filled out the forms. She listed the information she had learned from the mysterious letter written by Leokadia to someone in Israel. Her mother's married name was E. A. Zajdler. Her mother's maiden name had been Szapiro. She believed she had been handed over in a hospital ward in the town of Garvolin.

Back in Warsaw, Barbara resumed her search in the Jewish archives. She tracked down Zajdlers, but they did not fit the details of her mother's letter. She could not find any reference to a Dr. Zajdler who had worked in a hospital in Garvolin. And Szapiro—the Polish version of Shapiro—was such a common name it was virtually useless.

Then one evening she returned from work and found in her mailbox a letter from the Polish Red Cross. She raced up the four flights to her apartment and, inside, ripped open the envelope. The letter urged her to call the Red Cross immediately regarding her case.

It was too late to call. Lying, sleepless, that night next to her husband, Barbara considered the possibilities. Had her family, like so many others, perished in the Holocaust? Or had someone, by some miracle, survived—an aunt, an uncle, someone who could fill in the holes in her past?

The next morning, Barbara hastened to the Red Cross building with her husband. She gave the notice to a clerk, who disappeared into a back room. Barbara agonized as she waited. The clerk returned. "You've been to America, haven't you?"

"Yes," Barbara replied.

"And what do you expect us to do?"

"I am looking for my family."

The clerk disappeared again and returned with a sheet of paper—the form Barbara had filled out in New York had been forwarded to the Polish Red Cross in Warsaw. It was a false alarm. There was no news of Barbara's family. The clerk, unmoved, told Barbara to fill out more forms.

Three times since the end of World War II, Poland had waged war against its Jews. In 1946, they had unleashed pogroms that killed more than a hundred Jewish survivors of the Nazi death camps and drove thousands more to Israel. In 1956, a Communist-led anti-Semitic campaign had caused thousands more to leave the country, including Barbara's young friend Elzbieta. In 1968, another wave of Communist-sponsored anti-Semitism drove twenty thousand Jews out of Poland, including Leokadia's friend Maria Wisniewska; only a handful remained. In 1956 and 1968, Barbara had been a passive onlooker. The attacks did not affect her directly. She was a Catholic and a Pole.

But now she was a Jew. And the new freedom in Poland brought with it yet another wave of anti-Semitism. Every day on her way to work she passed a wall with the scrawled graffiti: "Jews to the gas chambers!" At Umschlagplatz, where 300,000 Jews from the Warsaw ghetto were convened for deportation to Treblinka in the summer of 1942, someone painted the slogan "A good Jew is a dead Jew." Surveys showed that some 30 percent of Poles held anti-Semitic views. When Jewish groups outside Poland criticized the growing anti-Semitism, Cardinal Josef Glemp, who had succeeded Karol Wojtyla, now Pope John Paul II, as the leading Catholic figure in Poland, warned: "My dear Jews, do not speak to us from the position of a nation raised above all others and do not present us with conditions that are impossible to fulfill. . . . Your power lies in the mass media which is at your disposal throughout many countries. Do not let this power serve to disseminate anti-Polish feeling." When Lech Walesa, the hero of the Solidarity trade union, decided to run for president, his supporters mounted a whispering campaign against his Catholic opponent, saying he was a "crypto-Jew." Walesa himself proudly announced that he was a "pure" Pole.

Unlike 1956 or 1968, Barbara could not now turn away from the anti-Semitism that was manifesting itself all around her. She began to fear the day that she would come home and find a six-pointed Star of David scrawled on her mailbox. She watched television programs about the small number of Jews left and predictions that soon there would be no Jews left in Poland at all. She thought about leaving for Israel. But the climate there seemed so hot and harsh. She considered leaving for the West, but she could speak only Polish. Perhaps if she had been younger . . .

When she visited New York, her hotel had been near the jewelry district, where Hasidic Jews, dressed in their distinctive black coats and black hats, with their long beards, had hurried along the street, talking and laughing. No one had given them a second look. Why could Poland not be like that, she thought, where Jews were not only legally protected but socially accepted?

There were moments when Barbara began to consider that Leokadia, the mother she had known for forty-three years, had perhaps been right to hide Barbara's Jewish background. It had made her life simpler and quieter, without all these complications.

Barbara thought, too, of her other mother. What had gone through the mind of this woman, still sore from childbirth, as she handed her newborn baby over to a stranger? Had she loved Barbara as Barbara had loved her son, if only for a few days? Had she, in the face of death, decided in a panic, laying Barbara in the arms of a stranger with a gold watch and perhaps some money? Or had she managed to muster a cool reserve to preserve her baby's life? Perhaps the small victory in knowing that a part of her would live on had emboldened her to give Barbara up.

And then her parents had vanished. Was there a chance her mother had escaped the fate that befell so many mothers like her? And if Barbara succeeded and found proof that her mother was still living, what would she say to this stranger?

*      *      *

In the spring of 1992, Barbara met Zigmund, an eighty-seven-year-old Polish Jew, at the archives where she had taken a part-time job. He came from Zelechow, the town Leokadia had visited before she returned to Warsaw with her baby. Barbara had been thinking about going to Zelechow. She remembered her mother talking of a friend there, Barbara's godmother. All the other avenues she had explored turned out to be dead ends: Her baptismal records had been falsified. She could not find any relevant records in the Jewish archives. The Polish and American Red Cross had been unable to help. Perhaps Zelechow would provide some answers.

On a cool spring day, Barbara and her husband climbed into their car with Zigmund. Barbara had developed an affection for many of the elderly Jews she had met; they were the last living link to Poland's rich Jewish history. A faint tug of anxiety pulled at Barbara as they motored through the countryside, and Zigmund tried to lighten the mood by telling Jewish jokes. The landscape they traversed had not changed in the fifty years since seventeen-year-old Leokadia traveled to Zelechow by train and horse cart with her lover: broad plains, a winding road, an occasional farmhouse.

The drive took about an hour. They entered Zelechow from the main road and paused before the massive church. Zigmund directed them to turn right. Past several blocks of newer residential houses, they came to what looked like an abandoned field, perched atop a small hill. It was the old Jewish cemetery, Zigmund explained. He had paid to have a fence put around it. Just a few tombstones were left, and the rutted ground was so choked with weeds that the cemetery looked more like a fallow, overgrown field.

Barbara, her husband, and Zigmund drove back to the church and then headed down the street that ran behind it to see some people whom the old man knew. Juga Street—the name seemed vaguely familiar to Barbara. The visitors from Warsaw got out of the car and approached the home of Zigmund's friends. Barbara was distracted, thinking about the name of the street. She had seen it somewhere—perhaps on a letter? Or had her mother spoken of it? Then suddenly it came to her. Her godmother lived on Juga Street.

Barbara asked Zigmund's friends whether they happened to know a Mrs. Pleskot.

"Of course," a young woman said. "She lived across the street. But she died six months ago. Her daughter still lives there."

The woman went to the phone and dialed a number. She didn't know quite how to explain, so she began simply.

"We have a lady here from Warsaw who just arrived—"

"Oh." The woman on the other end of the line interrupted. "It must be Basia, Bruno's daughter." Bruno! The name of Leokadia's lover. Her mother had said she was married to Bruno because of the baby.

Barbara hurried across the street. Her godmother had always hoped Barbara would visit, the daughter explained, and was puzzled that she and Leokadia had never come back to see her. Barbara had played in this house as a child back in the early 1940s, she was told. The woman remembered her father, Bruno, who had been born in Zelechow.

Barbara did not say anything. She did not reveal that Bruno was not her real father. She wanted to find out as much as this link to her past could tell her.

"My mother has died, and I am trying to find out more about the circumstances of my birth," Barbara said.

"Well, then," the woman responded. "Let's go to the church and check the christening record. My husband sings in the church choir. He knows everyone."

Barbara and the woman went to the church and sought out the priest. They checked the records, but there was no mention of Barbara. They checked 1943, when Barbara thought she was born. And 1942 and 1941. They checked under different names—Bruno, and Leokadia's maiden name, her godmother's name. Nothing.

Then Barbara told the family the truth. Her mother had never married Bruno. She had been given Barbara by a Jewish family, named Zajdler, just before the ghetto in Zelechow was liquidated.

There was silence. The husband, who had been so eager to

help, sank into angry silence. His face clouded with hostility. The daughter of Barbara's godmother tried to ease the tension. They knew about the Jews in Zelechow, of course. They lived in a house that had once been owned by Jews.

It was an awkward parting. But the two women promised to stay in touch. Barbara returned to Warsaw. She called her god-mother's daughter again a few days later and read to her from her mother's letter. Perhaps that would help jog her memory? Perhaps her godmother—Leokadia's best friend—had left behind in her papers and belongings some clue, some trace of what happened. The woman said she would look.

But when Barbara called back, the woman was harsh. "There is nothing," she barked over the phone. "There is nothing, no trace. Perhaps nothing happened at all." There was no good-bye, only a click.

The one link Barbara had with her mother's past was broken.

She found other family bonds straining as well. At first, when she discovered she was Jewish, she told everyone. She did not want to keep secrets, tell lies. She saw no reason to hide her past. Her husband and son and daughter-in-law, who had been with her when the phone call came five years earlier, had always stood by her. Her daughter-in-law's parents, who were devout Catholics, were enthusiastic about her search: "We could tell, even though you did not go to church, that there was always something spiritual inside you."

But her husband's family responded differently. At first they said, "You are still Barbara." But the relationship steadily cooled. Her husband said she was making too much of it. But Barbara thought differently.

The last time she had seen one of her husband's relatives, he had said: "You are who you are. Don't pay so much attention to the Jews. Give those Jews up."

Even her husband, Barbara sensed, had become a little weary of her endless questioning, her search to discover who she was and what it meant.

\*       \*       \*

Barbara returned to her part-time job at the Jewish archives. One day an elderly man came in with a search request. Barbara took the name and walked back into the records room, filled with catalogs of the Polish Jews killed by the Holocaust. She checked one of the catalogs, then moved on to the file cabinets filled with cards that recorded victims and their families. She pulled the blue card with the man's name. On the card, listed under relatives, was the name Estella Zajdler. Barbara's heart began to pound. She hurried to the man and asked him what he knew of Estella Zajdler. Did she have a baby? Was her husband a doctor near Zelechow? The man did not know. But his mother was still alive. Perhaps she would know. Please ask her, Barbara implored. The man called back; his mother remembered Estella Zajdler. She had never given birth to a baby.

That was it: the final cruel letdown. Barbara, who had become increasingly anxious, had been prescribed pills to calm her, but her doctor warned her that if she did not stop pursuing her past, she could end up in the hospital with a nervous breakdown.

Barbara stopped her search. But in Sweden, Maria Wisniewska, who had turned Barbara's life upside down with her New Year's Day phone call in 1987, continued to look for answers. Even as she approached seventy-five, Maria felt the need to honor the request of Barbara's adoptive mother, Leokadia, that she help find Barbara's birth mother. She had been tracking down every Zajdler who had lived in Poland before the war. She wrote letters, describing Barbara's predicament. Maria forwarded their answers to Barbara, who kept them in a living room cupboard in her small apartment:

> Dear Madame:
> I received your letter about the war history of Mrs. Barbara Asendrych, who recently found out her real name is Zajdler. Unfortunately, not as I think my relative, despite the coincidence of names. I know my father's family only two generations back, and only in fragments. And my grandfather Chaim Zajdler also died there at the beginning of the war, had some brothers and sisters whom I didn't know. I only know that there

was numerous family in Lodz called Zajdler, then they
changed the spelling to Seidler. I also know that some
of them participated in a company dealing with tea
trade.

Dear Madame:
Thank you for your letter. I have to confess with much
sorrow that I don't remember Dr. Zajdler, whom you
write about, and whose daughter you write about in
such a moving way. During my work at the doctors'
chamber, I met many doctors, and therefore I do not
remember their names, after all the 50 years.

Dear Madame:
Unfortunately I have no answer to your request con-
cerning Mr. Zajdler. I looked through the archives in
Lodz, where there are many people under the name of
Zajdler, but none of them was a doctor. I also checked
all the hospitals and places where doctors worked in
'38, but I didn't find anybody called Zajdler.

For all her searching and questions, her trips to Zelechow and
even to New York in search of her Jewish roots, Barbara had still
not traveled the three miles across Warsaw from her home to the
last remaining synagogue. She had wanted to go to the synagogue
for several years. But she was afraid—afraid that she wouldn't
know what to do, that the Jews there would throw her out.

The only functioning synagogue in Warsaw occupied a fenced-
in courtyard in the center of Warsaw—an island of what remained
of Jewish life. Next to it was the Yiddish theater, which had been
preserved by the Communists and featured Christian actors
putting on Yiddish plays for tourists and Poles. Poles listened to
translations on headphones. The theater was a popular spot, but it
had the atmosphere of a museum—like Colonial Williamsburg or
Plimoth Plantation, where vanished cultures are re-created.

The synagogue featured a gracefully arched entrance, but
people actually entered from the back, through a four-story concrete building that had housed the handful of officially approved
Jewish organizations. Going into the synagogue meant first
climbing up concrete stairs and entering a nondescript lobby that

looked like the drab entryway of any other Communist-era building in Warsaw. The synagogue was Orthodox. Men and women sat in separate sections. The stairs split. A dark stairway led up to the women's section in the balcony; a small set of three stairs down to the men's. There was no hint the synagogue lay on the other side.

It was a warm spring Saturday when a woman Barbara had met in the Association of Hidden Children called her at home. "I want to see you," the woman said. "Let's meet at the building." This term was accepted shorthand for the structure that housed the Jewish offices and the synagogue. Barbara assumed her friend just wanted a convenient meeting place.

She entered the lobby with its gray institutional floor and chipped walls. The porter waved her upstairs. "That's where you go," he said, barely acknowledging her. Barbara walked up the stairs. Her friend was waiting. Wordlessly, without realizing fully where she was, she followed her friend into the synagogue.

It was like walking from night into day. The walls were brilliant white; ornate golden chandeliers hung from the ceiling. Barbara stepped onto a balcony with curved wooden benches. Below, a dozen men were chanting and singing in Hebrew. Upstairs, in the balcony with Barbara, women were praying but also, Barbara realized, talking and gossiping.

Barbara had never considered herself particularly religious. She admired people who were devout, Catholics like her grandmother or like her daughter-in-law's parents. She had entrusted the religious upbringing of her own son to her grandmother to ensure that he was brought up a good Catholic. But she herself had stopped going to church when she was a teenager. Church failed to move her. Barbara had always believed her lack of faith was another one of her failings.

Now, looking down at the men praying, Barbara suddenly found it all very familiar and comforting. Though she spoke no Hebrew, the rhythms of the service, the melodies of the chants, did not seem strange or exotic. Barbara settled down on one of the benches and let the sounds wash over her. After fifty years, Barbara felt at home.

# Chapter Twenty-Two

# "It Never Lets You Go"

Like most Americans, like most Jews, I grew up familiar with the Holocaust. I had seen the grainy black-and-white news-reel pictures of emaciated bodies stacked like cordwood, as American, British, and Russian soldiers liberated the concentration camps. I had seen the movie *Shoah*, with its chilling scenes of Polish women chortling as they described how the Nazis had rounded up the Jews from their village and piled them into cattle cars; and the Polish boy grinning as he told how he watched the Jews peering out through narrow slits of the boxcars and then drew his finger across his neck as the trains headed for the gates of Auschwitz. I had read *The Destruction of the European Jews* by Raoul Hilberg and *The War Against the Jews* by Lucy Davidowicz; *Eichmann in Jerusalem* by Hannah Arendt and *Schindler's List* by Thomas Kenneally. I had interviewed survivors of the concentration camps. I had heard the tales of trees turned gray with ash from the crematoriums, boxcars that groaned with suffering when soldiers opened them at the end of the war and found them packed with Jews, left in the sun to die and rot. I had fallen into the poignant, uncomfortable silence that accompanied the display of a forearm with a number tattooed on the skin. I had not lost any immediate family in the Holocaust; most of my relatives had left Europe long before the Nazis began their extermination. Still, the details of the Holocaust were familiar to me when I arrived in Berlin a few days after the Berlin Wall fell.

But nothing prepared me for Berlin or Warsaw, Budapest or Prague—the Jewish life that had been destroyed and the Jewish life that had, miraculously, survived.

Traveling through East Germany, Poland, Czechoslovakia, and Hungary often felt like stepping back in time. In these countries, the clock seemed to have stopped in 1945. The buildings were old. There was a shabbiness and grayness everywhere. For decades, the Eastern Bloc had used high-polluting brown coal for heat, and the soot had settled everywhere. Entire countries were colorless—like black-and-white movie sets. The contrast was sharpest in Berlin, where the wall had divided East from West. After World War II, both halves of the city lay in ruins. Only the West Berliners had the money to rebuild. So they had done massive urban renewal, razing old buildings and putting up 1960s-style skyscrapers, covered with neon advertisements. East Berlin, aside from a few streets of postwar Stalinist apartment blocks, mammoth and grotesque, was a city of old buildings and little color. "It's amazing," said a friend, "how much difference advertising signs can make."

These black-and-white images, like time itself, had stood still, emblazoned in American minds. It was only after the wall was demolished that grains of color began to animate the gray still lifes. The more these countries opened up, and the more I traveled in them, the more the old images began to fade away and be replaced by more complex ones. Forty-five years of hidden Jewish life began revealing itself, teeming with vitality and contradictions, told in complex layers by Jews, their friends, and their enemies. The details filled in the old gray picture, leaving a richer, more colorful portrait.

I wanted very much to solve the mystery of Barbara Asendrych— to find some trace of her birth parents and the story of what had happened in 1942 or 1943, just before the Germans began deporting Jews from Zelechow to the concentration camps. Like Barbara, I traveled to Zelechow and spoke with the priest and townspeople. But the past had vanished.

This was the greater tragedy of Barbara's story. Like Zelechow, which had once been 70 percent Jewish, with a thriving rabbinical seminary and a prosperous shoe industry, Barbara represented the intermingling of Poles and Jews. She could have been a great source of pride to the Poles—a Jew given refuge from a common enemy. But instead Barbara was a prick to the conscience of the Poles—a reminder of all those who had not given refuge to Jewish children, who had turned away as their neighbors had been rounded up. And she was an oddity and an embarrassment to Jews, some of whom could not believe that a Pole would save a Jewish child, while others could only blame the Poles for their role in extinguishing Jewish culture. Barbara felt unconnected, and Catholicism had not served any of her needs. And until she was finally induced to set foot in Warsaw's synagogue, she was too nervous and uncertain to attend, fearful that she would be mocked by Jews who saw how little she knew.

Barbara could not forgive Leokadia for what she had concealed. But that anger pushed away the reality that, for all her faults, Leokadia had saved Barbara from the Nazis and the Communists and protected her in the way that she felt was best. What choice did Leokadia have? Had it been known that Barbara was Jewish, she might well have been persecuted and forced to flee, like her friend Elzbieta in 1956 or Maria in 1968.

Like so many of their fellow Poles, like so many Eastern Europeans, Barbara and Leokadia were victims of Nazism and Communism. In a different Poland, a free Poland, Barbara might have found out about her real family and her background. She might have embraced Judaism earlier. In a different Poland, a free Poland, Leokadia might have been thanked for the person she was—a Christian who saved Jews, even if not from the purest of motives.

If it were not for the chance envelopes left among her mother's papers, Barbara would never have known she was Jewish. The Polish destruction of Jewish life after the war would have claimed another victim.

Would the Poles have minded? No sooner had Communism collapsed in Poland than anti-Semitism reemerged, as it had right after the war and again in 1956 and 1968. It evidenced itself in unlikely places. I was in Warsaw soon after the Solidarity government had taken power. One morning a Polish man turned to me in the hotel elevator with a joke that had been making the rounds in Warsaw.

"Do you know how many Jews there are in the cabinet?" he asked.

"No," I answered.

"Fifteen, plus an Arab," he said with a grin, explaining that the name of the new minister of industry was pronounced like the Polish word for "Arab."

In fact, there were no Jews at all in the Polish cabinet. There were very few Jews left in Poland at all.

Traveling throughout the country, hearing the jokes, seeing the anti-Semitic graffiti, I found it easy to agree with the Polish writer who had told me, "The Jews have given up on the Germans. But they still hate the Poles." Poles and Jews have been yoked together by one of the world's most profound and painful relationships. They shared the same country for almost a thousand years. Like siblings, they passed through stages of love and hate, rivalry and affection. The millions of Jews who lived in Poland produced the richest flowering of Jewish literature, religious teachings, and humor the world had ever seen.

The relationship between Poles and Jews ended disastrously in the Second World War when Poles mutely watched while their Jewish population was annihilated by the Nazis. That war never really ended for the Jews. Anti-Semitic campaigns and purges during the Communist years, and even after Communism, had continued systematically to drive Jews out of Poland, until only a handful of elderly, frightened Jews were left. The anger and betrayal that Jews felt toward Poland remained—and remains—a living, breathing thing, even fifty years after the end of World War II.

And yet I was optimistic about the Poles. One morning in 1993, I attended a ceremony commemorating the fiftieth anniversary of the Warsaw ghetto uprising, when Jews bravely battled the Nazis and resisted being deported to the gas chambers. Under

Communism, the commemorations had become politicized; Solidarity had boycotted the ceremony and conducted its own observance. But here in a free Poland, Poles were united in paying their respects to the Jews. Members of the Polish army solemnly laid a wreath at the monument honoring the Jewish fighters. President Lech Walesa escorted the last surviving resistance fighter, a member of Solidarity and a newly elected member of the Polish parliament. In the crowd stood many Americans, muttering in disbelief that the Polish feeling of remorse seemed genuine. The Poles just wanted Western investment, said one; the Poles still hated the Jews, said another.

Surely, some did. But I also believed that Poland wanted to join the West and that many Poles—certainly Polish intellectuals and political leaders—recognized that in modern Western society, anti-Semitism was unacceptable. There were Poles, admittedly a minority, who mourned the loss of the Jews and what they had meant to Polish culture. In the privacy of people's homes, and in the occasional comments of priests and others, anti-Semitism would rear its head again in Poland. But I believed that the more Poland became integrated into the West and its young people were exposed to Western values, the more it was capable of leaving its anti-Semitic past behind.

And what of the Jews? Could Poland, once home to more than three million Jews, have a Jewish future with the six thousand who remained? Of course not, scoffed foreign visitors, brandishing surveys that showed one-third or more of Poles held anti-Semitic views. But a few years after the Berlin Wall fell, Jews in Warsaw opened a nursery school; soon after, I was invited to attend a Sukkoth party in the courtyard of the synagogue. Dying communities, a friend of mine observed wryly, do not open nursery schools. On my last trip to Poland, I visited Barbara and asked about her family. Though she had taken her son, now a young married man with a daughter of his own, to a Jewish retreat to learn more about Judaism, he did not seem very interested. The reemergence of her roots, it seemed, would die with Barbara. But then one day Barbara's granddaughter came home from elementary school with some drawings. Poland had instituted mandatory religion classes in its schools, and because Poland was a Catholic country, students were taught Catholic dogma. The assignment that week had been to color in a picture of a church altar with a cross and a chalice and other Catholic regalia. Barbara's granddaughter had carefully colored in her assignment. Then she had added a menorah to the altar. And on the border she drew row after row of Jewish stars.

No one could say for sure what this would lead to. But neither could anyone dismiss it and say it would come to nothing.

Klaus Gysi was surely the most complex person I met in my journey, a man of many experiences and many identities. The last time I visited him, he was eighty and visibly slowed by a stroke. He walked laboriously across his living room, past the shelves jammed with books, to a small balcony and pointed across the street. There, just on the other side of where the Berlin Wall had once stood, was a building. Once, it had housed one of Berlin's largest Jewish publishing houses, and Klaus's uncle had worked there. That world had vanished, Klaus said sadly.

"But you know," he said, "this being Jewish—it never lets you go."

Was this the real Klaus? Or just another mask put on by a political chameleon who had prospered by always bending his views, even his identity, to suit different audiences?

I doubted if I would ever know. But it was a curious phenomenon that after the Berlin Wall fell, many Jewish Communists in East Germany suddenly found religion. They convened at Irene Runge's cultural gatherings—which she had initiated in the 1980s—and traded stories about their hardships as they were being toppled from power. Having lost faith in one ideology, they now found some solace in the Judaism they had denied for so long.

But what, then, explained Gregor's appeal to non-Jewish German voters? He was, after all, a short, bald, chain-smoking Jewish Communist—or, to use his own preferred phrase, Democratic Socialist. One Sunday afternoon, when I told a West German friend that I was going to hear Gregor speak, she asked eagerly if she could come along. This elegant, well-traveled woman would never have considered voting for Gregor Gysi. But still he fascinated her. "He has such charisma," she said as we headed off to the speech.

Gysi discovered that, as a politician, he was perfectly suited to the western television and political culture he had scorned and feared for so long. He became a fixture on German political talk shows—often broadcast at prime time—where his quick wit and sharp intelligence made him a master of the sound bite. His speeches and rallies always drew large crowds, often including many who had no intention of voting for him but were eager to hear him speak. Gossip magazines wrote admiringly of his magnetic hold on women voters, who spoke lovingly of his sensual lips and quick mind. In Parliament, opponents heaped abuse on him, jeering his speeches with catcalls. But Gysi relished the battle, and responded with well-timed barbs of his own. The Social Democratic Party, Germany's liberals, tried to woo Gysi to switch sides and join them.

Gysi's popularity baffled and enraged many members of the German political and journalistic establishment. He was still a Communist, they fumed, a fossil from a discredited regime. His party might have a new name but in the minds of many German conservatives, it still bore the legacy of forty-five years of crimes. Helmut Kohl, the conservative German chancellor, refused to shake Gregor's hand.

Though many Germans did not realize it, and Gregor himself was uncomfortable with the fact, his appeal lay in the fact that he represented what Germany had lost in the Holocaust. Gregor's was a voice, an accent, that had not been heard in East or West Germany since the shattering of glass on Kristallnacht in 1938. To an American, certainly to an American coming from New York or Chicago or Los Angeles or Cleveland, Gregor was familiar—a smart, quick-thinking left-wing Jewish intellectual. But in Germany he was unique, like a bird, long thought extinct, that suddenly reappears amid the clouds over the skyline. German politicians were serious, products of a system that valued loyalty and connections over creativity and charisma. It was a system that produced more competence than flash.

Most German humor was crude or broad, primitive slapstick. German television shows were full of pratfalls and fat men embarrassing themselves as they angled to meet slim, sexy women. Gregor's humor was deft and ironic—a cultured and daring humor that had flourished in Berlin during the Weimar period, before Hitler came to power.

In a different Germany, a Germany where the Nazis had never come to power, there still would have been thousands of men like Gregor in Berlin and around the country in arts and culture, at newspapers and in business. Few would have been as left-wing as Gregor; many would have been more religious. But this Germany, for forty-five years, had been a Germany virtually without Jews. In his own way, Gregor was filling part of the hole rent in German life by the annihilation of the Jews.

In the spring of 1991, Gregor kept one of his election pledges: his first visit overseas as head of the Party of Democratic Socialism would be to Israel.

On board the plane, Gregor was unaccustomedly nervous. He fidgeted and smoked incessantly. Accompanying him on the trip was his friend and top political adviser, André Brie, a fellow East German whose father had also been Communist and Jewish. The two men talked about their fathers. They agreed that they had defined themselves as German Communists rather than Jews—and Gregor now regretted that he knew so little about Jewish culture and religion. He feared arriving in Israel unprepared. Stacked on the seats next to the two men were piles of literature and books on Jewish religion, Jewish culture, and Israeli history that Gregor had brought along.

The plane landed in the shimmering heat of the Middle East. Brie was surprised at how dry the land was; he had never fully realized that Israel was in the Middle East. Gregor headed for a conference where he delivered a speech that attempted to win over the Israelis to the new, reformed Communist Party that Gregor insisted had broken with the old East German Communist Party which had denounced Israel for decades. The Israelis were skeptical. They could not easily forget that East Germany had trained and protected Palestinian terrorists.

The next day, the two men went to Yad Vashem, the memorial to the six million Jews killed in the Holocaust. They walked slowly past the exhibits documenting the Nazi horror, then came to the real object of their trip: the memorial room containing records of the six million Jewish victims. In silence, Gregor paged through the records until he found the name of his great aunt, the kindly woman who had apologized she did not have cake to offer Klaus and Irene when they came to her home in 1943 to help her pack for "resettlement." There were other Gysis as well, the relatives Klaus had lost in the war.

Gregor finished his search and stepped out into the sunlight. Anger and grief churned inside him. To see the names of his relatives listed in stark black and white—it took him hours to regain his composure. Putting aside his official duties, he and Brie walked for hours. Around them they stared at the Hasidic Jews—in broad-brimmed hats, black frock coats, and beards and side-curls—hurrying along their way. For the first time, Gregor sensed the enormity of what Germany had destroyed.

The trip brought him an odd kind of peace. During his election campaign, he chafed at people who wanted to label him a Jew; he was stung by the anti-Semitic attacks against him. Now, however, he found his Jewish background easier to deal with. He began to fill his bookshelves with books on Jewish life and learning and shared the family lore about Erna Gysi and Klaus's relatives with his own son.

Though he had sparred much with his father, Gregor had become a lot like him. Some charged that Gregor had turned out to be all too much like his father. Charges swirled around him that he had betrayed some of the dissidents he had defended to the Stasi, the East German secret police. Gregor denied the charges, even taking those who spread the rumors to court to make them stop. In elections he and the Party of Democratic Socialism, building on the continued discontent in the former East Germany, continued to hold on to their Socialist niche in parliament.

Increasingly Gregor invoked the memories of the famous German Jewish Communists of the 1920s, Rosa Luxemburg and

Karl Liebknecht, whose cosmopolitan, outward-looking Communism had first attracted his grandmother and his father—the Communism that spoke of equality and social justice before, as Gregor saw it, it had been curdled by Stalin and by the Communists' drive for power. Many Germans dismissed Gysi's beliefs as a fantasy, but for Gregor it was not just a political mission but a family one—as if to prove that the lives of his grandmother and father had not been wasted.

"The world has nothing to do with the Jews," Estrongo Nachama declared when the Berlin Wall went up. No matter what the politics of the moment, he would not be deterred from his work, or his prayers at the synagogue, or his singing.

True to his words more than thirty years later, Estrongo remained angry about the right-wing violence and anti-Semitism that followed the fall of the wall and the unification of Germany. But he continued to sing at the synagogue every Friday night and Saturday morning, to preside over funerals and keep in touch with the sick and elderly, especially over in East Berlin, where he had traveled for so many years. The pace of bar mitzvahs picked up, many of them Russian Jewish boys coming to him for lessons as they approached thirteen. They knew very little about Judaism, but still, here they were, standing deferentially in front of his small office—in the same synagogue to which, all those years ago, he had carried firewood, just as he walked the streets of Berlin to recruit Jews to come and pray.

Now in his seventies, Estrongo was increasingly in demand to sing throughout Germany and overseas. He rarely turned down an invitation. His voice never faltered.

One evening, Andreas invited me to hear his father perform at the Schauspielhaus in the former East Berlin. The greatest concert hall in the city, it was fifteen miles from the Sachsenhausen concentration camp, where Estrongo had spent the final days of the war. Two years earlier, the entire German government had assembled there to hear Beethoven's Ninth Symphony on the eve of Germany's official unification.

Onstage, Nachama sang Jewish prayers and liturgical music.

His tenor voice filled the hall, enveloping the audience with its power. When the concert ended, the audience applauded, demanding encores. Nachama sang again. The audience rose to its feet. Nachama sang a Yiddish folk song. Pounding their feet in approval, people demanded, "More! More!"

Nachama had run out of music to sing. He riffled in vain through his music scores. Then he looked up, stepped to the front of the stage, and began singing "Hava Nagila." He waved to the audience to join in. Back and forth across the stage he strode, encouraging the crowd, his barrel chest straining against his dark suit. He bounded up and down the stage, a young man again, the audience clapping and singing along, reaching out to an audience, opening his arms to the world.

I didn't know whether to believe Sylvia. I found myself questioning the shades of gray behind the Iron Curtain, the compromises people made or I would have made in similar circumstances. In speaking to people throughout Eastern Europe, it was clear to me that the Communists understood how to manipulate the chemistry of human ambition. Courageous dissidents like Prague's Vaclav Havel were rare. There were, to be sure, venal people in Eastern Europe, who eagerly sold out others for money and advancement. There were heroes, like Havel, or like Tamas Raj in Hungary, who stood courageously against Communism and paid a heavy price. And then there were all the others, caught within a system, filled with desire for a better life for themselves and their children. The Communists were not good at making cars or stocking stores with food, but they knew how to exact what they wanted from people—by threatening their children, promising travel overseas and places at university. Many in Eastern Europe, especially bright young people, coped with the secret police by treating them as if they were government bureaucrats: Simply give them a report, a few names, and get them off your back. No one knew that one day the wall would collapse and all the daily compromises would be revealed. In the 1990s, the decisions made in the 1960s, 1970s or 1980s appeared in a different light.

Still, Prague pulsated with the energy of Jewish life reborn. A new rabbi—a former dissident—took the pulpit at the historic synagogue in the former ghetto. Jews set up societies to discuss Jewish culture and another to discuss Israel. The most popular pop band in Prague took the name "Shalom" after the bandleader learned that his family was Jewish. To talk with Jews in Prague was like talking with Jews in New York or Chicago as they debated: Just who is a Jew? Was a Jew someone born of a Jewish mother, as Jewish law traditionally declared? If so, then Prague's Jewish community was tiny, with an average age of seventy. But what of the Jews showing up in Sylvia's basement—some with a Jewish father, others with a suspected Jewish grandmother. How were they to be defined? For forty-five years, the Orthodox Jews helped hold Eastern European Jewry together by their determination to attend synagogues and keep Jewish traditions alive. But now Prague brimmed over with new Jewish traditions, indeed, with new Jews, all searching for ways to connect with their Jewish past and build a Jewish future.

Tamas Raj served a successful term in parliament. He denounced anti-Semitism and appeared regularly on television news shows, always wearing his yarmulke, showing that Jews in Hungary, along with Catholics and Protestants, had cast their lot with the new freedoms. He won compensation for many elderly Jews who had suffered under the Nazis but never received adequate pensions from the Communists. And he helped form an international parliamentarians' committee against anti-Semitism, which drew support from all the new democracies in Eastern Europe.

After four years in parliament, however, Raj decided not to run again. He almost certainly would have won. But now that democracy was safely ensconced in Hungary, Raj believed that priests and rabbis did not belong in government. Their place was in their churches and their synagogues. It was a sign of Hungary's Jewish vitality that after Raj retired from politics, there were still six Jews in parliament. Budapest's 100,000 Jews constituted the largest Jewish community in Eastern Europe. It was the one place where a Jewish future was assured.

Just as he was about to leave politics, Raj was asked to become rabbi of the Dohany Synagogue in the center of Budapest—the synagogue I had seen on my first visit, with its soaring towers and seats for 2,500 Jews. It was a sweet victory for a man who had been stripped of his job in Szeged twenty-five years earlier because he was seen as a troublemaker. But Tamas turned the job down, after quibbles over some of the details of the appointment—such as whether other rabbis would be allowed to speak at the synagogue. It was his stubbornness and commitment to what he saw as the right thing to do that had strengthened him during his years of dissidence. And that stubbornness remained, even in a new Hungary.

Raj returned instead to his small congregation and started a fund-raising drive to fix his temple's leaky roof. He planned a series of lectures around the country and set up a small publishing house concentrating on Jewish books for children—books that would explain the rudiments of Judaism to children, but also to parents who were thirsty for such knowledge after all these years. He joined the board overseeing one of Budapest's blossoming Jewish schools. Suddenly, after so many years of drought, there were many job opportunities for Tamas Raj.

Soon after leaving parliament, Raj moved with his family into a new apartment just a few blocks from where he had grown up. It was a grand place, with high ceilings. He filled it with his cherished books. Off the living room, behind a set of French doors, lay Raj's study. Behind his desk he placed a smaller version of the large ark that houses the Torah in Jewish temples. Into that wooden ark, delicately carved, painted white, he carefully set the family Torah. The name of Tamas's great-grandmother was embroidered on the protective cloth. It was the Torah they had hidden under a pile of blankets in the hand cart they rolled past the Nazis when his family fled their home to the safe house provided by Raoul Wallenberg. After the Communists seized power in Hungary after the war, the Torah had lain in the bottom of his mother's closet. It had remained there for all the years Tamas spent in Szeged. It was there when the Communists banged on his mother's door and arrested him. And it lay in the dark closet during the fifteen years that Tamas lived

with his mother, unable to get regular work, because he had battled with the Communists.

For fifty years, ever since the Nazis roared into Budapest on the
motorcycles that so fascinated little Tamas, that Torah, like Hungary's Jews, had been in hiding. Now it rested in a proper place of
honor. It, too, had found a home.

After three years in Berlin, I still found myself uneasy about Germany. The danger was not so much for the Jews. Germany was
not about to revert to Nazism, and if the Jews were ever threatened, they had the means to escape. What troubled me was the
xenophobia expressed against foreigners, refugees, and immigrants, even Turkish immigrants who had lived in West Germany
for thirty years. After the fall of the Berlin Wall, the wave of right-
wing attacks in East Germany commanded the most attention.
But just as many occurred in West Germany. In reaction to the
growing violence, several hundred thousand Germans began
holding candlelight demonstrations. But in a poll conducted by a
German magazine, 35 percent of Germans—more than one in
three—said they "understood" the motives behind the right-wing
violence and, presumably, supported it at some level.

One day, after covering an anti-refugee riot in Rostock—
Molotov cocktails were thrown at Romanian and Vietnamese
refugees, while other Germans looked on, cheering—I returned to
the site of the riot and met two teenage boys loitering outside a
burned-out building. Germans nearby went about their daily rou-
tines, shopping and ordering bratwurst from a colorful pushcart.
The boys regretted they had missed the action the night before.

"If I got one of those foreigners, I'd push him down on his knees
on the street," one of them, a fifteen-year-old, said, munching on a
hamburger, bouncing from foot to foot.

"Yeah," his friend chimed in. The heads of both boys were
shaved, a defiant fringe left in the back, the mark of neo-Nazi
skinheads.

"I'd push him down on the street and make him put his mouth
on the curb," the fifteen-year-old continued.

"Yeah, on the curb," agreed his friend.

"And then," said the first, pulling his foot back and snapping it forward, "I'd kick him real hard in the head."

His friend chortled. "In the head."

The resurgence of anti-Semitism engulfing Europe after the fall of the Berlin Wall was not about Jews at all. The real question was one of modernization, change, becoming a diverse society— whether it was adjusting to the two million Turks who lived in Germany or the 100,000 Jews who lived in Hungary.

Nationalism in Germany and Eastern Europe has historically been more extreme, violent, and explosive than in Western Europe or in the United States. It is a more neurotic nationalism: all these nations concentrated into a space the size of New England, all having endured long spells of foreign rule and recent conquest. Their passions were constantly in collision with each other. The nationalism and ethnic pride that we in America have domesticated and turned into annual festivals and parades is real and violent in Eastern Europe.

In 1968, during the upsurge of anti-Semitic campaigns in Czechoslovakia and Poland, the writer Isaac Deutscher wrote that "anti-Semitism invariably reflects or foreshadows a diseased condition in European civilization. Its rise and fall is perhaps the most sensitive index of Europe's moral and political sanity."

The rise of anti-Semitism was an important indicator of that sanity because Jews were a Rorschach test for tolerance, for the ability of all these countries to change and enter the late twentieth century. If Andreas Nachama, Gregor Gysi, Tamas Raj, and Barbara Asendrych could find a home in the new democracies and live their lives in peace, that would be a good indicator that these countries were likely to prosper in peace. If they had to flee—like Gregor's grandmother in 1937, or Barbara's mother's friend Maria in 1968, or Tamas's brother, Ferenc, in 1977—the future for these countries, and all of Germany and Eastern Europe, was grim.

As the rubble from the fall of the Berlin Wall settled and the ugly passions that had been kept locked behind the wall for so long roamed free, the question was simple: Which way were Germany and Eastern Europe headed? Toward tolerance and prosperity? Or toward the downward spiral of hatred and nationalism that anti-Semitism foreshadowed?

Were Germany and Eastern Europe once again going insane?

Not this time. Despite the rise of anti-Semitism and extremism after the fall of the Berlin Wall, the Nachamas did not flee West Germany. Gregor Gysi did not wilt under questions about his Judaism. The right-wing party, Tamas Raj's nemesis in Hungary, was defeated at the polls. Barbara Asendrych did not leave Poland.

The year Communism collapsed, 1989, turned out to be as epochal for Germany and Eastern Europe as 1945, the year Nazism was defeated. Germany, which had long been divided, was now united. Countries that had fallen under the shadow of Communism were now free. The Soviet Union's domination of Eastern Europe had disappeared. By 1992, so had the Soviet Union. The defeat of Germany in 1945 had brought hope to all of Eastern Europe, especially to Jews staggering out of the concentration camps and emerging from hiding. So had the fall of the Berlin Wall in 1989.

But unlike 1945, the five years after the epochal changes of 1989 had not witnessed a reaction against the Jews, despite the spasms of anti-Semitism. In a united Germany, Klaus Gysi's son, Gregor, was serving in the Bundestag, the German parliament, and complaining about the blizzard of celebrity that put him on German talk shows.

In Czechoslovakia, Alena's daughter, Sylvia, made her living taking tourists around to Jewish sights in Prague and talked about going to America to study to be a rabbi.

In Hungary, five years after the fall of the Berlin Wall, Tamas Raj was both a rabbi and a member of a democratically elected parliament in Budapest.

In Warsaw, Barbara Asendrych, conscious of her Jewish parentage, could begin, however tentatively, to understand what it was like to live as a Jew.

In West Berlin, five years after the war, an emaciated Estrongo Nachama had picked his way through the ruins of the city to find a functioning synagogue. By 1950, a sapling had taken root in the great Oranienburger Strasse synagogue's shattered lobby and had begun its slow reach toward the sunlight. By 1989, after four decades of Communist neglect, the tree's upper branches reached toward the roof line. Now the tree was gone, chopped down as part of a restoration project. The glittering gold dome of the synagogue had been replaced, its golden Star of David visible for miles around, the synagogue itself set to reopen soon.

The spasm of anti-Semitism that gripped Germany and Eastern Europe right after the fall of the Berlin Wall had died down. In this part of the world, its soil soaked with the blood of murdered Jews, it was impossible to say that the danger had passed forever. The future of Jews in Germany and Eastern Europe depended, as it always had, on the economic and political stability of the countries in which they lived. If Germany, Hungary, Czechoslovakia, and Poland continued on the road of peaceful democracy and prosperity, Jews there would most likely thrive. They would never recapture the role they had had earlier in this century, when 40 percent of the lawyers in Warsaw were Jews, when middle-class Jews thronged a hundred synagogues in Berlin, when Jews sat on the boards and in the executive offices of Hungary's major banks and railroads. There were more Jews in Warsaw or Budapest before World War II than there are now in all of Eastern Europe. But neither would Jews be reduced to a few elderly men and women gathering at the synagogue on a Friday night. Whether it was Gregor Gysi running for parliament or Tamas Raj speaking to cheering crowds or Sylvia Wittmann gathering her young friends in a basement to celebrate the Friday-night Sabbath, Jews would not fade away. They would again restore a Jewish accent to Germany and Eastern Europe— not as broad an accent as that of their parents and grandparents, but an accent and an influence nonetheless. The refilling of that great gaping hole that had once been the European Jewish community had begun.

In truth, the fate of Germany's and Eastern Europe's Jews would not be known for another fifty years. In 1918, when Andreas Nachama's grandfather, Siegfried, returned to Berlin with his German army medals at the end of World War I, who could have predicted that twenty years later he would be driven to suicide by the anti-Semitic rage of the Nazis? In 1953, when Tamas Raj's father snuck through the back streets of Budapest, fearful of being spotted by the Communists, to attend his son's bar mitzvah, who would have guessed that in forty years young Tamas would be a member of parliament, proudly wearing a yarmulke on his head? If the hidden history of the Jews of Eastern Europe revealed by the fall of the Berlin Wall proved anything, it was that Jews and Jewish life were far more resilient and adaptable than anyone had ever thought.

So while Jews might be anxious about the future, they lived in the present. In Warsaw, the number of young Jewish children had grown so fast that the Jewish community opened a nursery school, the first Jewish nursery school in Poland in fifty years. In Berlin, the Jewish community reopened the old Jewish high school that had been closed by the Nazis. The laughter of students again filled its hallways. Prague's Jews debated the merits of their new rabbi, and some considered starting a new, more liberal congregation. In Budapest, reconstruction of the Dohany Synagogue, which I had seen on my first visit, was nearing completion. On the Jewish High Holidays, every seat was filled. Across the street, a theater featured a Jewish film festival.

On one of my last trips to Poland, I asked an American rabbi assigned to help the Jewish community there to explain the persistence of Jewish life in these countries despite the horrors of Nazism and the persecution of Communism stretched over fifty years. How could he explain the determination of Tamas Raj, the stirrings of Gregor Gysi, the awakening of Sylvia Wittmann, the search of Barbara Asendrych?

"I don't have to explain it," he said with a smile. "I'm a rabbi. I believe in miracles."

# Acknowledgments

**M**ore than five years elapsed between the first idea for this book and delivery of the final manuscript—enough time to accumulate many debts of gratitude.

My greatest thanks go to the five families who shared their memories and feelings with me in hundreds of hours of interviews. It was one of the wonders of the heady years right after the fall of the Berlin Wall that the people of Eastern Europe were so open to the journalists—strangers—who dropped into their lives. It was as if their stories had been bottled up for forty-five years and now, at last, had a chance to pour forth.

I could not have gathered these stories without a corps of talented and empathic translators. It is difficult enough to get people to share the intimate details of their lives; it is even more difficult through the barriers of different languages and cultures. Although most of my translators were not Jewish, their support and interest never flagged, even when it meant excavating the hidden, and often painful, history of their countries.

Rarely have I had the privilege of working with a colleague as resourceful, talented, and multiskilled as Claudia Himmelreich in Berlin. Whether tracking down an elusive citation, evaluating the treatment of Jews in the former East Germany, or stopping the car to buy flowers in the hope of opening the door of a recalcitrant interviewee, Claudia showed unfailing judgment, insight, and commitment. She was indispensable to this book and to our time in Berlin. I will treasure her friendship always.

In Warsaw, Magda Iwinska and I began discussing the tortured history of Poles and Jews soon after the fall of the Berlin Wall. We started as colleagues and soon became friends, and Magda opened her home and family to me. A topic that many Poles find discomforting Magda approached with empathy, curiosity, and enthusiasm. I learned much from Magda, and without her extraordinary skills I could not have unearthed Barbara Asendrych's extraordinary story. Whatever optimism I have about Poland, and the future of Polish-Jewish relations, comes from Magda.

In Budapest, Magdi Seleanu helped plant the seed for this book by taking me to visit the new Jewish schools that blossomed across the city soon after the collapse of Communism and by sharing with me her own rediscovery of her Jewish roots. She welcomed me into her home and to meet her friends, and tirelessly pursued with me the twisting trail of Tamas Raj's story.

In Prague, Dagmar Oberreigner helped research the reemergence of Jewish life after the "Velvet Revolution" and put me in touch with several key figures. Jody Becker assisted with an early stage of the research and introduced me to Sylvia Wittmann.

In Berlin, thanks also go to Edward Serotta, who generously supplied some of the photographs for this book, along with his endless stream of history, insight, enthusiasm, and laughter. My thanks, too, to friends and colleagues John Tagliabue, Paula Butturini, Tyler Marshall, Petra Falkenberg, Marc Fisher, Katie Hafner, Andreas Brie, Henryk Broder, and Christian Caryl.

In Warsaw: Konstanty Gebert, Fred Kempe—whose story for the *Wall Street Journal* led me to Barbara Asendrych—and Michael Shudrich.

In Prague: Tomas Kraus, Arno Pajik, Tomas Brod, and the wonderful Iva Drapalova.

In Boston, Ferenc Raj, Tamas Raj's brother, who deserves a book of his own one day, was generous in recollections of his family. My thanks also to Wil Haygood, Ross Gelbspan, Nina Giovannelli, Leonard Zakim, Bill Prindle, and Steve Fayer for spiritual sustenance.

The *Boston Globe* sent me to Berlin to open the Berlin bureau and were enormously supportive of both my reporting there and my decision to do this book. My thanks to my old friend Tom Ashbrook, to Jack Driscoll, Al Larkin, David Greenway, Matt Storin, and John Yemma.

Larry Sternberg and his colleagues at Brandeis generously provided me with a year-long fellowship and the use of the university library. Andy Markovits of the University of California at Santa Cruz and Harvard's Center for European Studies read the manuscript and offered several helpful suggestions as well as his bountiful goodwill. I am grateful for both.

At Viking Penguin, I was fortunate to find editors who cared about this topic, and this book, as much as I did. Barbara Grossman came up with the original idea for the book in New York around the same time I was mulling the topic in Berlin. We never parted ways after that, and I am glad. Her support, good humor, and terrific editing eye buoyed this book, and my spirits, along. Beena Kamlani adopted this book like a wayward child and, like a good parent, criticized, nudged, corrected, and shepherded the book into adulthood. Together, Barbara and Beena provided editing that most people say does not exist anymore in publishing. It does with them.

As always, Michael Carlisle provided sage advice, jokes, friendship—all that and suggestions that shaped the book from its title to its final structure.

Barbara Howard lived with this book from its outset, listening to me talk about it during its early stages and editing it when it was finally done. She shared the adventure of living and reporting in Berlin and our continuing adventure back in Boston. More than she knows, her thoughts, comments, and observations shaped this book. She is many things to me. This book is for her.

Molly and Ben can't read this yet. But when they do, they should know that I wrote this bearing them in mind—and with them never far out of earshot. This is part of their heritage too. I hope that one day, when they return to Central Europe, they will find the Jewish life described here sprouting into full bloom.

# Notes

Introduction
4 *Berlin before Hitler*: Sarah Gordon, *Hitler, Germans and the "Jewish Question"* (Princeton, N.J.: Princeton University Press, 1984), pp. 7–49.

5 *Germans were the most frequent recipients of the Nobel Prize*: Bernt Engelmann, *Germany Without Jews* (New York: Bantam Books, 1984), pp. 45–58.

7 *700,000 Jews left in Eastern Europe*: Paul Lendvai, *Anti-Semitism Without Jews* (New York: Doubleday, 1971), p. 25.

Chapter One
14 *Estrongo Nachama . . . left his office*: Details of Estrongo Nachama's life and activities on November 9 are drawn from a series of interviews with Nachama, his wife, Lilli, and his son, Andreas.

23 *the Gysis were finishing dinner*: Details of Klaus Gysi's life and activities on November 9 are drawn from a series of interviews with Gysi, his wife, Birgid, his former wife, Irene, his son, Gregor, his daughter, Gabriele, and friends and coworkers.

25 *Barbara Asendrych was at home*: Details of Barbara Asendrych's life and activities on November 9 are drawn from a series of interviews with Asendrych and her husband, son, and daughter-in-law.

26 *Tamas Raj rarely let politics*: Details of Tamas Raj's life and activities on November 9 are drawn from interviews with Raj, his wife, his brother, Ferenc, friends, coworkers, and members of his congregation.

28 *Sylvia Wittmann was heading back*: Details of Sylvia Wittmann's life and

activities on November 9 are drawn from interviews with Wittmann and her mother, father, and friends.

Chapter Two
37 *The mansion sat on the edge:* Details of Klaus Gysi's childhood and years in hiding in Berlin are drawn from interviews with Klaus Gysi and Irene Gysi.

40 *The Jewish romance with socialism:* Lendvai, pp. 47–86.

46 *the contempt Marx had for his fellow Jews:* Robert Wistrich, *Antisemitism: The Longest Hatred* (London: Methuen, 1991), pp. 49–53; also discussed at greater length in Robert Wistrich, *Revolutionary Jews from Marx to Trotsky* (New York: Barnes & Noble Books, 1978).

60 *Many of the writers who returned:* Robin Ostow, *Jews in Contemporary East Germany* (London: Macmillan, 1989), pp. 1–9.

Chapter Three
65 *The death march from the concentration camp:* Details of Estrongo and Lilian Nachama's childhood, their experiences during the war, and their life in Berlin right after the war are drawn from a series of interviews with Nachama, Lilian, their son, Andreas, and friends and colleagues.

69 *Jews first arrived in Berlin:* Edward Serotta, "Travelling Through Time in Europe and the Middle East: Past, Present and Future" (Publication in conjunction with the United Jewish Appeal, 1993), pp. 3–24.

70 *No place better reflected:* Ibid.

72 *"symbolized a modernity that many Germans found profoundly threatening":* Ron Chernow, *The Warburgs* (New York: Random House, 1994).

Chapter Four
81 *"Gary Cooper. John Wayne. Bette Davis."* Details of Alena Schmula Wittmann's life and experiences under the Nazis and Communists are drawn from a series of interviews with Wittmann, her mother, her husband, Vaclav Wittmann, and her daughter, Sylvia.

Chapter Five
87 *There was no question:* Details of Tamas Raj's life and experiences under the Nazis and Communists are drawn from a series of interviews with Raj and his brother, Ferenc.

87 *resisted German demands that they ship Jews:* Kati Marton, *Wallenberg* (New York: Ballantine, 1982), pp. 56–62.

92 *"That commerce is alive":* Quoted in Peter Meyer, et al., *The Jews in the Soviet Satellites* (Syracuse, N.Y.: Syracuse University Press/The American Jewish Committee, 1953), p. 403.

93 *The mood in Hungary was beginning to change:* Ibid., pp. 409–50.

93 *"We are hated because we returned":* Ibid.

94*"My hands are tied":* Ibid., p. 429.

Chapter Six
97 *Leokadia Burzynska:* Details of Leokadia's story are based on interviews with her daughter, Barbara Asendrych, and her friend Maria Wisniewska Wiltgren.

98 *Zelechow had been founded in the fourteenth century:* The history of Zelechow is based on interviews with local priests and professors, and on the memorial (Yizkor) books compiled by the Jewish community of Zelechow after the war and housed in the YIVO center in New York.

99 *the history of Poles and Jews:* Meyer et al.

101 *The Nazis marched into Zelechow:* Interviews with local professors and priests; memorial books housed at YIVO.

102 *knocked on the door of the rectory:* Interviews with local priests.

105 *Jews seemed to wield more power:* Lendvai provides the most comprehensive survey of this period.

Chapter Seven
116 *The gap between West Berlin and East Berlin:* Except where noted, details of Klaus Gysi's life and feelings under the Communists are drawn from a series of interviews with Gysi, his first wife, Irene, and their children, Gabriele and Gregor.

119 *an article in* Pravda *that attacked Israel:* Lendvai, p. 19.

119 *Arthur London . . . was berated by the prison warden:* Lendvai, pp. 253–54.

120 *East German Communist Party issued a sixty-page report:* Ostow, pp. 3–4.

123 *One of those arrested was Walter Janka:* Details of the Janka episode are drawn from a letter from Walter Janka to the author dated Sept. 1, 1993; Janka's autobiography, *Die Unterwerfung;* interviews with Klaus Gysi; Klaus Gysi interview with German television interviewer Guenter Gaus, reprinted in Guenter Gaus, *Porträts in Frage und Antwort* (Berlin: Verlag Volk und Welt, 1991); Marcel Reich-Ranicki, "A Fanatic One Can Talk To," *Die Zeit,* Jan. 28, 1966.

125 *"only lack of paper and hard currency":* Generalanzeiger, Jan. 14, 1966.

126 *"understood that in culture":* Reich-Ranicki, *Die Zeit.*

126 *Gysi was the worst kind of opportunist:* Interview with Stefan Hermlin.

126 *"We are so close to the Kremlin":* Generalanzeiger, Jan. 14, 1966.

127 *"that everything had to turn out like this":* Reich-Ranicki, *Die Zeit.*

127 *To grow up as Klaus Gysi's children:* Except where noted, details of Gregor and Gabriele Gysi's childhoods are drawn from a series of interviews with Gregor, Gabriele, and their parents, Klaus and Irene Gysi.

130 *Being Jewish gave Gregor the privilege:* Irene Runge and Uwe Stelbrink, *Gregor Gysi: "Ich bin Opposition"* (Berlin: Dietz Verlag, 1990).

131 *"Some optimists even think":* Reich-Ranicki in "Die Zeit," Jan. 28, 1966.

132 *five-year-old Gregor was walking:* Autobiographical manuscript by Gregor Gysi, in author's possession.

133 *summoned to his school principal's office:* Ibid.

134 *Gregor took an internship as a cattle breeder:* Ibid.

137 *The law school convened:* Ibid.

139 *Klaus Gysi decided to visit his son:* Ibid.; interviews with Klaus and Gregor Gysi.

Chapter Eight
141 *The singer from Auschwitz:* Details of Estrongo Nachama's life and feelings and those of his son, Andreas, are drawn from interviews with Estrongo, Lilian, and Andreas Nachama.

143 *most Germans "seemed to look away":* Inge Deutschkron, *Bonn and Jerusalem* (Philadelphia: Chilton, 1970), pp. 1–2.

Chapter Nine
149 *Alena Schmula never lost her affection:* Details of Alena Schmula Wittmann's experiences under the Communists are drawn from interviews with Wittmann, her mother, her husband, Václav Wittmann, and her daughter, Sylvia Wittmann.

158 *the Nazis, carrying out a grand plan:* David Atshuler, *The Precious Legacy* (New York: Summit Books, 1983), pp. 17–38.

Chapter Ten
164 *Tamas Raj's bar mitzvah:* Details of Tamas Raj's experiences and feelings under Communism, except where noted, are drawn from interviews with Raj and his brother, Ferenc Raj.

167 *agreed on Louis Stoeckler*: Meyer, et al., chapter on Hungary; interviews with Hungarian historians who began researching Stoeckler's role and fate after the collapse of Communism.

171 *Szeged reflected the success*: Interview with officials and historians in Szeged.

172 *the old synagogue in Szeged was hopping*: Interviews with members of Raj's Szeged congregation.

Chapter Eleven
182 *Leokadia was still young and pretty*: Details of Leokadia's and Barbara's experiences and feelings under Communism, except where noted, are drawn from interviews with Barbara Asendrych and Maria Wisniewska Wiltgren.

184 *the anti-Semitism that had swept across*: Lendvai, pp. 90–239.

185 *Maria embodied many of the stereotypes*: Details of Maria's story are drawn from interviews with Maria Wisniewska Wiltgren.

189 *anti-Semitism flared anew in Poland*: Lendvai, pp. 90–239.

Part III
193 *"What is that Jew from Galicia doing here?"*: Ibid., pp. 279–80.

195 *"True enough, the country is calm"*: Vaclav Havel, "Open Letter to President Husak," reprinted in Havel, *Living in Truth* (New York: Faber and Faber, 1990).

Chapter Twelve
196 *For more than thirty-five years*: Details of Klaus Gysi's life and feelings under Communism, except where noted, are drawn from a series of interviews with Gysi, his first wife, Irene, and their children, Gabriele and Gregor.

198 *Klaus seemed oddly at home in Rome*: Interview with Günter Gaus.

198 *a professor standing at the doorway*: Autobiographical manuscript by Gregor Gysi.

198 *Gregor was overcome by the realization*: Ibid.; interview with Gregor Gysi. Further details of Gregor's feelings and experiences, unless otherwise noted, are drawn from a series of interviews with Gregor Gysi.

201 *"The disgusting crime did not arouse my sympathy"*: Autobiographical manuscript by Gregor Gysi.

201 *In one celebrated murder trial*: Interview with Lothar de Maziere, Gregor Gysi's law partner.

202 *exasperation at being a defense lawyer*: Ibid.

202 *Gregor . . . was overwhelmed*. Autobiographical manuscript by Gregor Gysi; interview with Gregor Gysi.

203 *asked to defend . . . Havemann*: Ibid.

205 *"You will report only to me"*: Interview with Horst Dohle, Klaus Gysi's chief of staff at the Office of Church Affairs.

205 *Klaus launched into a speech*: Ibid.

206 *"God will exist"*: This and other official statements from Gysi during this period are drawn from copies of files maintained by Radio Free Europe, in author's possession.

206 *"Where is my gefilte fish?"* Interview with Andreas Nachama.

207 *"It doesn't matter what he does"*: Ibid.

207 *"That's a typical father's compromise"*: Interview with Lothar de Maziere.

207 *found Gregor slumped against the wall*: Ibid.

208 *Gabriele . . . found herself increasingly at odds*: Interview with Gabriele Gysi.

209 *Klaus was becoming more . . . pessimistic*: Klaus Gysi television interview with Günter Gaus.

210 *Gysi tried to smooth over disagreements*: Interview with Bishop Albert Schoenherr.

212 *he bombarded them with questions*: Interview with Horst Dohle.

214 *Irene Runge organized*: Interview with Irene Runge.

214 *"Susannah gives chocolate"*: Irene Runge, "Susannah." Copy in author's possession.

216 *Gregor was asked to attend*: Interview with Birgid Gysi, who attended the meeting.

217 *"Every abuse of power"*: Gregor Gysi, *Einspruch!* (Berlin: Alexander Verlag, 1992).

218 *The Communist Party, in a new spirit of openness*: Jonathan Kaufman, "How the Wall Fell," *Boston Globe*, Nov. 9, 1990.

220 *Gregor . . . went home to sleep*: Interview with Gregor Gysi; interview with Gabriele Gysi.

Chapter Thirteen
222 *In 1972, Andreas Nachama left*: Details of Andreas Nachama's experiences and feelings are drawn from a series of interviews with Andreas Nachama and his wife, Sarah Nachama.

228 *Estrongo was proud*: Interview with Estrongō Nachama.

229 *Once, on a trip to Magdeburg*: Ibid.

Chapter Fourteen
232 *The last customers had left*: Details of the experiences and feelings of Alena Wittmann and Sylvia Wittmann are drawn from a series of interviews with them.

Chapter Fifteen
242 *Tamas Raj pondered his next move*: Details of the experiences and feelings of Tamas Raj come from a series of interviews with Raj, his wife, and his brother, Ferenc.

247 *The ceremony filled*: Timothy Garton Ash, *The Magic Lantern* (New York, Vintage Books, 1993), pp. 47–60.

Chapter Sixteen
249 *Leokadia had been lying*: Details of the experiences and feelings of Leokadia and Barbara Asendrych are drawn from a series of interviews with Barbara Asendrych, her husband, son, and daughter-in-law, and Maria Wisniewska.

Part IV
259 *"In Poland it took ten years"*: Ash, p. 78.

Chapter Seventeen
262 *Gregor was handed a note*: Autobiographical manuscript by Gregor Gysi.

264 *An artist visiting Klaus*: Interview with Klaus Gysi.

265 *"I'd like to read about myself also being blue-blooded"*: Quoted in Runge and Stelbrink.

265 *the words hit him like stones*: Interview with André Brie, Gysi's campaign manager and friend.

268 *"There would be only one problem"*: *Stern*, May 8, 1990.

268 *"Unity requires unification"*: Answers to a questionnaire from the Deutsches Historisches Museum, February 1991.

269 *Klaus Gysi telephoned his son:* Autobiographical manuscript by Gregor Gysi; interview with Lothar de Maziere.

Chapter Eighteen
270 *Estrongo Nachama had always drifted above:* Details of the life and feelings of Estrongo Nachama and his son, Andreas, are drawn from interviews with Estrongo, Lilian, and Andreas Nachama.

Chapter Nineteen
279 *Sylvia Wittmann had gone into business:* Details of the experiences and feelings of Alena Wittmann and Sylvia Wittmann are drawn from a series of interviews with them.

Chapter Twenty
286 *Raj spoke of the Hungarian David:* Details of the experiences and feelings of Tamas Raj are drawn from a series of interviews with him.

Chapter Twenty-One
290 *Barbara . . . took a part-time job:* Details of the experiences and feelings of Barbara Asendrych are drawn from a series of interviews with her.

292 *"My dear Jews":* Quoted in Wladyslaw T. Bartoszewski, *The Convent at Auschwitz* (New York: George Braziller, 1991), pp. 109–10.

Chapter Twenty-Two
314 *"anti-Semitism invariably reflects":* Isaac Deutscher, *The Non-Jewish Jew and Other Essays* (London: Oxford University Press, 1968).